THE WORLD OF A TINY INSECT

錄于此一樣人間世荒涼劇可嗟山風秋嘯兔鶴也山多兔車春瘴

夜肥蛇遇山有蛇肥遇日雪爛可食大璞空文玉山有文石人寒灘漲鐵沙

者謂有金寒鐵氣孤城莽寥落嵐翠萬重疊霧雨朝

蘭佩纖纖小蘭花可作不與常居人喜佩之謂竹葉上與竹相類也男宜清分處木

花處州者最佳故名自蕭然遠塵世雅合住仙家煨芋山茅灃

來教山林故自嘉清風振崖谷高樹溺煙霞及他林彬香溫巖

蔄衣不食四十許人以不尚飢年也常如炊煙寒水末紉約幾人家來者乞兒老檜冬夏一

桓以芋不為能食致米春雲水碓斛邑中且資生之具然此為潤美既挽枯柱水以有

民以資不為能食致米

因以海紜者有嵐溪宜種竹山能宜台兔居人不致人諸不祥也有邽台研去以為

爭而頌紜者種之沙暖利培穣傾其汁林而居人後人不識培種法採取即以筥煮利之盡

種之沙暖利培穣春風鬧鶯粟花藍衣歌采采涉險履嶺呀衣

者益鮮益可惜連畦畛

薄益鮮益可惜連畦畛春風鬧鶯粟花藍衣歌采采涉險履嶺呀衣

如日石衣深藍或翻味類禾耳而澀之性逗瘴結而成者頗不易有厚

赤日麻布色深藍或翻味類禾耳而澀之性逗瘴取之頗不易有厚

之遇蛇虎或目眴尚異味誅求者當登歊阻爲得石骨寒毛髮殘生狷恊

之難也或目眴尚異味誅求者當登歊阻爲得石骨寒毛髮殘生狷恊

The WORLD of a TINY INSECT

A MEMOIR OF THE
TAIPING REBELLION
AND ITS AFTERMATH

by **ZHANG DAYE**

Translated, with an introduction,
by **XIAOFEI TIAN**

UNIVERSITY OF WASHINGTON PRESS
Seattle and London

Printed and bound in the United States of America
Design by Thomas Eykemans
Composed in Chaparral, typeface designed by Carol Twombly
20 19 18 17 16 15 14 13   5 4 3 2 1

UNIVERSITY OF WASHINGTON PRESS
PO Box 50096, Seattle, WA 98145, USA
www.washington.edu/uwpress

LIBRARY OF CONGRESS CATALOGING-IN-PUBLICATION DATA
Zhang, Daye, 1854–
[Weichong shijie. English.]
The world of a tiny insect : a memoir of the Taiping rebellion and its aftermath /
Zhang Daye ; translated, with an introduction, by Xiaofei Tian.
     pages cm
ISBN 978-0-295-99317-1 (hardback)
ISBN 978-0-295-99318-8 (paperback)
1. China—History—Taiping Rebellion, 1850–1864—Personal narratives.
2. China—History—1861–1912.
3. Zhang, Daye, 1854–
4. China—Biography.
I. Tian, Xiaofei, 1971– translator, author of introduction.
II. Title.
DS759.35.Z53613 2014   951'.034092—dc23   2013035414

The paper used in this publication is acid-free and meets the minimum
requirements of American National Standard for Information Sciences—
Permanence of Paper for Printed Library Materials, ANSI Z39.48–1984.∞

Frontispiece: A page from the manuscript of *The World of a Tiny Insect*
in the collection of Taipei's National Central Library.

CONTENTS

ACKNOWLEDGMENTS

I STILL remember how I first stumbled upon this remarkable late-nineteenth-century manuscript. When I was browsing a catalogue of Qing dynasty manuscripts that have never been printed, the title—*The World of a Tiny Insect*—caught my eye. Thinking that it might be a rare work of entomology from premodern China, I sought it out and opened its pages. Little did I expect that it would turn out to be another kind of rare work; it grabbed me immediately, with its violence, its pain, and its profound compassion for human cruelty and foolishness. From then on, I embarked on a journey retracing the footsteps of the "tiny insect" in his labyrinthine passage through time and space. While the discovery was serendipitous, my work on this manuscript related closely to my long-term research interest in travel writing, memory, trauma, and manuscript culture. Subsequently, I gave a presentation on my finds at the Manuscript Culture Conference I organized at Harvard University in May 2010. I am grateful to the participants of the conference for their input, especially Waiyee Li, for giving an illuminating discussion of my paper, and Judith Zeitlin, for her astute insights.

I am much obliged to Professor Xia Xiaohong of Beijing University for helping me search for the excerpted manuscript copy in the library collection of the Institute of Modern History at the Chinese Academy of Social Sciences. Although the search did not turn up the manuscript, I appreciate Professor Xia's time and efforts in the scorching summer of Beijing.

I thank Hannibal Taubes, senior student of Harvard College majoring in East Asian Studies, for being one of the first readers of my draft translation, and for his enthusiastic, helpful comments, in an Independent Study course on Chinese travel literature we did together in the fall semester of 2012. We both learned a great deal in that course.

A special note of appreciation is due my colleague Peter K. Bol for his generous offer of help in creating the map that graced this book, at a particularly busy time right before a new semester began. Occasional grumbling could never conceal Peter's chivalrous nature, for which I am thankful as much as for his expertise in GIS.

I am grateful to the two anonymous readers for their detailed reports, which were extremely helpful in my revision of the manuscript. I am also deeply indebted to the superb editorial team at the University of Washington Press: Kerrie Maynes, Mary C. Ribesky, Marilyn Trueblood, Tim Zimmermann, Rachael Levay, and, last but not least, Lorri Hagman, whose warm encouragement and sage advice were instrumental in bringing this book to print.

While one's family always deserves thanks for enduring a time-consuming project, I want to thank my husband Stephen Owen especially for always being available for consultation on a better turn of phrase, and for reading through my translation and offering feedback. When I was working on this project during a sabbatical leave in the fall of 2011, my infant son, George, kept me company every day and opened up a new world of wonder and love to me that I could never have imagined possible without him: I am forever in his debt.

X.F.T.

THE WORLD OF A TINY INSECT

Map of Author's Travels

TRANSLATOR'S INTRODUCTION

THE nineteenth century was a bad century for the Manchus, who established the Qing dynasty in 1644 and ruled over China until 1912. Internal and external problems beset the once powerful, prosperous empire. Among other things, the Qing government had to handle the Opium Wars with the Great Britain, the armed uprisings of the Hui Muslims and other ethnic peoples, and natural disasters, famines, bureaucratic corruption, and economic stagnation. But the most horrific tragedy that befell the country in the nineteenth century was the Taiping Rebellion (1850–64), led by a failed civil service examination candidate who claimed to be the son of God and the younger brother of Jesus Christ.[1] Along with the contemporaneous Nian Uprising that broke out in north China, the Taiping Rebellion caused an immense loss of life, devastated large parts of the wealthy and cultured southern provinces, and dealt a near-fatal blow to the already weakened Qing regime. More than twenty million people, mostly civilians, died during the fourteen years of one of the largest civil wars in human history. This book, *The World of a Tiny Insect* (henceforth *The World*), is an autobiographical work that, at its core, contains a lengthy recollection of the author's traumatic childhood experience in one of the southern provinces most ravaged during the Taiping Rebellion.

....

1   There are many historical narratives of the Taiping Rebellion in the English language. Interested readers may refer to Jonathan D. Spence's *God's Chinese Son: The Taiping Heavenly Kingdom of Hong Xiuquan* (New York: W. W. Norton, 1996), or to a more recent publication on the subject, Stephen R. Platt's *Autumn in the Heavenly Kingdom: China, the West, and the Epic Story of the Taiping Civil War* (New York: Alfred A. Knopf, 2012).

As might be expected, there are many accounts of the Taiping Rebellion by people who lived through it; what sets *The World* apart from most of them is the fact that it recounts the turbulent period as experienced by the author as a very young child. When his hometown was captured by the Taiping army in the autumn of 1861, the author of *The World* was seven years old. In the next two years, he and his mother were constantly on the run, hiding from the "Longhairs" (i.e., Taiping soldiers, so called because they refused to wear the braid ordained by the Manchus), the "Shorthairs" (i.e., local bandits), and the imperial troops. During this time, he witnessed gruesome deeds of violence and cruelty as well as macabre scenes of death, including the suicide of a family member right before his eyes; he himself almost died a number of times, from terrifying encounters with the Longhairs, the Shorthairs, and even other civilians who also just wanted to survive, as well as from struggles with starvation and illness.

Compared with people who experienced the rebellion as grown-ups, our author had an unusual perspective. Sometimes, as a curious little boy who still only half-understood what he saw, he actively sought out opportunities to observe sights shunned by adults; and perhaps because he was a small child, he remained more or less invisible to those who were engaged in acts of violence, and managed to stay out of harm's way. But the psychological damage caused by those nightmarish experiences was more difficult to avoid and proved long-lasting. The images and memories remained with him, haunting him so much that he felt compelled to tell his tale thirty years later. And a remarkable tale it was: shocking and horrifying in its grisly detail, poignant in its compassion and grief over the senseless killings and deaths.

The author of *The World* is a man named Zhang Daye, Zhang being his family name. He hailed from Shaoxing, a city with a long and illustrious cultural past, in the fertile, scenic, and sophisticated southeastern province of Zhejiang. Nothing is known about him outside *The World*, which both reveals much about him and discloses little. We know, for example, the date of his birth, which was January 29, 1854; and we know his nickname and baby name; and yet we do not know his "style name" or "courtesy name," by which a premodern Chinese man was known among his peers, and which furnished an important piece of information regarding his identity. We know that his father served in some middle-level official post in Jiangsu Province; at one point, the author remarks that his father was on good terms with Wan Qingxuan (1818–1898), a late Qing official who was recognized for his administrative accomplishments but is now better known as the maternal grandfather of Zhou Enlai (1898–1976), the premier of the People's Republic of China (PRC). And yet, while the author gives the names of several of his uncles, cousins, family acquaintances, and personal friends, he never mentions the name of his father even once. When the Taiping army occupied Shaoxing, one of its highly ranked commanders, Yu Guangqian, lived in the author's family house throughout the occupation period, a fact that suggests that it was one of the best residences in Shaoxing. In short, what we can gather from *The World* is that Zhang Daye was a well-educated member of the old literati elite from an apparently well-connected family located in one of the richest and culturally most active areas of the country, even though we do not know whether he was married and, if he was, whether he had any children. Judging by the dates provided therein, *The World* was composed from 1893 to 1894. It apparently never went into print, but was circulated as a handwritten, hand-copied manuscript, possibly among family members and friends. Now the only complete manuscript copy is in the collection of National Central Library in Taiwan, where it was photo-reprinted as part of a series of Qing manuscripts in 1974.[2]

The level of detail regarding some aspects of the author's life and the vagueness or total silence regarding others make this work a rather idiosyncratic autobiography. Indeed, idiosyncrasy characterizes the work as a whole. It is, for instance, difficult to place this work in the scheme of traditional Chinese literary genres, because it is a mixture of many different kinds of writings: "account of self" (*zixu*); travelogue (*youji*); "miscellany" or "random notes" (*biji*) that, among other things, introduce bits and pieces of local knowledge; sociopolitical discourse (*yilun*); and poetry (both *shi* poems in regular meters and song lyrics in irregular meters). In modern library or book store classification, it might be shelved under "nonfiction: memoir." It begins, however, with a statement that, in its striking reference to the birth of a "world," highlights the constructed nature of a textual universe that is the work itself:

. . . .

2   Zhang Daye, *Weichong shijie* [The world of a tiny insect], in *Qingdai gaoben baizhong huikan* [A collected series of a hundred Qing dynasty draft manuscripts], vol. 55 (Taipei: Wenhai Chubanshe, 1974).

In the nineteenth year—the *guisi* year—of the Guangxu era, beginning
when the Emperor [i.e., the Guangxu Emperor, r. 1875–1908] took the
dragon throne, on the sixth day of the fourth month [May 21, 1893],
this tiny insect took a trip to Tiantai. Thus the world came into being.
I suppose the fruit of bodhi was about to ripen.

With the remark that "the world came into being," this opening recalls
the cosmic context in which we find the openings of several classical Chinese novels, such as *Journey to the West* or *The Dream of the Red Chamber*,
and accentuates the fictional dimension of all autobiographical narratives despite their inevitable reference to reality.

The World is an extraordinary text for a number of other reasons. Produced in the twilight years of the Qing regime, it is noteworthy in its
intense concern with ostensibly local problems as opposed to national
problems, as it dwells in loving, poignant detail on the landscape, the
people, the customs, and the situations of various counties in Zhejiang.
While scholarly attention has focused largely on late-Qing intellectu-
als and radicals intensely engaged in issues of nationhood and revolution, here we see someone who was much more interested in what was
happening in one region than in "China" as a (nascent) nation. In some
ways, the author of *The World* might well be regarded as "provincial," and
indeed he was not only so but also very self-consciously so. In the preface
to this work, he refers to himself as a "tiny insect" in a big world:

Unable to see the sun, the stars, great mountains, and large rivers,
when it sees a cup of water and a burning torch, it is startled and filled
with admiration, thinking that perhaps they are none other than the
so-called sun, stars, great mountains, and large rivers. It leaps with
excitement, looks up, cries out, and writes down in private what it has
seen.

The self-conscious humility with which Zhang wrote these words is
borne out by the fact that he apparently never traveled beyond the two
adjacent provinces of Zhejiang and Jiangsu; nevertheless, his humility is
offset with a keen sense of the relativity of "large" and "small," and the
very first sentence of the preface states, "From the cry of a tiny insect,
one can hear the sound of a vast world." Zhang goes on to express the

hope that, in the legendary tradition of "collecting the songs" from the common folk and presenting them to the Son of Heaven so that the Son of Heaven will know what was happening in the realm, the cry of this "tiny insect" might be found useful by a sage ruler in the management of the affairs of the world. Clearly the author intends for this account to represent something larger than a single person's life, and by challenging the common notion of what constitutes "greatness," he endows the perspective of one ordinary individual with an extraordinary dignity. We might also note that the dragon belongs to the category of insect in traditional Chinese taxonomy, albeit the most august of insects and a symbol of the emperor, and that the opening remark of this book, cited earlier, balances the "tiny insect" with none other than the imperial dragon itself. In other words, as the tiny insect's embarking on his journey and the emperor's taking of the dragon throne (*long fei*, literally, "the soaring of the dragon") are set in parallel with each other in the opening statement, the little insect at the lowest level of the social hierarchy acquires a nobility of stature from the rhetorical contrast. And yet, in a further twist of the pious hope of being useful to the imperial rule, the author observes, "What one takes to be a whole world is nothing but wavering hot air and floating dust." This remark, together with the comment that even the world of a bee or a mosquito has "ruler and subject, father and son, husband and wife, brothers and friends," just as in the human world, undermines on a spiritual level the earnestness of his political aspirations. Thus oscillating between sentiments that might be termed practical and those that might be termed philosophical, the standpoint of the author has a complexity that is matched only by the account's generic idiosyncrasy and hybridity. What ultimately emerges from the account is a profound compassion for various kinds of human suffering at a chaotic time, not the least of which were the shock and pain experienced by the author himself during his tumultuous childhood.

With this observation we come to the most striking aspect of this work, one of the few detailed accounts of traumatic childhood memories—indeed of any childhood memory—in the otherwise rich and diverse premodern Chinese literary tradition. *The World* is an exemplary piece of trauma writing, not just because of the grisly violence of the child's experience, but also because of its unusual structure. The figure of travel is useful here for two reasons. One reason is the importance of the travel theme in this work: it opens with the description of a trip that is said to have been the genesis of *The World*, and subsequently relates the author's life story as being threaded together almost entirely by travel, which begins, in chronological terms, with his flight from the Nian rebels and then from the Taiping army as a child. In adulthood he traveled for family business or for livelihood, and during these travels the author would go on outings to local scenic spots. Thus *The World* is full of depictions of journeys within journeys. The other, more important, reason for using the figure of travel to conceptualize *The World* is the way in which the narration evokes a dream landscape that turns nightmarish with the narrator's experience of the Taiping Rebellion. The unfolding of *The World* is characterized by apparently free association, but underlying the stream-of-consciousness narration is a haunting recurrence of words, images, and motifs that serve as memory triggers, much like road signs in an intricate labyrinth. The recurrence of these words, images, and motifs mimics the way in which traumatic memory works. Finally, the generic hybridity of *The World*, in addition to its structural quirkiness, bespeaks the disorienting effect of trauma that poses a challenge to conventional narrative modes.[3]

Memory is subject to interference, even as one attempts to "fix" it in writing, for writing is likewise susceptible to changes in the environment. In the following pages, I will discuss the peculiar structure of *The World*, and conclude with a description of the afterlife of this work in the twentieth century, when the distortion of cultural memory resulted in further violence and trauma. Nowhere is the distortion embodied so clearly as in the ideology of textual preservation and transmission. It is fascinating to note that the only modern typeset edition of this late Qing manuscript is a small excerpt of the section on the author's childhood memories of the Taiping Rebellion, and yet, all of the macabre details involving the Taiping army have been cut out.

....

3   In her article "Chaos, Memory, and Genre: Anecdotal Recollections of the Taiping Rebellion," Rania Huntington argues that the form of *biji* ("miscellanies" or "random notes"), as a genre noted for "its brevity, miscellaneous content, and problematic relationship to history and fiction," is in a privileged position to give shape to memory, "particularly the memory of the anonymous third person," in accounts of the Taiping Rebellion. *Chinese Literature: Essays, Articles, Reviews* 27 (Dec. 2005): 61. Zhang Daye's memoir incorporates, among others, the *biji* type, but, in contrast to *biji*, it has an overarching narrative structure.

The Structure of Memory

The World of a Tiny Insect is a book of mourning and remembrance. It is about death, loss, fear, and violence; it is also about coming to terms with the painful memories of a traumatized childhood. Divided into three parts, it has a remarkable structure that mimics the workings of personal memory, especially traumatic memory, and invites the reader to directly participate in the process of remembering as well. Just as traumatic memory is the kind that keeps coming back in flashbacks and fragments, *The World* is characterized by its carefully constructed repetitions and fragmentation, fraught with macabre images, paranoia, and emotional excess. If fragmentation describes its episodic and anecdotal narrative style, then its repetitiousness is manifested both in content (e.g., journeys are repeated, and the same places are visited time and again) and in form, so that underneath its apparent desultoriness, we recognize a recurrence of narrative elements that keeps the book together as a whole.

As we see in the opening passage of the book cited earlier, the account begins with "a trip to Tiantai." By and by, the author reveals that he undertook the trip to pay his final respects to a deceased friend named Yuan Jichuan (1839–1893), though he also took the opportunity to visit people and sights along the way. The author's use of formal dating at the beginning of the day-to-day account of the trip, along with the allusion to the birth of the "world" and to the ripening of the bodhi fruit (a Buddhist symbol of spiritual enlightenment), endows the journey with a personal significance that transcends its immediate purpose.

Although he did visit Tiantai during the trip, it is worth noting that Zhang's destination was, as a matter of fact, the city of Shaoxing. To refer to his trip as "a trip to Tiantai" foregrounds the importance of Tiantai, which is both the name of a town in Zhejiang and that of a mountain range famous for its breathtaking scenery and as a major religious site of Buddhism and Daoism. But first and foremost, "a trip to Tiantai" evokes the story of Liu Chen and Ruan Zhao, which originated in the early fifth century and has been part of the Chinese cultural lore ever since.[4] In the

....

4   Liu Yiqing (403–444), *You ming lu* [Records of worlds of darkness and light], in *Han Wei liuchao biji xiaoshuo daguan* (Shanghai: Shanghai Guji Chubanshe, 1999), 697.

story, Liu Chen and Ruan Zhao, while picking herbs on Mount Tiantai, had a romantic encounter with two goddesses; they eventually left the human world for good and presumably became immortals themselves. In *The World*, however, the trip to Tiantai begins with an ominous occurrence. Almost as soon as Zhang and his travel companion embark on their journey, they encounter four sinister-looking men who share their ferry boat. "Two of them spoke with a Hu'nan accent, and looked like soldiers." Apprehensive that these men are up to no good, Zhang devises an elaborate plan to stay out of trouble. The account of the first two days of the journey ends with a sigh of relief for escaping potential danger.

There is no knowing whether the perceived threat was real or merely a psychological drama played out in our author's mind—as we shall see, he certainly had good reason for being paranoid. What matters here is the rhetorical function served by such an incident. Zhang and his fellow traveler are figured as the latter-day Liu Chen and Ruan Zhao, who, instead of meeting two beautiful goddesses, stumble upon four menacing strangers. Zhang also discovers that Tiantai, a mountain of otherworldly beauty, is now stationed with soldiers defending against "mountain bandits." When Zhang and his companions pass through the town of Tiantai, they have a run-in with a soldier that again threatens to turn deadly. The darkness of the modern situation represents an ironic reversal of the idyllic, if imaginary, past, and sets the tone for the entire book. The incongruity between past and present is reinforced by a story of thwarted desire on the third night of the journey, when Zhang's porter interrupts his dalliance with a local courtesan. This failed erotic venture with a small-town prostitute forms a further contrast with Liu Chen and Ruan Zhao's romantic encounter with goddesses, and highlights the author's description of his trip as a "trip to Tiantai" as a deliberate discursive choice.

The opening sections of *The World* thus contain several images and motifs that will recur throughout the book: the menace posed by strangers suspected of being bandits (*zei*); the hardship and perils of being on the road; the disappointing present as opposed to a romanticized but

....

For a complete English translation of Liu Chen and Ruan Zhao's story, see Karl S. Y. Kao, ed., *Classical Chinese Tales of the Supernatural and the Fantastic: Selections from the Third to the Tenth Century* (Bloomington: Indiana University Press, 1985), 137–39.

lost cultural past. The term *zei*, meaning "bandit" or "robber," consistently used to refer to the Taiping soldiers in the book, has a particular resonance. That two of the menacing men sharing their ferry boat speak with a Hu'nan accent and look like soldiers is another meaningful detail: the Xiang Army was organized from existing local militias of the Hu'nan region to suppress the Taiping Rebellion; it played a major role in crushing the rebellion, but also gained notoriety for slaughtering and pillaging the city of Nanjing, the capital of the Taiping Kingdom, after capturing it. The Xiang Army was largely disbanded after the Taiping Rebellion, and many of the former Xiang soldiers joined gangs. Thirty years after the Taiping Rebellion, society was still feeling its reverberations.

In the incident involving the local courtesan, Zhang notices a poem written on the wall after the courtesan has left. The first two couplets read,

> It's been thirty years since I last visited
>   this mountain road by the stream,
> Black dog, red sheep—
>   the world has changed.
> With a goblet of ale, I still like to invite people
>   to a game of "finger battle";
> And yet, even in the midst of chatting and laughing,
>   a war is raging in my heart. . . .

"Black dog," originally used to indicate the shifting shape of clouds, is a figure of change. "Red sheep calamity" (*hong yang jie*) refers to the catastrophe that was believed to befall a nation and its people in the *dingwei* year (the year of the sheep), which occurred every sixty years according to the sexagenarian cycle in the traditional Chinese calendrical system. Since the surnames of the two leaders of the Taiping Rebellion, Hong Xiuquan (1814–1864) and Yang Xiuqing (d. 1856), may appear in combination as "Hong/Yang" and thus pun with "red sheep" (*hong yang*) in Chinese, the Taiping Rebellion was also known as the "Hong Yang Calamity." "Finger battle" is a drinking game, while "a war in the heart" is a metaphor for concerns weighing heavily on one's mind.

The trip to Tiantai in many ways serves as a powerful memory trigger for Zhang: along with the word "bandits", phrases such as "red sheep," "finger battle," and "a war in the heart," as well as images of soldiers and ex-soldiers, work like prompts that evoke memories of violence and death, and prepare the way for part 2 of the book, in which Zhang recalls his childhood experience during the Taiping Rebellion. Even the first couplet of the poem on the wall echoes his circumstances uncannily, for by the time he undertook the trip, it had been thirty years since the Rebellion.

At Tiantai, Zhang visited several Buddhist temples, and stayed at the Temple of True Awareness for two nights. He describes his late-night reflection on life and death, as well as a conversation with the abbot at the temple. In traditional Chinese poetry, temple visits are always depicted in an enlightenment narrative, with the poet's physical progress toward a Buddhist temple, usually one located in the mountains, configured as a metaphor of spiritual progress. Significantly, in the poem composed and presented to the abbot before his departure, Zhang begins with a comment on memory: "Shadow matters, dusty past: my memory has grown hazy." And yet his book is nothing but a record of memory. "But what is it to remember?" asks Paul Ricoeur. "It is not just to recall certain isolated events, but to be capable of forming meaningful sequences and ordered connections. In short, it is to be able to constitute one's own experience in the form of a story where a memory as such is only a fragment of the story."[5] To remember is to sort out; to write down one's remembrance is to make sense of one's life and exorcize the demons that impede one's spiritual progress. In *The World*, "memory as such" is woven into a large tapestry that is the author's life, which in turn is set against the larger background of national events and dynastic fate. The life story of the author, and national history, are thus the two grand narratives that, as double frames, help the author process his micro-memories, especially those from his childhood.

The day-to-day narration of the trip concludes with Zhang's expression of a desire to retire to a quiet life at Tiantai. Then the author turns to an account of the local customs of the Taizhou Prefecture, of which Tiantai was one of the six counties. The account is interspersed with melancholic anecdotes and poetry. One anecdote, for instance, relates the strange profession the author encounters at a ferry, where the boatmen

....

5   Paul Ricoeur, *Hermeneutics and the Human Sciences: Essays on Language, Action, and Interpretation* (New York: Cambridge University Press, 1981), 153.

have hired a woman who is good at crying and lamenting to maintain peace among the contentious ferry passengers. The last passage of part 1 describes two kinds of birds in the mountains of Xianju, another of the six counties of Taizhou. Each bird, according to local legend, had been transformed from a girl who had died a tragic death. Part 1 ends with the following remark: "When those birds cried on a clear and quiet night, it nearly broke my heart." The crying of the woman on the ferry boat and the crying of the birds echo each other; the birds also evoke the two menacing strangers from Xianju at the beginning of part 1, "whose dialect sounded like bird talk." Such verbal resonance contributes to a network of elegiac but also violent imageries that haunt the book.

Part 2 forms the centerpiece of the book. The main body of this section is an autobiographical account that begins with Zhang's birth and then focuses on the years between 1861 and 1863, when he and his mother fled Shaoxing and sought refuge in various places in Zhejiang. This section opens by picking up where part 1 leaves off, reiterating the author's decision to move to Tiantai and live out his life in reclusion. At this point, he reveals that he has turned forty, the age of "having no doubts" according to the *Analects*. This may be considered the Confucian counterpart of the Buddhist metaphor of ripening bodhi fruit mentioned in part 1, once again underscoring the book as the product of an important turning point in the author's life. Indeed, in the late nineteenth century, when the average life expectancy for men in China did not exceed forty,[6] turning forty might very well seem tantamount to confronting the finitude of life face-to-face, and feeling compelled to find meaning and coherence in one's experience. And yet, "to be capable of forming meaningful sequences and ordered connections" requires the intervention of time. The temporal distance of thirty years enables the author of *The World* to adopt a new perspective, gained from age and maturation, on his troubled childhood. In many ways, as we will see, it also enables the author to understand the meaning of an earlier event, in a case of what psychologists term "deferred action," in which an earlier event obtains traumatic power over the author as he recalls it. In such a

....

6   For data on average life expectancy for men in China in the nineteenth century, see William Lavely and R. Bin Wong, "Revising the Malthusian Narrative: The Comparative Study of Population Dynamics in Late Imperial China," *Journal of Asian Studies* 57, no. 3 (Aug. 1998): 714–48.

case, writing the earlier event down is an act of conjuring up and exorcizing the demon at the same time.

Part 3 of the book continues the autobiographical account, and turns from the Taiping Rebellion to the contemporaneous Nian Uprising. Zhang was a teenage boy living with his father at Yuanjiang (modern Huai'an, Jiangsu) when a major leader of the Nian army, formerly a Taiping general, attacked the city; Zhang witnessed the defense of Yuanjiang firsthand. It was also at Yuanjiang that he first learned to write poetry. He recalls with some irony how his father dismissed poetry as useless and instructed him to read the political writings of two former statesmen instead:

> I respectfully retired and read them, and henceforth my actions went against the times, until I find myself in serious straits today. Although I am despised by the world, I suppose I will be able to face my father in the underworld one day and tell him that I have not greatly disobeyed him.
>
> After my father passed away, my family's financial situation became increasingly stressed, so I began to travel for my livelihood.

Part 3 subsequently focuses on those travels. At one point, Zhang compares himself to a donkey marching around and around a millstone, covering a great deal of ground but never going beyond its narrow confines. With this self-mocking simile, he brings the narrative full circle in the following pages, recounting his journey to Xianju in 1887 to take up a post, where he struck up a friendship with a local sheriff named Yuan Jichuan. Yuan had played a key role in defending Xianju against the attack of bandits in 1883, and the last section of part 3 is devoted to a discussion of the problem of bandits, both at Xianju and in general. The book ends with a discourse on the difficulty of governance.

The most striking feature of the last sections of part 3 is their constant echoing of the opening sections of the book. The book begins with a trip to Shaoxing, with a stop at Tiantai; it closes with a trip to Xianju, again with a stop at Tiantai. The trip in part 1 ends with Zhang's expression of a desire to retire to Tiantai; in part 3 we are told that he had first entertained such an idea during his trip to Xianju. For each trip he had hired a native of Tiantai as his porter, and in each case the porter turned out to be a delightful travel companion. The purpose of Zhang's trip in part 1 was to pay final respects to the deceased Yuan Jichuan; the highlight of his sojourn at Xianju in part 3 was his friendship with Yuan. While part 1 gives a brief sketch of Yuan's life, part 3 recasts the biography in a long poem. An obsessive concern about the problem of "bandits" in part 3 resonates with both part 1 and part 2; indeed, it is a prominent motif throughout the book, demonstrating the long-lasting effect of Zhang's childhood trauma.

The cycle of continuous return, so to speak, does foreground change. One remarkable incident that takes place during Zhang's sojourn at Xianju involves his seeing the dancing corpse of an executed "bandit" outside the city gate, which so shocks and frightens him that he flees for his life. This forms a sharp contrast with the anecdotes narrated in part 2, in which Zhang as a child feels no fear when coming into close contact with dead bodies. Indeed, Zhang himself comments with wonder on his earlier fearlessness. Maturity is measured by the advent of fear in the face of death, a fear compounded with, and intensified by, pity. It is also an allegory of the belatedness of trauma.

The reverberations in part 3 create a curious rhetorical effect for the reader. When relating his journey to Xianju, Zhang gives a thorough description of the places he passed through, and the reader recognizes these places to be the same as those visited on his trip in part 1. With this realization, seemingly casual remarks made in part 3 take on significance in the narrative context of Zhang's life. To offer one particularly striking instance: he mentions that he planned to visit Guoqing Temple on Mount Tiantai but was unable to do so. This leads us back to part 1, in which Zhang tells us that on May 25, 1893, he (finally) toured Guoqing Temple in the rain. A monk acted as his guide, but the temple was under renovation: "Many craftsmen were working in the temple, and there was nothing really worth seeing. The former sacrificial hall for Fenggan had been converted into the Hall of Three Saints, including, besides Fenggan, the pair Hanshan and Shide. Its decor was not particularly attractive either."

This is decidedly an anticlimax, but it is an anticlimax in retrospect that occurs at the very beginning of the narrative. The reappearance of Guoqing Temple near the end of the book makes the reader pause and recall its earlier mention. Compelled to "look back" in terms of the chronology of reading to a "future" in terms of the author's lived time, the reader is jolted out of the linear progression of the narrative and, like the author himself, undertakes a journey in remembrance. If trauma has been compared to haunting—that is, the dead refuse to stay buried, then *The World* is not only haunted but also reproduces the effect of haunting on the reader, who strives to grasp the specter of a vaguely familiar name.

Writing Trauma

As we have seen, *The World* structurally mimics the contour of memory: often triggered by accidental happenings and images, memory is evoked by free associations and works in a stream-of-consciousness manner; it does not necessarily observe chronological order but presents events clustering around a topic. The structure of the book mimics traumatic memory in particular. Rather than an event that simply happened in the past, a traumatic event cannot be localized in one specific time and place, because it keeps coming back to those who are traumatized. As many researchers working on trauma recognize, there is a belatedness not only in the manifestation of the effect of the traumatic event but also in the very experience of the traumatic event itself. In many ways, trauma is a form of memory because it always exists only as memory; and writing trauma, as Dominick LaCapra puts it, "involves processes of acting out, working over, and to some extent working through in analyzing and 'giving voice' to the past."[7]

Zhang frequently comments, with a sense of wonder, on how he had known no fear when he was a child. This seems to testify to the Freudian concept of deferred action, as the occurrence of trauma is displaced to a much later point in time than the moment of the occasioning event. In one instance, Zhang eagerly went to watch a battle between the Taiping army and the local militia, a situation from which adults would most likely have stayed away. After the battle was over, he poked around the dead bodies, and went from a passive observer to an active participant, even reproducing the violence he had just witnessed by kicking and trampling those Taiping soldiers who "were not quite dead yet," and who to the little boy were the bad guys fully deserving such treatment. As he

....

7   Dominick LaCapra, *Writing History, Writing Trauma* (Baltimore, MD: Johns Hopkins University Press, 2001), 186.

observes his former self's observation of the battlefield scene, the distance between the little boy and the forty-year-old author writing the account is psychological as well as temporal. Looking back, the latter both identifies with the boy and feels alienated from him. In many ways, this is an allegory of the difference between the author of the text and the autographical subject. As the critic Leigh Gilmore says in *The Limits of Autobiography*, "The autobiographical 'I' is not the self in any simple way, it is necessarily its rhetorical surrogate."[8]

In arguing for the possibility of memory falsification due to heavy emotional investment, David Henige states in *Oral Historiography*, "Facts and events may be remembered but the attitudes we had toward them at the time may have been forgotten and replaced by new viewpoints."[9] "Facts and events," however, may very well have been "replaced" by new versions as well, especially when these "facts and events" are being represented in *their* rhetorical surrogates. The narration of the battle scene is in a straightforward style that shows a good literary education but is not overtly embellished in any way; but the battle cry of the Taiping rider—"Good brothers, charge, kill! Be careful! If we fail, we die. Charge, kill, good brothers!"—is represented in vernacular Chinese. Forming a startling contrast with its framing narrative, written in Literary Chinese, it shows the rhetorical self-consciousness of the author.

In one of the most grisly accounts of violence, Zhang again goes beyond being a mere observer:

> I once saw a woman at Lu's Dike who came with several bandits from the east. They were laughing and joking with one another, and seemed quite jolly. Then suddenly she said, "Dong Er, you heartless man!" One bandit asked, "What do you mean?" The woman laughingly dumped on him. In a fit of anger, the bandit drew out his sword. The woman said with a chortle, "Why, just try and kill me!" Even before she finished her words, he cut off her arm. The bandits were still laughing as the arm was severed. Then they took off her clothes, exposed her breasts, cut them off, and threw them away. Still laughing aloud, they left. I went

....

8   Leigh Gilmore, *The Limits of Autobiography: Trauma and Testimony* (Ithaca, NY: Cornell University Press, 2001), 88.

9   David P. Henige, *Oral Historiography* (New York: Longman, 1982), 110.

over to look at the breasts: they were covered with blood, and inside they were filled with something of a pale red color like pomegranate seeds. I picked one up to take a closer look, and it seemed to be quivering in my hand. I was seized with a great terror and went home.

In a brutal reaction against the woman's attempt to domesticate the man by treating him as a "normal" person and a "normal" lover, the men not only dehumanize the woman by dismembering her but also desexualize her by cutting off her breasts. The passage is notable for the five mentions of laughter, which intensify the horror of the crime. What is most striking about the account turns out to be the response of the little boy: he is drawn to the mutilated woman by the same impulse that led him to scrutinize the dead men wrapped in banners, and once again he cannot help poking and touching, as a young child is wont to do. His curious examination of the dying woman produces a macabre close-up represented in a shocking verbal image: a severed breast that looks like an opened pomegranate. Even more than the plain narration of the act of violence itself, this visual detail, rare in the classical Chinese tradition, captures the terror of the incident. Seen through the eyes of a child, the scene is further mediated, and intensified, by the memory of the adult that enables the image to take on its full traumatic power across the abyss of time. This is best demonstrated by the author's reference to the pomegranate, a fruit of numerous seeds that symbolizes fertility in Chinese culture ("seed," *zi*, puns with "son," *zi*); on a more literary level, "a pomegranate[-colored] skirt" (*shiliu qun*), an old poetic phrase, is a conventional metonym for a woman. By zooming in on the severed breast, which through the use of the image of a pomegranate takes on a synecdochic quality, the narrative textually mimics the fragmentation of the woman's body and the destruction of her humanity, and induces the reader to personally experience the traumatic nature of the incident by bringing her face-to-face with the horrific picture. The representation of the incident thus focuses squarely on the terror of the boy rather than on the pain of the woman;[10] and yet the woman's physical wounds are

....

10   For a discussion of the experience of pain of the female body at the turn of the twentieth century, see Dorothy Ko, "The Subject of Pain," in *Dynastic Crisis and Cultural Innovation*, ed. David Der-wei Wang and Shang Wei (Cambridge, MA: Harvard Asia Center, 2005), 478–503.

nonetheless kept open in the little boy's psychological wound that leads to the compulsory textual replication of the mutilation.

Zhang's ensuing comment on the fickleness and cruelty of the rebels, though seemingly falling short of the complicated, entangled significations of sex and violence of the happening, represents an attempt to make sense of the senseless brutality. The same gesture at healing, long after the victims of the physical violence were dead, continues through the remembrance, as in the anecdote about the two Feng brothers. One of the brothers, Feng Zhiying, joins the Taiping army and is executed for some offense; his head is hung on a pole, and the other brother, Feng Zhihua, proceeds to steal the head to give it a proper burial. Zhang goes along with him and witnesses a scene as ghastly as it is poignant. As the brother burst into tears, he "wept too, not quite understanding where *my* tears had come from." Once again Zhang observes, with a sense of detachment and wonder, the child's lack of comprehension of his own emotional response to what happened. The comment he makes—"It broke one's heart to see brothers separated by death like that"—furnishes a belated explanation of his reaction, but the significance of the explanation lies outside of the immediate, literal implication of its content, for the *endeavor* to understand "what happened" matters more than any interpretation the adult comes up with.

In dealing with an autobiographical account relating traumatic experience, one common question posed by the reader is that of veracity. Oftentimes the initial impulse is to ask, "Did this truly happen?" Such a question, though understandable, may be essentially misplaced. The self represented in an autobiographical account is, first and foremost, a self constructed in language. Verbal habits, rhetorical conventions, and literary tropes all intervene in the process and contribute to the composition of the autobiographical subject, especially in the case of a well-educated author, such as the author of *The World*.

The self in the text is, furthermore, conjured up from the past, and in Zhang Daye's case, from when he was a little child. Early childhood memory, instead of a fixed object, should perhaps be viewed as a complicated process developed over time and vulnerable to the interference of many external and internal factors. Citing Pierre Janet, the influential French psychiatric theorist, psychologist Bruce Moss describes how "accurate personal memory retention" can be especially problematic with young children because "memory functioning demands the ability to deal with mental events at a level of some complexity." When experiencing a complicated event that a child lacks the mental sophistication to understand, she or he will have trouble articulating the event, just as "we do not know how to make a veridical post-dream recitation because we are simply unable to encode and construct our dream experiences into satisfactory narratives."[11] In *The World*, sometimes traces of the past are retained, just like fragmented dream images, but the adult self writing the text needs considerable resources—the knowledge, for instance, of "what was going on" at the time of the event, acquired long after the event was over—to weave the images into a satisfactory narrative. In such a case, the "veracity" of a remembered event becomes an intricate matter.

One of the earliest of Zhang Daye's memories of violence furnishes a good example. This incident took place when he, his mother, and several other female family members were staying in a village near Shaoxing, hiding from the Taiping soldiers, in the winter months of 1861.

> There was a Mr. Meng, who was a doctor from the city [i.e., Shaoxing].
> He brought with him his wife and a three-year-old son. One day, as
> we were hiding together, it rained, and the boy started to cry. An old
> woman holding prayer beads and reciting the Buddha's name detested
> the boy, for she was convinced that his cries would lead the bandits
> to us. She kept muttering about it while reciting the Buddha's name.
> Thereupon Mr. Meng tore the boy apart and killed him with his own
> hands. My grandfather's concubine tried to snatch the boy from him
> but failed; she was so shocked and distressed that she burst into tears.
> I was still very young, and had no idea what it was all about; I only
> remember seeing guts spilling out and blood flowing all over the place,
> and I was trembling with fright.

This account gives one pause, as one wonders what exactly is implied in the statement that the father "tore the boy apart and killed him with his own hands." A Holocaust survivor, who was very young while in Auschwitz, "did not actually remember some of the stories he was telling

....

11   Bruce M. Moss, *Remembering the Personal Past: Descriptions of Autobiographical Memory* (Oxford: Oxford University Press, 1991), 147.

but learned them from his fellow survivors."[12] One wonders if Zhang had similarly learned this story from one of the family members who were with him then, such as his grandmother. Nevertheless, although he stresses his lack of comprehension of the event at the time of its happening, much like in the other instances cited above, the image of "guts spilling out and blood flowing all over the place" seems stuck in his mind.

Speaking of the instability of memory in psychotherapy, Donald Spence writes,

> More than realized, the past is continuously being reconstructed in the analytic process, influenced by (a) the repressed contents of consciousness; (b) subsequent happenings that are similar in form or content; (c) the words used by the analyst in eliciting and commenting on the early memories as they emerge; and (d) the language choices made by the patient as he tries to put his experience into words. The past, always in flux, is always being created anew."[13]

Perhaps Zhang conflates that initial experience of violence with the blood and spilled guts he saw so often afterward; perhaps a family member's memory was narrated to him when he was younger and became embedded in his own memory. This account of the death of a little boy, supposedly taking place right in front of another little boy, seems to me to exemplify some of the essential aspects of trauma writing. Like the scene of the mutilation of the nameless woman, the image of guts and blood is a textual reenactment of the physical dismemberment and depersonalization of the child; incomprehensible and nightmarish, it keeps coming back to the author until he does his share to give voice to the muted boy. To verbalize this image is to give it a stable place in a narrative that makes sense of the senseless violence, to "keep it down," and to exorcize an elusive flashback that defies conscious recall or control. Insomuch as the image takes on a symbolic significance in terms of embodying the author's experience during the Taiping Rebellion, its

....

12   Henry Krystal, "Trauma and Aging: A Thirty-Year Follow-Up." In *Trauma: Explorations in Memory*, ed. Catherine Caruth (Baltimore, MD: Johns Hopkins University Press, 1995), 92.

13   Donald R. Spence, *Narrative Truth and Historical Truth: Meaning and Interpretation in Psychoanalysis* (New York: W. W. Norton, 1982), 93.

"psychical reality" is just as important as the "practical reality,"[14] and the venue through which the adult author "remembers" the incident hardly matters in this case.

Zhang not only witnessed violence done to people around him but also lived through many direct threats to his life during the two years on the run. Some of the dangerous situations in which he and his companions found themselves were compounded by macabre scenes. Once, during their flight on water, they were forced to turn back because the river was completely blocked by dead bodies. "There was an accumulation of white 'corpse wax' that was several inches thick. Maggots crawled into our boat and in an instant were everywhere. The stinky smell made us so sick that we thought we were about to die."[15] The visual image of death and the odor of decay were no less traumatizing than physical danger, of which there was no dearth.

By Catherine Caruth's definition, "trauma describes an overwhelming experience of sudden, catastrophic events, in which the response to the event occurs in the often delayed, and uncontrolled repetitive occurrence of hallucinations and other intrusive phenomena."[16] While this accurately describes one dimension of Zhang Daye's experience, the horrors of the Taiping Rebellion were also intimately bound up with the whole experience of growing up, with the simple pleasures of childhood and the mundane business of daily life. The rebellion became interwoven with the very texture of his existence, in terms of the long duration of the violence he experienced and its intensified effect on him at a particularly impressionable age. It is therefore very difficult to delimit the scope of trauma in his case.

Some pleasures, like pains, become such only in retrospect. Zhang relates how, trying to pick persimmons when hiding in the hills, he fell from the tree and hurt himself badly. "Thinking back," he writes, "I find it all very funny now." Other pleasures, however, turn into nightmares in

....

14   Sigmund Freud, *On the History of the Psycho-Analytic Movement* (New York: W. W. Norton, 1966), 16.
15   Corpse wax, also known as grave wax, mortuary wax, or adipocere, is a waxlike fatty substance that forms during the decomposition of corpses due to moisture.
16   Catherine Caruth, *Unclaimed Experience: Trauma, Narrative, and History* (Baltimore, MD: Johns Hopkins University Press, 1996), 11.

reminiscence. He recalls playing in a temple dedicated to the Ten Kings of Hell:

> I remember the statues and colored murals in the temple as being stunningly beautiful. There was a statue of a Wuchang demon that held an iron shackle to put around a person's neck. I was scared at first, but eventually got used to it. One day, I went there with some other children, and we saw the body of someone killed by the bandits. Together we lifted the dead man up and tried to get his neck through the shackle. The corpse was heavy, and fell flat on its back; the demon statue fell with it. We all laughed aloud, and then we started beating its legs. How naughty we were! I have no idea why I was not frightened.

It is not immediately clear whether the children were beating the legs of the corpse or those of the demon statue. In either case, it is a show of bravado that serves to exorcize fear and affirm the powerlessness of the corpse/statue despite its frightening appearance. Although in this case it is just a bunch of mischievous boys rather than cruel adult men, their laughter reminds the reader, in an oblique way, of the Taiping soldiers' laughter when they mutilated the nameless woman: it signifies a release of tension, a camouflage of the inner sense of horror at the aggressive absence of humanity. In some ways, the image of children reenacting an act of violence in a setting of death brings out the traumatic nature of the author's experience even more forcefully than any of those bloody incidents or macabre scenes, precisely because of the juxtaposition of child's play and a dead body, all surrounded by visual representations of hell.

The child's perspective, as mentioned earlier, is one of the things that make *The World* unique among accounts of the Taiping Rebellion. While the child observed a grand historical event on a reduced scale due to physical and mental limitations, he also had a rare point of view, both on a metaphorical and on a literal level, precisely because he was able to, as a young boy, "go up and down the cloudy peaks and climb the treetops, as agile and fast as a monkey." The book contains a remarkable eyewitness account of the Taiping army's well-known capture of Bao Village from a unique viewpoint. Bao Village of Zhejiang was where the local resistance to the Taiping army was the fiercest, lasting about eight months. According to *The Draft of Qing History* (*Qing shi gao*), when Bao Village fell, more than six hundred thousand people were killed, including numerous wealthy families from other parts of Zhejiang who sought refuge there.[17] But in the gaze of the child from the top of a mountain, the Taiping soldiers taking the road under the peak advanced "like ants," and Bao Village itself was "only about as big as a dinner plate":

> when it was taken, cannons were blasting off, but one could hear only a vague sound and see a thin strand of dark smoke. Tens of thousands of people sank into oblivion in an instant. I suppose Snow Shadow Peak is no more than two thousand meters high and about twenty leagues from Bao Village. If it had been higher, one would not have been able to see even the dark smoke. In one tiny speck, numerous tiny specks vanish; in numerous tiny specks, one tiny speck disappears. And yet, human beings continue to dream their great dream, and none wakes up from it. From past to present they have always been busy distinguishing favor from disfavor and gains from losses, harming and murdering one another. What ignorance! I turn around and see the mountain flowers in bright red blossoms as if they were smiling; the realm of happiness in nature and that of suffering in the human world are as far apart as clouds and ravines. As I look up at the blue sky, the white sun is shining forth with a dazzling light. It is all very sad.

In this passage the juxtaposition of two perspectives, child/past and adult/present, creates a curious effect: the tragedy of Bao Village, while spatially removed, seems to be very much present in temporal terms, demonstrating the eternal return of a traumatic event.

Throughout the book we find numerous lyrical descriptions of the haunting beauty of Zhejiang and Jiangsu's landscape. As Zhang observes in the passage cited above, "The realm of happiness in nature and that of suffering in the human world are as far apart as clouds and ravines." But when the two realms are placed side by side, a powerful effect is created: nature's beauty, even with its magnificent indifference to human suffering, takes on an elegiac aura. Zhang was, like every member of the Chi-

....

17   Zhao Erxun et al., eds., *Qing shi gao* [The draft of Qing history] (Taipei: Dingwen Chubanshe, 1981), 493.13654.

nese scholar elite, familiar with the Tang poet Du Fu's (712–770) poetry, and Du Fu's famous lines, written when the great poet was trapped in the capital behind enemy lines during the An Lushan Rebellion in 755, come to mind: "A kingdom smashed, its hills and rivers still here, spring in the city, plants and trees grow deep."[18] The cultural splendor of the capital of the Tang empire is vanishing all too quickly into the verdure of spring that threatens to turn the metropolis into a primeval, undifferentiated jungle. The eternal return of spring is both a comfort to the inconsolable poet and an ironic reminder of the ephemeralness of political order and human civilization.

With its loving depiction of the southern landscape, *The World* is written in the long tradition of premodern Chinese travel writings. The day-to-day account of Zhang's "trip to Tiantai" in part 1 can be traced back to Li Ao's (772–836 or –841) *Lai nan lu* (Diary of my coming to the south) from 809, the first travel diary in the Chinese literary tradition;[19] the composition of poetry upon encountering a scenic site is also well in keeping with cultural conventions. And yet, with its fragmentation and flashbacks of a remembered landscape as lyrical as it is nightmarish, as elegiac as it is violent, *The World* also stands at the nascence of the modern Chinese literary tradition: its immediate descendants are Shen Congwen's (1902–1988) *Congwen zizhuan* (Congwen's autobiography) and *Xiang xing san ji* (Miscellaneous sketches of travels to western Hu'nan), and its later successor is Gao Xingjian's (1940–) *Ling shan* (Soul mountain). The figure of the traveler is central in all of these accounts, and the landscape, with its astounding natural beauty and uncanny, often violent happenings, is as interior as exterior, much like in *The World*. Although far apart in history, these modern accounts eventually hark back, with profound differences highlighted by their similarities, to the great early medieval Chinese traveler and the "founding father of Chinese landscape poetry," Xie Lingyun (385–433), whose exile in Yongjia (Wenzhou of Zhejiang) produced luminary poems in which he seeks

. . . .

18   The poem is titled "Chun wang" (The view in spring). Stephen Owen's translation, in Owen, ed. and trans., *An Anthology of Chinese Literature: Beginnings to 1911* (New York: W. W. Norton, 1996), 420.

19   Translated by Richard E. Strassberg in *Inscribed Landscapes: Travel Writings from Imperial China* (Berkeley: University of California Press, 1994), 127–31.

meaning in a landscape that is as textual as it is physical.[20] Thus both looking back and looking forward, *The World* provides a link between the cultural past and modern times, with its cartography of trauma and of an aesthetic pleasure that is infinitely complicated by the recognition of social ills and human suffering.

The author of *The World* often whimsically refers to "the mountain god" or "the mountain spirit." Although he never earnestly believed that gods and spirits possessed the ability to confer blessings on human beings, laughing as he did at the old women praying to "mere statues made of mud" at a local temple, he was open-minded to the existence of forces beyond human comprehension, marveling at the strange happenings during the years of chaos. But ultimately he was preoccupied not so much with the supernatural as with the metaphysical dimension of Buddhism and Daoism, and the spiritual influence of both traditions is manifested in his preface and throughout the book itself. While the discourse on governance at the end of part 3 falls well within the sphere of what would be termed "Confucian," it is quite clear that the author finds consolation for his inner turmoil in Buddhist and Daoist doctrines, as can be seen in, among other episodes, his conversation with Abbot Minxi on the Tiantai Mountains and with the old Daoist priest on Weiyu Mountain in part 1. Zhang's travels might not have been compelled by a modern man's conscious search for the self, but they are permeated by a sense of spiritual restlessness and a mournful mood that characterize the particular historical moment he inhabited.

The Afterlife of the Manuscript

The human brain has one hundred billion neurons, and recording a memory requires adjusting the connections between neurons. Neurons send messages to one another across narrow gaps called synapses. While short-term memory involves relatively simple chemical changes to the synapses, long-term memories require neurons to produce new protein and expand the synapses to transform short-term memory into a mem-

....

20   Interested readers may refer to the chapter on Xie Lingyun in Xiaofei Tian, *Visionary Journeys: Travel Writings from Early Medieval and Nineteenth-Century China* (Cambridge, MA: Harvard Asia Center, 2011): 119–41.

ory that lasts days, months, or years. Neuroscientists have long believed that once a memory is built, its content becomes stabilized. The memory is, in their terms, "consolidated," and cannot easily be undone. Recently, however, researchers proposed a new theory about how memory works. To put it simply, every time a memory is being recalled, it involves building protein at the synapse, and the memory has to be re-formed in a process known as reconsolidation. The point is that memory becomes unstable every time it is recalled. This theory about memory finds resonance in the work of psychologists, who maintain that every time one retells a memory, the memory is subject to whatever is in one's immediate environment.

The work on memory in the field of neuroscience offers an excellent counterpart to the issue of memory regarding the text of *The World*. Memory is always in flux; when a memory is committed to paper, it is a form of consolidation. But writing itself goes through metamorphosis in response to changes in the external circumstances: it is changed in textual transmission through copying, excerpting, editing, anthologizing, and printing; ultimately it is also changed in the act of reading.

The large amount of material about the Taiping Rebellion that survives was, as Rania Huntington observes, due in part to the publishing boom in the last quarter of the nineteenth century in conjunction with "the rise of the periodical press and the impact of Western-style publishing houses."[21] *The World*, however, has survived only in manuscript copies. In the photo-reprinted version of the only complete copy that is still extant, a brief editorial preface describes it as a draft version copied out in the author's own hand. The handwriting, however, seems to be in diverse styles, and some marginal notes were clearly written by someone other than the author himself.[22]

....

21 Huntington, "Chaos, Memory, and Genre," 63.

22 One marginal note, for instance, correctly points out an erroneous character in the text. See Zhang, *Weichong shijie*, 116. This does not discredit the assumption that the version was copied in the author's own hand, since there are changes made to the text that could have only come from the author. It does seem to indicate that the author had copied out the text from an earlier draft, since an error caused by a similar graph is one of the typical copyist errors; alternatively, the manuscript might have been copied out by different people, including the author himself, as suggested by the difference in handwriting styles.

In the early 1950s, a manuscript copy of part 2 of the book was donated from a personal collection to the Third Branch of the Institute of History, also known as the Institute of Modern History, then at Chinese Academy of Sciences (CAS).[23] Later on, a very small excerpt from this copy was printed in *Modern History Materials* (*Jindaishi ziliao*), a series of publications of late Qing and early Republican historical sources put out by CAS. As far as I know, this is the only time that a part of *The World* appears in a punctuated, modern typeset edition, even though it is but a fragment of a fragment of the original. Subsequently, the manuscript copy of part 2 has, to all appearances, been lost.

The survival of *The World* in manuscript copies bespeaks the importance of manuscript tradition even on the verge of the revolution in printing, as many late Qing texts have never been published and still exist solely in manuscript form; it also situates this text squarely in a local, rather than national, setting. According to the editors' note to the excerpt in *Modern History Materials*, the manuscript copy kept by the Institute of Modern History at CAS had been donated by a Mr. Wang Yongyuan of Zhejiang Normal University.[24] The identity of Wang Yongyuan is otherwise unknown, but one can clearly see the local connection here. Not only is the content of *The World* characterized by its local flavor, but the circulation of the text itself also seems to be a largely local phenomenon, though a copy eventually found its way to Taiwan. When copying a manuscript, people tend to choose those parts that interest them the most rather than reproducing the text in its entirety. It should come as no surprise that part 2, with its sensational details about the Taiping Rebellion, might have been most often copied by people who came upon the manuscript.

Like personal memory, cultural memory also has gaps, suppressions, and distortions. If a reader in the early twentieth century might have singled out for copying the part of the work containing the most macabre details, then the printing of the excerpt of *The World* in mainland China

....

23 The Institute of History was later placed under the aegis of Chinese Academy of Social Sciences (CASS).

24 Zhang, *Weichong shijie jielu* [Excerpt from *Weichong shijie*], in *Jindaishi ziliao* [Modern history materials], no. 3, ed. Zhongguo kexue yuan lishi yanjiusuo disansuo [The Third Branch of the Institute of History at CAS] (Beijing: Kexue Chubanshe, 1955), 87.

shortly after the establishment of the People's Republic follows a very different principle. The Taiping Rebellion, commended for its "revolutionary" nature, had to be presented in the best possible ideological light. What this means is that, while the excerpt in *Modern History Materials* includes damaging reports about the government troops, the foreign forces, and the Shorthairs, it excises all of the violent details that reflect negatively on the Taiping soldiers. Instead, the editors' note stresses "the great discipline of the Taiping army" glimpsed in *The World*.[25] In this context, it is easy to understand the fragmentation of the incident about the Feng brothers in the excerpt: while the part about Feng Zhiying joining the Taiping army and then being beheaded for some offense remains, the part about his brother stealing his head, with its terror and pathos, is left out.

The editors also observe, "The work records many trivial family matters that have no value as historical material. They have all been expunged."[26] In addition to the warning that the author of *The World* "belonged to the landlord class" and that the reader must therefore beware of his "unrestrained slandering of the Taiping Heavenly Kingdom," disdain for the "trifles" of an ordinary person's family life is another editorial principle that characterizes Chinese historical studies in the 1950s. And yet, it is precisely the unpretentious account of Zhang's personal experience that, among other things, makes this work valuable, perhaps all the more so in the case of an author who was, instead of a prominent member of the literati or an important statesman, just a "tiny insect," for it enables us to see history from the perspective of someone who was, though not exactly "everyman," in some ways not untypical of the scholar elite in late-nineteenth-century China.

The World was written at the time when China had suffered defeat in the Sino-Japanese War of 1894–95 and was on the verge of great change. It was also around this time that accounts of violence and trauma during the Manchu Qing conquest of China, which first entered print in the second quarter of the nineteenth century, were being reprinted in multiple editions, creating what Peter Zarrow describes as "secondary memories"

. . . .

25　Ibid.

26　Ibid.

and "secondary experience of trauma," and inciting anti-Manchuism.[27] These accounts include the famous *Account of Ten Days in Yangzhou* and *Account of the Jiading Massacres*.[28] The author of *The World* might have read them; but if so, they certainly did not inspire any nationalistic sentiments in him. He was not a radical revolutionary; his concern was primarily with the local, not the national. Compared with *A Record of Life beyond My Due*, a seventeenth-century account of the author's traumatic experience in the Qing conquest that uses the Confucian virtue of filial piety as a narrative frame and the means of "working through," *The World* focuses on individual sentiments and values rather than the familial, even though Zhang's passionate interest in the problem of "bandits" and the issue of good governance betrays a sense of "survivor's mission" centering on social action.[29] Such a focus might have seemed too narrow to the PRC historians of the 1950s, but Zhang's perspective is both uniquely his own and, in many ways, perhaps not unrepresentative of a large portion of the Chinese population at the turn of the twentieth century.

If the shocking particulars of the civil war through the eyes of a child might have been the very reason why a reader had singled out part 2 of *The World* for copying, then the excision of all of the violent or "trivial" details in *Modern History Materials* demonstrates even more clearly that each version of a text of remembrance is literally a memory that remains

....

27 See Peter Zarrow, "Historical Trauma: Anti-Manchuism and Memories of Atrocity in Late Qing China," *History and Memory* 16, no. 2 (2004): 78, 74.

28 For bibliographical information on these two accounts, see Lynn A. Struve, *The Ming-Qing Conflict, 1619–1683: A Historiography and Source Guide*, Association for Asian Studies Monograph no. 56 (1998), 242–43, 251. For essays about literature, trauma, and memory during the Qing conquest, see Wilt Idema, Wai-yee Li, and Ellen Widmer, eds., *Trauma and Transcendence in Early Qing Literature* (Cambridge, MA: Harvard Asia Center, 2006).

29 Written by Zhang Maozi, *A Record of Life beyond My Due (Yusheng lu)* was translated into English by Lynn A. Struve and included in the *Hawai'i Reader in Traditional Chinese Culture*, ed. Victor H. Mair, Nancy S. Steinhardt, and Paul R. Goldin (Honolulu: University of Hawai'i Press, 2005), 531–38. For an insightful discussion of this work, see Lynn A. Struve, "Confucian PTSD: Reading Trauma in a Chinese Youngster's Memoir of 1653," in *History and Memory* 16, no. 2 (2004): 14–31. Identifying a "survivor's mission" and reestablishing connection with the social world is, according to psychiatrist Judith Herman, the third stage of recovery from trauma. Judith Lewis Herman, *Trauma and Recovery* (New York: Basic Books, 1992), 175.

sensitive to the interferences of the environment. In Tasso's epic *Jerusalem Delivered*, the Christian knight Tancred accidentally kills his beloved Clorinda in a battle; later on, in a magic forest, he unwittingly slashes his sword at a tree in which her soul is imprisoned. From the cut on the tree, blood gushes out and the voice of Clorinda is heard complaining that he has wounded her again. This episode is used by Freud to illustrate his claim that "there really does exist in the mind a compulsion to repeat."[30] In Zhang's case, the experience of trauma repeats itself not through the repetition compulsion in Freudian terms but through the conscious editorial cutting that leaves gaping holes in the body of the text—the wounds through which the voice of a tiny insect is trying to speak.

A Note on Translation

This book contains a daunting number of names of both places and people. I have used Pinyin romanization to transcribe the names of provinces (such as Zhejiang), cities (such as Suzhou), and administrative units (such as the Taizhou Prefecture); but for the names of smaller places, such as villages and mountains, rivers, and lakes, I have tried to preserve the sense of the names whenever I could, to make them more accessible to English readers. When the meaning of a place name is unclear or no graceful translation is possible, I have used transliteration in Pinyin instead.

When introducing a person in the text, the author usually refers to him by his style name (also known as courtesy name) and then gives the person's personal name as well as his place of origin, all in keeping with the Chinese biographical conventions of premodern times; for a woman he gives only the surname, as a woman's name is not supposed to be known outside of her family circle. When translating people's names, I have followed the Chinese custom by giving surname first and personal name second.

Zhang Daye had a large extended family. His father had a principal wife, née Chen, and at least two concubines, one of them being Zhang's biological mother, née Wang. He had several paternal uncles and many cousins. He refers to all of his female cousins as "sisters," and ranks them,

....

30   Sigmund Freud, *Beyond the Pleasure Principle* (New York: W. W. Norton, 1961), 24.

according to convention, by the order of birth in the same generation; thus his second uncle's daughter was his "ninth sister" while his fifth uncle's two daughters were, respectively, his "eighth sister" and "little sister." In the case of his "elder sister" and "fourth sister," it is impossible to know whether they were his sisters or female cousins (Zhang himself seems to have been an only son, judging from the fact that he had to take care of his father's funerary arrangements, but it is unclear whether he had any sisters or half sisters).

Zhang records with affection several of his family servants and hired hands, such as Ah Zhang, Lu Sanyi, Wenjing, Ye Ahsheng, Yatou, and a young orphan, Zhou, who was taken in by his father off the street and possessed an ambiguous identity as half adopted son and half servant. To Zhang, they were heroes who saved him from death or delightful companions who assuaged the loneliness of his travels. There is also an intense sense of guilt about his inability to repay the kindness of those who had helped and protected him during the years of chaos. *The World* is, in this sense, a register of gratitude, and lasting regrets, that Zhang owes to the dead. I have provided a list of the author's connections, including his kinsfolk, friends, and casual acquaintances met during his trips, as well as domestic servants and hired hands, in an appendix, to help the reader navigate the complicated familial and social relationships.

A note should be added about dates. As typical of premodern conventions, Zhang uses both the sexagenarian cycle in the traditional Chinese calendrical system and the ruling emperor's "reign title" to record a year; for instance, the year 1893 may be recorded either as the nineteenth year of the Guangxu era or the *guisi* year of the Guangxu era. The calculation of days and months is based on the Chinese lunar calendar; thus, the sixth day of the fourth month in the nineteenth year of the Guangxu era is May 21, 1893. I have converted all dates in the book into Western calendar dates, which are placed in brackets following the Chinese dates.

Two things must be pointed out here. First, according to traditional Chinese age reckoning, a newborn is considered one year old, and with each passing of a lunar new year, one year is added to the person's age, so that a person is two years old (or two *sui*) in the person's second year, and three years old (or three *sui*) in the person's third year, and so on. There is usually a gap of one year, sometimes even two, between a person's age by Western reckoning and the person's age by Chinese reckoning. In my translation, I have kept the Chinese reckoning used by the author to avoid further confusion. Second, the author sometimes misremembers dates. On one occasion, a marginal note points out the error; on another, the error lies in neglecting to update the reign title of the ruling emperor, so that when the text says "the seventeenth day of the third month in the *yihai* year of the Tongzhi era" (April 22, 1875), it should say "the *yihai* year of the Guangxu era," because Emperor Guangxu changed the reign title on February 6 that year (the emperor usually changed his predecessor's reign title not as soon as he took the throne but on the first lunar new year's day of his reign). At a time of dynastic change, loyalists to the overthrown dynasty sometimes chose to continue to use that dynasty's last reign title as a demonstration of their loyalty to the fallen regime. Zhang Daye's errors, however, seem to be no more than slips. Like many people in premodern times, he did not always have the most precise notion of time. At one point in *The World*, he claims that almost three thousand years had elapsed from the Taijian era of the Chen dynasty to his own day, while in reality a mere 1,300 years had passed. In the volume, I explain these errors in footnotes. I have also appended a chronology of the author's life at the end of the volume to help orient the reader in the temporal labyrinth.

In general, I have kept my footnotes as succinct as possible, but the sheer number of footnotes nevertheless shows the richness of the cultural lore with which a premodern Chinese reader would have been familiar in a work that is not particularly erudite. Throughout the manuscript there are many minor revisions. I have tried to add notes in cases in which the revisions substantially change the sense of the text, but have not noted those cases in which the revisions are merely stylistic.

One last thing to mention here is that the original book is divided into three parts (called "scrolls," or *juan*), but I have further divided each part into sections, based largely on content, and have added section titles, which appear in italics, to make it easier for the reader to find an episode.

PREFACE BY ZHANG DAYE

FROM the cry of a tiny insect, one can hear the sound of a vast world. To speak of a tiny insect and the world as relative to each other is why the Great Hero is capable of containing the ancient and modern times in himself, and his outlook alone is different from the masses of men.[1] That which is clear and light above us is heaven; that which is condensed and heavy below us is earth; sun, stars, great mountains, and large rivers are wedged in between. This is what we call "the world." Clouds are a world to the dragon; wind is a world to the tiger; the Sage is a world to the myriad things. Therefore, in the old days, when the former kings ruled the country, once the five grains were harvested, the kings had the common people share the same alleyways, and let men and women sing together if they had any grievance. Those who were hungry would sing of food; those who were fatigued would sing of labor. The government would provide for men over fifty and women over forty, and ask them to collect their songs and present them to the county; the county would in turn present them to the prefecture, and the prefecture would in turn present them to the capital, so that the Son of Heaven would know everything about the world without having to go outdoors.

What one takes to be a whole world is nothing but wavering hot air and floating dust.[2] When one looks at them from the point of view of what is large, they go back and forth continuously and blow each other

....

1   The Great Hero is an epithet of the Buddha.
2   The phrase "wavering hot air and floating dust" is from the first chapter of *Zhuangzi*, "Free Roaming" (Xiaoyao you). The following discussion about the relativity of large and small is filled with echoes of this *Zhuangzi* chapter.

about; when one looks at them from the point of view of what is small, they go east or west with the wind, appearing at sunrise and disappearing at sundown. But no matter which way one looks at them, they remain the same in being the world. The wings of a bee and the eyes of a mosquito are extremely small, and yet they are capable of flying and seeing. They have ruler and subject, father and son, husband and wife, brothers and friends: their happiness, anger, sadness, and joy are the same as in the human world. When you pour a cup of water into a hollow in the floor of the hall, a passing ant may take it to be a huge lake. How then do we know that it might see a burning torch and not take it to be the morning sun?

A tiny insect is a tiny insect. Unable to see the sun, the stars, great mountains, and large rivers, when it sees a cup of water and a burning torch, it is startled and filled with admiration, thinking that perhaps they are none other than the so-called sun, stars, great mountains, and large rivers. It leaps with excitement, looks up, cries out, and writes down in private what it has seen. This is also the intent of "collecting the songs." Wouldn't the Great Hero of this world consider the sound of a tiny insect to be on a par with the wonderful music of Emperor Shun and the dance of "Mulberry Grove"?[3] There might be something here of use to the Sage in his consideration of the world.

The above is the preface.

....

3   Shun was the legendary sage emperor in ancient times. "Mulberry Grove" was the title of a musical piece supposedly performed for the emperors of the Shang dynasty in high antiquity.

PART ONE

Trip to Tiantai

IN the nineteenth year—the *guisi* year—of the Guangxu era, beginning when the Emperor took the dragon throne, on the sixth day of the fourth month [May 21, 1893], this tiny insect took a trip to Tiantai. Thus the world came into being. I suppose the fruit of bodhi was about to ripen.

In the evening, together with a traveler, Mr. Pan, who was a native of Tiantai, I went out the eastern gate of Ningbo and boarded the ferry boat to Fenghua. When we got into the boat, there were four men there already. Two of them spoke with a Hu'nan accent, and looked like soldiers; the other two were from Xianju of Taizhou, whose dialect sounded like bird talk. They frequently eyed my luggage, and asked me where I was heading. I suspected that they were up to no good. Mr. Pan nervously whispered to me that they might be robbers. I quickly stepped on his foot to stop him from saying anything more. By the next morning, we were still over ten leagues away from the Great Dockyard of Fenghua. The currents were too fast for our boat to advance, so we got off the boat and took a raft instead. The four men took leave of us and were gone. Mr. Pan was delighted that we were now safe. I said, "Well, not yet, I am afraid." We arrived at the Great Dockyard, and reached Huanggongtai, and indeed, there they were, waiting for us to show up. Huanggongtai was the name of the transfer station.

After we ate our meal, the four men set out first. I asked them where they were going. They replied, "Xinchang." Alarmed and panicked, Mr. Pan said to me, "We will have to share the same mountain road with them. What should we do?" I smiled and asked the restaurant owner to find us nine able-bodied men. Once they were assembled, I asked them, "Aren't you all Taizhou people who are working as hired hands here?" They said, "Why, yes indeed." I said, "Well, the barley is yellow now and ready to be harvested. Would you like to come with me and visit your families?" They all said, "Sure." They proceeded to carry me with a bamboo sedan chair. On our way, we ran into some mountain folks who were traveling merchants, and invited them to join us. By the time we arrived at Xikou, we had with us a group of forty-five people. Mr. Pan said, "I think we are okay now."

I took out three hundred cash, bought five kilos of rice wine, and treated everyone to a drink; they all became tipsy. Continuing on our journey, we came to a stream. Those four men were indeed there first. Upon spotting them, Mr. Pan gave a holler to the folks traveling with us, who clustered around me as we all crossed the stream together. We made a great deal of noise. The four men did not expect to see us with so many people, and their countenances changed. They departed on a different route through the mountains.

This was one of those situations that, though one never knows, might have become quite sticky if something bad had happened and I had taken no precautions. It was truly hard to be on the road. As I looked into distance for a hundred leagues, the journey ahead seemed infinite, and I wondered where I would eventually end up.[1] That night, we stopped at Madaitou.

On the eighth, we got up early. We crossed the Shijie Range and entered the territory of Xinchang. Earlier, from the Great Dockyard all the way to Madaitou, the plain was flat and the fields fertile; green plants met the eye everywhere, and the mountain was not yet very steep. By now, however, cliffs were rising high, and remarkable trees stretched across

....

1   The author is alluding to a couplet from "The Supple Mulberry Tree" (Sang rou), one of the "Greater Odes" in the *Classic of Poetry*: "Here is a wise man, / whose insight reaches a hundred leagues." The ode laments the miseries of the common people and the death and disorder afflicting the empire. It contains the following lines: "Intense grief and worries fill my heart, / as I think on the condition of my land. / I was born at an inopportune time, / encountering the wrath of Heaven. / I go from west to east, / there being no peaceful dwelling place for me." These lines provide an apt commentary on *The World of a Tiny Insect*.

the sky. Mountain birds sang melodiously, and flowers blossoming by the stream were full of charm. The road seemed to bend nine times for every ten steps and presented all sorts of enchanting views. The local people were simple, honest, and courteous, entirely different from Ningbo.

Around noon we passed through the Jiaxi Range. Making a rapid descent of Mount Wan, we had lunch at Old Man Xu's restaurant by the Dragon King's Lake. The "lake" did not have a single drop of water in it. One cannot help wondering how it acquired its name—I suppose in the same way some of the "famous gentlemen" of this world got their reputations. Old Man Xu's given name was Dingmu, and his studio name was Zhiting. A Licentiate Scholar in his sixties, he was a remarkably kind and sincere man.[2] He told me that besides selling wine, he made a living by raising silkworms. He had one son and two grandsons, and his grandsons were already beginning to establish a reputation for themselves at the local school. I presented him with a couplet: "In old age, you take the 'red buddy' as an understanding friend; / with leisure and ease, you act as a host to the green mountains."[3] The old man was greatly pleased. He brought out a fine brew for us, and insisted that we spend the night at his place. I declined, saying that we still had a long way to go. We made a date for the future, and I took my leave.

After we turned the corner around the "lake," we rested briefly at Jiujianlou. That night, we stayed at the Glorious Advancement Inn at Banzhu. A young courtesan, who was rather pretty, tried to ingratiate herself with me. Just as she was tuning her musical instrument, Ye Ahsheng, a native of Tiantai who was hired to carry my luggage, barged in with his beddings and asked to share my room. He said, "I hear this place is weird. If one sleeps alone, one could be bewitched by some female demon and die." I laughed heartily at that. The courtesan lingered for a while and finally left. I looked around, and saw a poem written on the wall. It was as follows:

It's been thirty years since I last visited
  this mountain road by the stream,

....

2 Licentiate Scholar (*xiucai*) was an unofficial reference to all men qualified to participate in the civil service examination at the provincial level in the Qing dynasty.

3 "Red buddy" is an appellation of wine.

Black dog, red sheep—
  the world has changed.[4]
With a goblet of ale, I still like to invite people
  to a game of "finger battle";
And yet, even in the midst of chatting and laughing,
  a war is raging in my heart.[5]
A fallen blossom sticks to the grass,
  so awfully charming;
Fragile catkin turns into duckweed,
  always full of sentiments.[6]
Tomorrow, at the wayside rest stop
  for travelers to say farewell,
"In the morning breeze, under the sinking moon,"
  what a melancholy affair.[7]

It was signed, "An All Too Foolish Man of Heng Lake." This, I thought to myself, must have been someone who had been "bewitched" and almost died. But then perhaps he too was feeling the sadness of drifting at the far edge of this world.

On the ninth, there was a drizzling rain when we first got up. We crossed the Huishu Range. By now I have traversed the Huishu Range three times: years ago, when I first visited Xianju, I went there in spring, and returned in autumn; this time, I passed through in summer. I have seen the mountain in darkness and in light, in wind and in rain. Truly I must have a predestined relationship with the mountain spirit.

....

4 That white clouds can quickly turn into the shape of a "black dog" is a figure of change. "Red sheep calamity" (*hong yang jie*) refers to the national disaster believed to take place every six decades in the *bingwu* and *dingwei* years. The *dingwei* year is the year of the sheep, while *bing* and *ding*, according to Chinese cosmology, are governed by the element of fire, hence "red." Punning on the surnames of its two leaders, people sometimes referred to the Taiping Rebellion as the "Hong Yang Calamity" (see introduction).

5 "Finger battle" is a drinking game; "a war in the heart" is a metaphor for concerns weighing heavily on one's mind.

6 "Fragile catkin" is a traditional metaphor for courtesans.

7 "In the morning breeze, under the sinking moon" is taken verbatim from a famous song lyric about the separation of lovers, "To 'The Sound of Bell in the Continuous Rain'" (Yu lin ling), composed by Liu Yong (987–1053).

At first, I did not know the name of the hills on either side of the road. I saw only myriad peaks soaring and dancing, a dark green permeating the sky, furling and unfurling above the clouds like pennants and streamers. I marveled at their beauty. This time I asked some wayfarer, who told me they were called the Plantain Mountains. I recognized the ingenuity of the ancients in coming up with such a name. If, some day, I could visit the mountains after a snowfall and thus get to see the Wangchuan painting in the real landscape, wouldn't that be wonderful?[8]

The road was very slippery in the rain, and the sedan carriers complained bitterly. So I started climbing on foot. Generally speaking, it is better to travel on foot when going uphill. When one gets tired, one can take a little rest and look around. The sights below and on either side are all marvelous, something that cannot be seen from behind the closed curtains of a sedan. When going downhill, however, it is better to sit in the sedan chair, so that one can look down from an elevated point of view, and clouds and streams are as in plain sight as two eyebrows facing each other. As one gradually approaches them, one sees their wonders even more clearly. It is regrettable that few mountain viewers have realized this.

The rainy atmosphere became thicker and thicker after we crossed the Huishu Range. Viewed from afar, the peaks of Tianmu Mountain seemed to have sunk into an ocean of fog. The rocks and soil of nearby mountains and valleys were all of a crimson hue. As profuse white clouds surrounded and encircled them, I felt as if I were watching a congregation of flames, which was quite a remarkable sight. After going on a few more leagues, we arrived at the Coldwater Way Station. By and by the terrain became more level, and the sky began to clear up. Dark green pines seemed to be dripping azure. A slender stream was gushing forth, and a cool breeze blew in our faces, refreshing and lifting our spirits. It was as if the divine beings of nature were beckoning us. We then crossed the Guan Range, which is connected to Black Summit Mountain. Black Summit was dense with rich vegetation and even more precipitous and perilous than the Guan Range. The scenery changed with every step and was beyond words. This was what I talked about in a poem I once composed:

....

8   Wangchuan refers to the Tang poet and painter Wang Wei (701–761). One of his paintings, now lost, featured a green plantain, a tropical plant, in snow.

Looking down from the mountaintop,
Vast and hazy, all I can see is a blue mist.
Descending gradually, I come to the level ground,
Suddenly the vista opens up into a grotto heaven.

By the time we went over Three Mao Bridge and reached Clear Stream Village, the terrain again gradually leveled out. Then we were in the town of Tiantai. There were troops stationed there to defend against mountain bandits. When we were passing through, a soldier was hunting pheasants with his shotgun. One of my sedan carriers, while relieving himself at the roadside, was startled and grunted about it. The soldier flew into a rage, took out his saber, and threatened to stab him. At that, everyone present was stirred to indignation. I quickly dismounted and intervened. Finally the sedan carrier was forced to kneel down and kowtow to the soldier, and only then did the soldier let him go.

Even bandits might be moved by human feeling; how can these soldiers be so impervious to courtesy? The people of Taizhou are often seized by soldiers for some trifle and then beheaded as "bandits"— just as in this case, I suppose. When those who are malevolent carry the weapons of destruction, and, moreover, possess power and authority, nobody cares for the destitute and miserable common folk, even if they have done nothing wrong to deserve the way they are treated. Isn't it extremely foolish for these poor folks to try to reason with them?

At Tiantai, I stayed with Mr. Pan, the man with whom I had traveled.

On the tenth, I toured Guoqing Temple in the rain.[9] The color of the mountains, reflected in the glistening stream, was of a darker green than spilled kohl. My sedan carriers had all left; only Ye Ahsheng followed me with my bags. A monk named Xiaoran acted as my guide and showed me around. At the time, they were constructing statues of the five hundred Arhats. Many craftsmen were working in the temple, and there was nothing really worth seeing. The former sacrificial hall for Fenggan had been converted into the Hall of Three Saints, including, besides Fenggan,

....

9   Guoqing Temple, to the north of the town of Tiantai, is well-known for being the head temple of the Tiantai Buddhist sect that was founded by the monk Zhiyi (538–597). It was first built at the turn of the seventh century, and has been repeatedly destroyed and rebuilt throughout history.

the pair Hanshan and Shide.[10] Its decor was not particularly attractive either. So I set out.

We passed the Golden Ground Range. The rocks on the roadside all looked as if they had been hewn with an ax, just as in Ma Yuan's paintings;[11] they were quite different from what we had seen before. Squirrels came and went on top of the pine trees that reached into the clouds.[12] So secluded and beautiful, the scenery hardly seemed to be of this mortal world. But it was freezing cold, so we went to Stūpa Temple.

Stūpa Temple was none other than the Temple of True Enlightenment, where the mummified body of Master Zhizhe of the Sui dynasty was preserved.[13] His Dharma descendant, Master Minxi, whose studio name was Huafeng, was a native of Huangyan. An enlightened monk with profound insight, he had just started a lecture series on *The Lotus Sutra*. He presented me with a copy of *The Unofficial Biography of Master Zhizhe*, and I spent the night at the temple.[14]

The chanting of sutras and the intoning of hymns echoed past midnight. Unable to sleep, I got up, lit the lamp, and peered out the window. The rain had stopped, and the clouds opened up to reveal a bright moon. I turned around to look at Ahsheng: he was sound asleep. So I went out, and took a stroll on the temple grounds. In a flash, I seemed to see life and death as bubbles on water. As long as one remained ignorant of the wisdom of Buddhism, everything seemed to be fine; but once one grasps it, wouldn't that person regard somebody like me as one of those people running about wildly like a headless person and, as the Buddha says, deserving nothing but pity? Even so, staying within the mortal world or going beyond its confines serves people in different ways. In benefiting oneself and benefiting others, one should always aspire to do good. If one could achieve this, then one would understand that the doctrines of

....

10   Fenggan was an eighth-century Chan monk who stayed at Guoqing Temple. It is said that he regularly associated with the eccentric poet-monks Hanshan and Shide, and authored poetry himself.

11   Ma Yuan (ca. 1160–1225) was a renowned landscape painter of the Southern Song dynasty.

12   Two characters at the beginning of this sentence are illegible in the manuscript.

13   Master Zhizhe refers to the monk Zhiyi.

14   This biography was written by Master Zhizhe's principal disciple and successor, Guanding (561–632).

Ni Hill and the Pure Land shared the same intent.[15] Taking Confucius's sagely teachings as the principle of function, but regarding Buddhism as the home to return to: if one could act like this to while away this glorious age, then wouldn't he be able to enjoy himself wherever he was going? As I pondered in this manner, my spirits were considerably lifted.

On the eleventh day, I visited the Correct and Extensive Temple, and viewed the Stone Bridge Cascade. When I first set out, I climbed Buddha's Mound and looked into the distance. The sun had not yet risen, and the mountains on all sides were in a haze. I was right in the midst of clouds, whose vapors were sinking below me.

We crossed the Daxingkeng Range, and passed Wild Boars Grove. The grove was named after a boulder stretching out in an irregular shape, which seemed like many big boars speeding toward the flat mountain ridge. Some were raising their heads; some were crouching; some were falling down; some were getting up. Complete with bristle and tail, they crowded together in tens and hundreds. But when you took a closer look, it turned out to be one gigantic boulder, which was just under one-fifth of an acre long. What a remarkable sight! The mountain god must have conjured up this illusion to entertain himself.

At times ascending into the clouds and at times descending into a deep ravine, after traveling another twenty leagues we arrived at the Correct and Extensive Temple. The sun shone through, bringing warmth to the clouds; flowers blooming in seclusion lent charm to the rocks. Fine, towering trees touched the sky; there were lovely plants all the way and a sweet brook flowing alongside the road. As a breeze was blowing, birds twittered here and there. This was truly a blessed place, which I had not expected to be able to find in the human world.

As we reached Tanhua Pavilion, a monk named Qiutan came to greet us. A native of Kuaiji, he was a calm and relaxed man who commanded respect. After lunch, he showed me the way to Stone Bridge Cascade. Comparing it to dancing snow and spewing cloud would not suffice to describe its beauty. As I sat in front it with my eyes closed, I felt as if I

....

15   Ni Hill is in Confucius's hometown, Qufu of Shandong. It is said that Confucius's
     mother had prayed there and then given birth to Confucius, hence Confucius's
     personal name was Qiu (meaning "hill") and his style name was Zhongni. The
     Pure Land is a Buddhist paradise inhabited by buddhas and bodhisattvas, or,
     more specifically, by the followers of Amitâbha Buddha.

were being carried away by the six gigantic tortoises bearing immortal mountains, swaying and soaring above the three isles and ten continents in the heavenly wind, completely transported to another realm.[16] After a long time, Qiutan took me back to the temple, and treated me to a fine tea.

"The wonderful scenery of this mountain cannot be exhausted even in several months," he said to me. "You could, for instance, view the cloudscape from Huading Mountain, where you can also find the 'minor holy site' of the Buddha; or you could enjoy the moonlight on Jasper Terrace—that is where Prince Qiao has left his traces.[17] Peach Blossom Fount is the dwelling place of transcendent beings; Tongbo Compound is where the feathered folks gather.[18] Would you like to linger here awhile? If you can come back in autumn, the 'bones' of the mountain will be all exposed, which is an especially extraordinary sight."

I was wide-eyed and could form no response, for I suspected that my soul had been captivated by the mountain spirit. Afterward, we went back to the Temple of True Enlightenment and stayed another night. "The old monk made a date with me for the autumn; / I think back on the flying cascade for a full ten days." As I recited the couplet by my old friend Qian Bochui (named Zhenxun) of Leqing, my heart was even more filled with yearning.[19]

On the twelfth, I rose early in the morning and paid my respects to the Buddha. Abbot Minxi spoke to me at length about the causes and conditions for calming my mind and setting my heart at ease. I presented him with a poem:

Shadow matters, dust objects:
    my memory has grown hazy;

....

16   According to legend, six gigantic tortoises carried five immortal mountains on their backs in the ocean. "Three isles and ten continents" refers to the immortal land in Daoist lore.

17   Prince Jin (or Prince Qiao) was the crown prince of King Ling of Zhou (d. 545 bce), who, according to legend, became an immortal.

18   "Feathered folk" is a term for Daoist immortals.

19   Qian Zhenxun (1867–1931), better known as Qian Bochui, was a late Qing poet. He passed the Provincial Examination in 1888, and held a series of teaching positions in the state-operated prefectural schools in Zhejiang.

Through this life of a hundred years, I have always
 felt ashamed of my unrestrained nature.
I aspire to rely on the power of the Buddha
 to understand ultimate Truth;
And, riding a gust of wind from heaven,
 ascend to the upper realm.
Once I gain a glimpse of the Dharma Assembly
 in the midst of the rain of flowers,[20]
My heart, the very source of the numinous spirit,
 will attain the round halo.[21]
After I fill up the ocean of suffering,
 I wish to come back here,
To be near the cloud of compassion,
 and guard the lecture hall.

A person like Abbot Minxi is someone whom I do not know how to praise.[22]

After I took my leave, I went to see Crimson Wall Mountain. The mountain was not very big, but it had all kinds of marvelous sights imaginable. On the top there was an "Immortals' Pool." It was a round hole with a circumference of no more than one square foot, but its depth was immeasurable. I scooped up some water and sipped it—it was so cold that my teeth chattered. There were also Golden Coin Pool, Piercing Sword Cliff, and various caves named Purple Cloud, Brushing Cloud, Drinking Rosy Vapors, and Jade Capital. The sight known as "dancing snow of the cold cliff" was the most outstanding: it was a stalactite spring, flowing down from the top of the crags, and scattering into numerous droplets.

Purple Cloud was the deepest of all caves, and was well over one-third

. . . .

20 A "Dharma Assembly" is a gathering for the purpose of reading the Buddhist
    scriptures, preaching or worshipping the Buddha. In Buddhist lore, gods and
    spirits would scatter fragrant flowers as large as cart wheels in admiration of Bud-
    dha's teaching.
21 A round halo surrounds the head of a Buddha. Acquiring a round halo signifies
    the attainment of enlightenment.
22 This echoes the *Analects* 8.1: "Confucius said, 'Taibo may be said to possess the
    utmost virtue. He declined the throne three times, and yet the people did not
    know how to praise him [because he never flaunted his virtue]."

of an acre wide. A Daoist nun had a house built next to it and practiced self-cultivation there. I inquired about her, and learned that she was the great-granddaughter of Master Qi Cifeng.[23] Widowed at a young age, she lived alone with a son, and supervised his studies herself. She was accomplished in poetry and painting, and gave herself the studio name Lady Scribe of the Jade Capital. She was a remarkable woman, and I paid her a visit. I asked her, "Since you, madam, live here alone, aren't you afraid of tigers and wolves and brutal men of force?" She replied, "Our humble region does not have brutal men of force; as for tigers and wolves, my son is skilled in the martial arts." I was even more amazed. Her son was a rather delicate young man. I asked him his name; he told me. I then asked him his age; he said, "I am twenty-one." Next I asked him about his learning, and this time he only smiled and did not answer—because what he studied was the Daoist canon.[24] I marveled at the mother and son for a long time.

After coming down from the mountain, we saw a rest stop by the road. Next to it was the tomb of Tian Heng's retainers. *The Historian's Record* states only that Tian Heng's five hundred retainers committed suicide on an island, but does not specify where it was.[25] *The Account of Famous Sights* says that Tian Heng's island is near Cloud Terrace Mountain of Haizhou, but without adequate research, its exact location remains unclear. Upon seeing the tomb, I believed that this place must have been part of the ocean in the old days.

On the thirteenth, I set out for Shaoxing. Going out of the little south gate, I boarded a boat, and Ahsheng followed along. In a short while, we went by the Shrine of Zhang the Perfected Being at the Hundred Pace

....

23 Qi Cifeng was Qi Zhaonan (1703–1768), a native of Tiantai. He was a scholar official and poet.

24 That is, what he studied was an unconventional subject, unlike the Confucian canon.

25 Tian Heng (d. 202 bce) was a nobleman of Qi who rebelled against the Qin dynasty. He sought refuge on an island off the eastern seashore of China with five hundred followers. After Liu Bang (d. 195 bce) became emperor, he summoned Tian Heng to court. Tiang Heng committed suicide on his way to the capital. Tian Heng's five hundred retainers, upon hearing the news, all killed themselves. *The Historian's Record*, the first comprehensive history of China, was authored by Sima Qian (ca. 145–86 bce).

Stream.[26] I once passed the shrine by land, and wrote a poem to commemorate the occasion:

> Today the immortal is nowhere to be seen;
> Quiet, forlorn, this high tower is left behind.
> Incense and candles still continue
> > under the care of a remote descendant;
> The imperial writing is preserved
> > on the grand stele.[27]
> The sound of pines—the emptiness of the wind;
> Shadow in the pool: purified of deep autumn.
> Vaguely, the numinous traces are distant;
> In the green mountains, sorrow at twilight.

Journeying by water, however, was even more delightful. Travel truly brought many pleasures.

After passing through Hundred Pace Stream, we turned west. The currents became swifter, striking against the jumbled rocks and producing silvery waves, evoking the tidal bore of Qiantang. As for the section of the river that was open and wide, it had both the austerity of Yan Guang's Rapids and the pure and sumptuous beauty of Tonglu.[28]

Soon after, the river turned around a peak, and level fields, all neatly laid out, came into view. The distant mountains were like a woman's dark-green eyebrows; trees with fragrant blossoms were shrouded in a light mist. This was the even and vast terrain of Wuxing. Having fully appreciated the scenery, I brought out *The Unofficial Biography of Master Zhizhe* and started reading. It seemed to be but an instant before the sun's shadow shifted, and my body was refreshed by a cool air. I got up and took in the landscape, which showed a thousand charming aspects, all bathed in a spiritual beauty, perhaps because it was suffused by a moral influence. All of a sudden I felt as if I had transcended the dusty

....

26   Zhang the Perfected Being refers to Zhang Boduan (983–1082), an influential Daoist master who was a native of Tiantai and passed away at the Hundred Pace Stream, located at the boundary between Tiantai and Linhai Counties.

27   The Yongzheng Emperor of the Qing (r. 1723–1735) composed a stele inscription for the shrine and wrote it out himself.

28   Both Yan Guang's Rapids and Tonglu are scenic sites in Zhejiang.

world—a feeling that was impossible to express with brush and ink.

At dusk we arrived at Shaoxing. The city was built following the contour of the mountains, its precipitous city wall overlooking the river. In terms of beautiful scenery and strategic position, it ranked number one in eastern Zhejiang. General Liu Tianxing from Hefei, whose studio name was Youzhi, was in charge of the banner garrison in defense of Taizhou and was stationed in the city. Li Xiaju (named Chengqi) of Jiangning was his secretary. Both were my old friends, and I stayed with them. I was going to send Ahsheng home the next day. Ahsheng had attended on me for a while now, and had become attached to me. I gave him money, and he would not take it until I forced him. Xiaju said with a chuckle, "What a Kingdom of Virtuous Men!"[29] I found Ahsheng a truly likable fellow.

On the fourteenth, I got up early and went with Xiaju to Fenshui Bridge to pay my final respects to a deceased friend, Mr. Yuan Jichuan. This was in fact my reason for undertaking this trip. Mr. Yuan's personal name was Shunjin. He was a native of Fenyang of Shanxi, and had served as the district jailor of Xianju County. I first met him when I went to Xianju in the *dinghai* year [1887]. He was generous, honest, and plainspoken, and had in him something of a knight-errant of the ancient times. He was especially devoted to ethics. His family was once extremely wealthy, trading silk and tea with the Russians for generations. At the beginning of the Tongzhi era [1862–74], the government was engaged in border demarcation negotiations with Russia at Yili.[30] That went on for a long time, and Mr. Yuan lost all of his capital. Thereupon he paid with grain for a position in the government, and received an appointment at Zhejiang. The mountain folks, living in an out-of-the-way area, were impoverished, and there were many cases of theft and robbery. Mr. Yuan assisted the worthy magistrate, Mr. Yu Jieshi of the Xi County of Anhui, to set things in order, and together they exerted themselves day and night. They founded an institute for scholars, established an orphan-

....

29 The Kingdom of Virtuous Men is a legendary country in which people all treat one another with deference and yield to one another with no argument or contention. It appears in the ancient *Classic of Mountains and Seas* and is also featured in a nineteenth-century fantasy novel, *Flowers in the Mirror* (*Jing hua yuan*), by Li Ruzhen (ca. 1763–1830).

30 The negotiations began in 1862 and ended with the signing of the Protocol of Chuguchak (Tacheng) in 1864.

age, provided for widows and widowers, and repaired city walls. They worked at it like tending the field: watering, fertilizing, so that summer heat could not scorch and winter cold could not freeze. The local people adored them.

Magistrate Yu's successor was, however, overzealous in his governance, which caused the bandits' besiegement of the city in the *guiwei* year [1883]. Mr. Yuan sent out scouts and searched for informants; he also personally led soldiers and civilians in defense, and swore to guard the city with his life. With a brilliant strategy, he captured two major bandit leaders, Guo Zhongqi and Pan Xiaogou, and executed both of them. When someone planned to escape from the besieged city, he slew a bandit with his own hands as demonstration. "Now look," he said. "If you do run away, I am a real man, and I am not going to spare you." Someone like Mr. Yuan, who upheld the Three Guides and Five Virtues in society, could truly vie with the sun and moon for glory.[31] And yet, after the siege was lifted, the civil and martial officers of the county were all promoted out of normal order, and Mr. Yuan was made only expectant appointee for the assistant magistrate.[32] Since ancient times, rewards have not gone to those who toiled. This might simply be the way of things.

Mr. Yuan was a plain-looking man. He loved to wear green-colored clothes. He walked in a laid-back, sloppy manner, like a clown in operas. Xiaju and I always poked fun at him. He did not mind our teasing but rather enjoyed it, and would even sing a so-called *bangzi* tune from operas for laughs. He also loved to make paper rolls, keep them in his sleeves, and hand them out to people—there always seemed to be an endless supply of those paper rolls, which was hilarious.[33] Occasionally he served as the acting police chief of Taiping County, and was hoping to become assistant magistrate there. At the time, I was going to go to Hangzhou, but came down with a nearly fatal case of malaria. Mr. Yuan found me a doctor who cured me. After my recovery, he gave me a large

....

31 The "Three Guides" refers to the relationships between ruler and subject, father and son, husband and wife, with the former acting as the latter's guide; the five virtues are benevolence, righteousness, propriety, wisdom, and trustworthiness.

32 An expectant appointee was a qualified man for whom there was no vacant official post, but who was promised to occupy the first appropriate vacancy.

33 Handing out paper rolls seems to be a personal idiosyncrasy, for which I have not been able to find any explanation.

sum of money, urged me to leave for Hangzhou, and promised to help me get my affairs in order. But then I happened to have an emergency and spent all of the money. He never reproached me. In the past, Guan Zhong lied to his friend Bao Shu, and yet Bao Shu understood his motivation and forgave him.[34] How could I compare with someone like Guan Zhong? And yet Mr. Yuan cared for me more than Bao Shu. When seeing him again in the underworld one day, how will I be able to face this good friend of mine? He would of course never reprove me, but the feeling of guilt in my heart is unbearable.

After having been parted from him for a long time, I was yearning to see him again. Last winter, it turned out that he was reappointed to be district jailor at Lin'an [i.e., Hangzhou]. He was immensely pleased. He wrote to me, saying, "I am getting on in years. I have not seen you for a while, and often feel frustrated because of it. Now I am only too happy that we can finally set a date for our reunion." Who would have thought that not long after that he would depart from this world?

Xiaju told me that Mr. Yuan had left Xianju on the sixth of the second month; he arrived at Shaoxing on the sixteenth, and went to Huangyan on the eighteenth to bid farewell to the local gentry. He fell ill when he reached Three Rivers Mouth, and died on the twenty-second [April 8, 1893]. He had always been very careful about his health, as if he were already old and fragile, but he had been particularly energetic when he undertook this trip, during which, however, he passed away. Wasn't this the hand of fate!

Mr. Yuan was fifty-five years old at the time of his death; he had no son. He had adopted Shouchang, the son of his fifth younger brother, as his own, but Shouchang was still very young and had remained in Shanxi. This was in fact just an agreement he had made with his brother, and he had never met the child. His wife, Madame Li, had a rheumatic condition; when it acted up, it was like epilepsy. Mr. Yuan had two concubines; one of them, Madame Zhang, was faithful and chaste. After Mr. Yuan passed away, a mercantile man named Wu Molin from Taiping County falsely spread word that Mr. Yuan had promised to give Zhang to him.

....

34 Guan Zhong was a famous statesman of the State of Qi from seventh century bce. Bao Shu was Bao Shuya, a minister of Qi, best known for his friendship with, and understanding of, Guan Zhong.

Zhang was infuriated, and cut her throat with a pair of scissors to show her determination not to marry Wu. Wu was frightened and fled; Zhang was eventually resuscitated. Only such strength of will can save powerless and defenseless people from being bullied and injured by monsters like Wu Molin. Mr. Yuan may rest in peace now.

On the fifteenth, I toured the Eight Immortals Crags, and climbed Headband Mountain. There was nothing worth recording. I heard that there was a mountain called Cloudy Peak that was quite beautiful, but did not want to brave the hot weather. Indeed, after having seen the wonderful sight of Stone Bridge Cascade of Tiantai, even if there were pretty scenery at Cloudy Peak, I felt like "having come back from the Five Sacred Mountains."[35]

That evening, General Liu held a dinner party in my honor. Years ago, when I had first gone to Xianju, my best friends had been Jichuan and Xiaju. Hence the couplet in my poem remembering them: "Speaking of my close friends within the four seas, / There is Li, and there is Yuan." Besides the two of them, I also got along well with Pan Yiting of Liuzhou, whose name was Honggui; General Liu was another good friend I made at Xianju. General Liu had never studied the classics, but he loved to converse with people about the past and the present. He often obliged his friends to talk about the Warring States, the Three Kingdoms, and the various romances of previous dynasties for enjoyment. He knew the principles of right and wrong as well as the reasons for success and failure well in advance, so that even those who were very well-read could not best him in argument. In the old days, he had invited me to go on an outing to South Peak with him several times, and I wrote the following poems to commemorate the occasions.

(1)
The general, so hospitable,
Has made a date with me for drinks.
Goblets of ale, golden waves glistening;
Clouds greet the sword and pendants, cool.

....

35   This was a saying of the great traveler and travelogue writer Xu Xiake (1586–
      1641): "After having come back from the Five Sacred Mountains, one does not
      want to view any other mountain."

Singing loudly, I am almost carried away;
Dancing while tipsy: he tolerates my wildness.
Toward dusk, I return to my lonely guest lodge,
Cherishing the memory of the joy we shared.

(2)
The cloudy hills move the general to a merry mood,
More than once, he has set a sumptuous banquet there.
On a leisurely day, we delight in expanding our feelings;
In a clear breeze, the guests follow the lead of a worthy man.
Mountains and groves present their charm;
As seasons change, time flows by.
We must not waste a fine hour—
Let the boat transporting ale come frequently.

From these poems one may see how captivated I was by the general's cha-
risma. His sincerity, honesty, and complete guilelessness were all part of
his nature. We had a good time at the dinner party.

Afterward, I boarded Huangyan's ferry boat. At midnight, we moored
at Eight Leagues Post Station and waited for the tide. We reached Three
Rivers Mouth at dawn. Three Rivers Mouth marked the boundary of
Linhai, Huangyan, and Haimen. It looked like Shanghai's Poplar Bank,
but was more grand and majestic. I arrived at Huangyan at twilight, and
stayed with Mr. Shen of Shanyin. It rained that day.

On the seventeenth, I visited the former residence of the Wang family
in the Eastern City. That was my birth mother's home. After the devastation of the war, almost everyone of the family had died. I found their
graves at the foot of Square Hill, and, with a small sum of money, made
sacrificial offerings as well as repaired the tombs.

On the eighteenth, I toured Weiyu Mountain. There is a Daoist monastery built by Emperor Huizong of the Northern Song there.[36] Seven to
eight leagues from the South City Gate, it is what the Daoist canon refers
to as "the second Grotto Heaven."[37] When I was going there that day, the

....

36 The Huizong Emperor (1082–1135) was famous for his promotion of Daoism. The
    Daoist monastery at Weiyu Mountain is called Dayou Gong.
37 According to Daoist lore, there are altogether "Ten Great Grotto Heavens" where
    immortals reside.

sky was just clearing up from a drizzling rain, and the mountain was in a haze. As I traversed the fields, I felt an expansiveness of spirit. The locals were planting wheat, and I stopped to talk to them. They were all simple and honest folks. Beyond the level fields there were many orange trees, all laid out in neat rows. Not a single blade of grass grew underneath. This was because orange trees were not compatible with many plants; if there were grass around it, it would have turned into brambles, so all of the grass had to be cut down.

After I got to the mountain, I sat down at a roadside inn and took a rest. Looking into the distance, I noticed dark green pines and cypresses surrounding a soaring tower, and that turned out to be the Pavilion of Overlooking the Void. I followed a footpath to get closer, and noticed that it was rather rundown and looked as if it were going to collapse at any moment. In it there was a Daoist master named Yunya. He was over eighty years old, with a long beard hanging over his stomach, but had a youthful face despite his age. Whenever a visitor came, he would show him the so-called Feather Mountain Cave. The space inside the cave was so small that it could contain only one sitting mat; it was pitch black in there. I heard that it led all the way to the ocean, but I did not have time to find out whether this was true or not. There was also a "cinnabar well." Its water was glossy and rich like oil, and tasted sweet. So I sat down and took time to savor it. The master asked me where I came from, and I gave him an honest reply. Then I proceeded to ask him about books on making the elixir.

"Those books," the master said, "all lead people astray. The only worthwhile ones are *Harmony of Difference and Equality* and *Enlightenment to the Truth*.[38] Even *Enlightenment to the Truth* cannot be entirely trusted. *Harmony of Difference and Equality*, on the other hand, is very eloquent, but so peculiar and profound that, if one does not comprehend its true meaning, then reading it would be a waste of time."

I asked, "What, then, is 'the dark gateway'?"[39]

With a chuckle he said, "The dark gateway—that is not something easy to explain. But don't you know about the 'swaying and creaking'?[40]

....

38   *Harmony of Difference and Equality* (*Zhou Yi Can tong qi*) is a Daoist work attributed to Wei Boyang of the second century. *Enlightenment to the Truth* (*Wuzhen pian*) was authored by Zhang Boduan (see note 26).

39   "The dark gateway" refers to the way to enlightenment.

40   This is a phrase from the *Zhuangzi* chapter "The Discourse on Thinking of All

Master Zhuang's words are worth mulling over. *That* would not be so difficult, would it?"

Upon hearing this I rose from my seat and bowed to him. The master said, "You, my dear sir, are someone who has a purpose in mind. Keep working at Confucian and Buddhist teachings; then the Daoist truth will not be difficult to manifest of its own accord."

I talked with him for a long time before I took my leave. By then the sun was already setting over the mountains, and an evening mist rose on all sides and permeated the landscape.

On the nineteenth, I went to Square Hill again to examine the Wang family cemetery, and made a record of all of the graves. Then I sat down in the shade to take a rest, and gazed at the Yandang Mountains in the distance. Watching the hills emerging and vanishing in clouds and mist, I felt a pang in my heart. I bowed to the mountain god, asking him, "If I go through a transformation, and put on a plain cloth robe, with a staff in my hand; then another transformation, wearing a wide-brimmed bamboo hat and a pair of straw sandals; then yet another transformation, holding a cane made of *jili* wood and carrying a shoulder pole, coming to you and roaming with you—will you take me in?"

At the time, there were numerous orange trees under Square Hill; I could not even see the end of them. I regretted only that it was not late autumn and so I was unable to witness the marvelous sight of a colorful grove, laden with orange fruits, like a piece of cloud brocade. I lingered there for a long time before I returned to the city.

I set out after lunch, and boarded a boat again. Toward evening, I reached Three Rivers Mouth, and from there I was going back to Shaoxing. As I turned around to look at Square Hill, it seemed as close to me as my own eyelashes. Now that the Wang family cemetery had been repaired, I could report back to my mother, which would certainly bring her some comfort.

The next day I arrived at Shaoxing at dawn, and paid a visit to Chen

....

Things as Being on the Same Level" (Qiwu lun). A teacher describes to his student
the working of "Earth's flutes"—wind blowing at the multitudes of fissures of
a large tree and making them bellow. He proceeds to compare human beings to
such trees and describe human emotions as the music that rises from our being.
The discourse is a contemplation of the subjective consciousness that governs all
of the emotions and their arbitrariness.

Yuan. A native of Linhai, Chen Yuan was skilled in bamboo carving. He would take a huge, thick section of Moso bamboo, pare it down to a flat surface, make it into a screen or a fan, and carve figures on it. The image had a fluid strength and was suffused with an ancient aura, and had no trace of brush and ink.[41] I once obtained a fan made by him, on which was carved an image of Su Dongpo wearing a bamboo hat and wooden sandals.[42] Dongpo looked casual and unrestrained; his beard and eyebrows were so vivid that it was as if he were coming to life. I had thought that Chen Yuan must have been someone from the past who had long been deceased; then I discovered, to my surprise, that he was a contemporary who lived in a place called Willow Bridge. His house was just a couple of rooms with low ceilings, which faced a vegetable garden. He stayed in day and night, and never stopped working on his carvings. It was both his livelihood and his passion. He was very happy meeting me, and showed me all of his best works. He also told me about his life, and was pleased that he enjoyed a good reputation among the gentry. I inquired about his age, and he said that he was fifty-seven. I said, "Aren't your eyes beginning to get dim?" He said, "Not at all." I said, "Given your talent, you should go to big cities. Why do you just grow old in hardship like this?" He said, "Other people yearn for big cities; but if you want me to forsake my wife and children, leave my hometown, fill my mind with worries, and enslave myself for the sake of fame, I would rather die." Now, wasn't Chen Yuan someone whom Zhuangzi would consider as having an "intact spirit"?

On the twenty-first, I toured East Lake with Xiaju. East Lake was outside the east city gate and extended about one and a half acres. On the lakeshore was an academy. A winding scarlet bridge led to a pavilion on an isle in the midst of the lake. I ascended the pavilion and looked into the distance: near and far, different shades of green seemed to infuse my sleeves. This was because Headband Mountain was facing the pavilion, and Pine Heights was in the background; the screen formed by pine trees was just like a painting.

Xiaju told me that the scenery was particularly fine with the lotus

....

41　By "brush and ink" the author refers to the more artful and delicate mode of literati painting.

42　Su Dongpo was Su Shi (1037–1101), a famous Northern Song poet, writer, and calligrapher.

flowers in blossom; the only regrettable thing was the lack of willow trees on the dikes. Behind the academy there was a Shrine of the Loyal Recluse, built to honor the man known as the "Woodcutter of the East Lake," a martyr who died during Emperor Jianwen's dethronement in the early Ming.[43] There was a couplet in the shrine, which read, "Remaining anonymous for a thousand years, he was loyal, and yet successfully concealed himself; / Carrying moral integrity and righteousness on his shoulders, how could we regard him as a mere woodcutter?" The woodcutter was but an illiterate commoner, and yet he was able to establish a name for himself, just like such worthies as Fang Xiaoru and Jing Qing.[44] Seeing this, how could people place much value on a well-to-do life with a fine carriage drawn by handsome horses?

The weather was hot and humid. We heard the sound of thunder, and hastened to turn back. As soon as we returned to the city, the rains came down like arrows.

As I planned to return to Ningbo on the twenty-second, I paid another visit to Fenshui Bridge and bid farewell to Jichuan's spirit tablet. His concubine was so grief-stricken that it was impossible to describe in words. Since I could not offer her any real consolation, I stayed only a little while. Looking upon the curtains hanging in front of Jichuan's spirit tablet, I felt I could still see his face and hear his voice. Thinking upon the past, I could not help my tears.

In the afternoon I visited the garden of Mr. Hong near the south city gate. The Hong family used to be prominent, but has since declined. Nevertheless, Xiaju told me that their collection of antiques, calligraphy, paintings, and books was still one of the largest in the prefecture. So we went together to take a look. But the master of the household was not in, and none of the womenfolk could entertain guests. Their garden had been turned into a vegetable plot. We could still see the old groundwork of the long corridor and winding walkway, and let out many sighs over

....

43   The Jianwen Emperor (1377–1402) was the second emperor of the Ming dynasty. He reigned for four years before being dethroned by his uncle, Zhu Di (the Yongle Emperor, r. 1402–1424), and was said to have died in the palace fire after Zhu Di's army took the capital. A woodcutter at East Lake committed suicide upon hearing of the death of the Jianwen Emperor.

44   Fang Xiaoru (1357–1402) and Jing Qing (d. 1402), two of the Jianwen Emperor's ministers, were executed by the Yongle Emperor for refusing to submit.

such a melancholy sight. I recalled that, when I was living at Suzhou, I once chanced upon the former garden of a local grandee. The garden was overgrown with weeds and looked quite forlorn. Only some white lotus flowers were still blooming in the pond. I lingered there awhile, and noticed that a rock by the pond used for fulling clothes seemed to have some inscriptions on it. Upon closer inspection, I saw a painted fan carved on the rock, and the painting was none other than the imperial brushwork of the Kangxi Emperor.[45] This, then, was what happened to distinguished old clans. Now that the Hongs had managed to preserve their family collection, they were truly doing much better than most.

That evening, Xiaju treated me to dinner and drinks. We sat and talked all night. I set out at the break of dawn.

At noon I passed by Three Rivers Mouth and continued on toward Haimen, as I was going to take the sea route. The waters flowed free in the wilderness, and jumbled hills were multilayered. The scenery in the area near the seashore was expansive and peculiar. Horse Head Mountain was especially remarkable: it stretched across the river to midcurrent, with a galloping momentum. It looked frighteningly ferocious, as if it were going to bite people. After dark, we were suddenly overtaken by a violent storm. Fierce tidal waves were rushing forward angrily; lightening slashed the sky, followed by fearsome thunders. One seemed to hear ghosts cry. I once wrote a poem about the night rain, which contained the couplet, "Life and death—tears shed for a dear friend; / Grief surges: the tidal bore of the great river." I had not expected to encounter such a scene again at this moment. Thinking about how almost half of my friends were already on the register of the dead, and reflecting upon my own life, I felt as if I were wandering in a city of mirage. Silently reciting that couplet over and over, I could not help raising my head toward heaven and heaving a long sigh.

At midnight, we moored at Peng Island and spent the night there.

On the twenty-third, I arrived at Haimen. The city of Haimen was built by the Junior Guardian Qi of the Ming dynasty as a defense against Japanese pirates.[46] There were fish, salt, mussels, and clams everywhere

....

45 The Kangxi Emperor (r. 1661–1722) was the fourth emperor of the Qing dynasty.

46 Junior Guardian Qi refers to Qi Jiguang (1528–1588), a famous Ming general best remembered for his fight against Japanese pirates. "Junior Guardian [of the Heir Apparent]" was an honorific title of great prestige.

in the city; their stench filled the streets. There were several small hills, which were rather bare and not worth viewing. In terms of its strategic importance, Haimen was the gateway to Taizhou, and the outside screen of Ningbo.

On the twenty-fourth, I boarded the steamboat named *Weiyuan*. At first it moved slowly; then, in an instant, it went as fast as wind. Like thunder and lightening it transcended the gray waves of the sea. Islands in the distance could barely be made out over the vast waters. I leaned against the railing and gazed at the scenery, and found it quite entertaining. We passed by Rocky Bank in the afternoon. People's dwellings were all built on the hill to avoid the tides. From afar, the houses seemed to rise into the clouds, and their terraces faced the sun. Ancient pines and extraordinary rocks spread high and low amid the houses, which were magnificent with their golden and emerald colors. It was the brushwork of General Li the Junior.[47] That evening we moored at Qitou.

The next morning we reached Dinghai. Dinghai was also known as Zhoushan. Toward the end of the Ming, Prince Lu ruled as regent here.[48] This was the place where, as Master Huang Lizhou said, as the sun set over rough waters, ruler and minister faced each other, and members of the gentry gathered and conversed on a remote and desolate isle in the midst of jumbled reefs.[49] Reflecting on *The Record of Remembrances* and reciting the poem about "gathering ferns," I thought of the previous dynasty, which had gone by like a fleeting dream.[50] As the millet grew

....

47 The Junior General Li was Li Zhaodao (fl. 8th century), the son of Li Sixun (651–718), the Senior General Li. Both father and son were well-known painters and excelled in the "golden and green landscape" (*jin bi shanshui*) style.

48 The Prince of Lu was born Zhu Yihai (1618–1662). He was a member of the Ming royal house. After the capital Beijing was captured by rebels and the Chongzhen Emperor (1611–1644) committed suicide in 1644, the Prince of Fu (1607–1646) was enthroned in Nanjing and established the Southern Ming regime, and the Prince of Lu was stationed at Taizhou, Zhejiang. A year later, the Southern Ming fell, and the Prince of Lu was made regent.

49 Huang Zongxi (1610–1695), a native of Zhejiang who was born in the late Ming dynasty and lived into the early Qing, was an eminent scholar and thinker as well as a Ming loyalist.

50 *The Record of Remembrances* (*Sijiu lu*) was one of Huang Zongxi's many works. "Gathering Ferns" (Cai wei) is a poem from the *Classic of Poetry* that describes a military campaign against the northern non-Han tribes.

lushly, I could not help feeling regret that the various lords, who were like swallows building their nests precariously on a curtain, managed state affairs as if they were child's play.[51]

There was a cemetery for palace ladies. I wanted to pay a visit, but was unable to do so.

In a couple of hours, I arrived at Zhenhai. Golden Rooster Mountain and Treasure Gathering Mountain seemed to be greeting me. By the time I reached Ningbo, it was not yet noon. I hurried home, saw my mother, washed, unpacked, and dealt with various things, which came one after another.

I have not yet become satiated with the pleasure of my friends' company or with the enjoyment of mountain and ocean. Whether to stay within the confines of this mundane world or to go beyond them: this is a choice as grave as the matter of life and death. How can I procrastinate any longer? From this point on, I would like to break free from the fetters. I can come and go in a bamboo sedan chair or a little bamboo boat, and manage the orange grove of Blue Creek and the tea plantation at Crimson Wall: that is surely not a task for an extraordinary man. In the following pages, I shall set down, for my own review and benefit, the gains and losses of the governance of the local areas, the good and bad of their customs, as well as what crops are suitable or unsuitable for planting in different places and what the local people like and dislike.

An Account of Taizhou Prefecture

Of the ten prefectures of Zhejiang, Ningbo is the richest, and Taizhou the poorest. The two places are adjacent, but they are exactly opposite in every way. The people of Ningbo are good at accumulating wealth. Every day they devote themselves to financial dealings and management, which is certainly an excellent way of preserving abundance and maintaining peace. Taizhou, on the other hand, used to have a reputation as "the land of Zou and Lu."[52] After the devastation of the Fang Guozhen

....

51   That the millet grew lushly is an allusion to another poem from the *Classic of Poetry*, "Lush Millet" (Shu li), in which, according to the traditional interpretation, an official laments the ruined capital of the Zhou, now overgrown with millet.

52   The State of Zou was the homeland of Mencius, and the State of Lu was the home-

uprising toward the end of the Yuan dynasty, the sound of music and the recitation of classic texts had long ceased.[53] Nevertheless, within just a few dozen years of the uprising, Taizhou produced Fang Xiaoru: this was a clear indication of the fine morals of the locality.[54] Today, however, Taizhou is regarded the gathering place of bandits.

When a young man turns out to be unworthy, it is the shame of his father and elder brother; but his father and elder brother love him no less. If he misbehaves, they might punish him, edify him, try to bring him to his senses with tears in their eyes, but I have never heard of chasing him down and killing him off whether he is deserving or not. Isn't a government official sent by the Son of Heaven to act as a parent to the people? And yet, a number of years ago, the "Incident of the Army of Huangyan Pacification" took place. It was truly shocking.

Before the incident, the harvest had been poor for several years in a row, and many travelers were robbed in the area between Shaoxing and Huangyan. The prefect, whose name shall remain unmentioned, was a forceful and capable man. It so happened that the former county magistrate of Huangyan was also a butcher in his heart.[55] The two of them schemed together and set up an army regiment, which they called "the Army of Huangyan Pacification." They encouraged the local people to volunteer for conscription, saying, "Now that the seashore region has disturbances, anyone who wants to render a service to the community should join the army. This is the time for you to establish accomplishments." When a volunteer came, they would first question him about his former experience at killing.

"Have you ever been a bandit?" They asked.

The man replied, "No."

"Then can you strike and stab?"

"No."

At this, they said, "You have never been a bandit before, and you don't

land of Confucius. "The land of Zou and Lu" refers to a civilized, virtuous place.

53 Fang Guozhen (1319–1374) was a rebel leader from Taizhou.

54 Fang Xiaoru was a Confucian scholar who was executed for his loyalty to the deposed Jianwen Emperor of the Ming (see note 43).

55 The prefect was named Liu Ao (1829–1887), a native of Hu'nan. He was the prefect of Taizhou from 1864 to 1872. The county magistrate of Huangyan was Sun Xi, whose term was from 1868 to 1873. The incident described here took place in 1869.

know how to kill; you are going to ruin our plan. What use do we have for someone like you?" They subsequently dismissed him.

When another volunteer came, they repeated the questions, received the same answers, and dismissed him just as before. After this happened a few times, all of the volunteers would admit to having been bandits. The two officials were overjoyed. They got five hundred men this way and had them sign a confession; then, one day, they took them by surprise and slaughtered them all, and described them as captured bandits in their report.

A noble man studies the Way and loves people; when he hears a case and passes a verdict, he feels grief and pity upon learning the criminal's motives rather than complacency and joy.[56] These two officials, on the contrary, conspired and tricked people into making fake confessions. The *Poems* describe a noble man as "congenial, gentle and easygoing"—how could they bear to devise a plan like this?[57] The prefect was even recommended for a promotion because of what he did, and rose by two ranks. Someone composed the following couplet about him: "How pitiful that the blood of numerous common folks / Dyed red the cap badge on the head of the turtle."[58] What misery! But in the end he was demoted and died in disgrace. The county magistrate of Huangyan went broke because of his obsession with a femme fatale and met a sudden death in a traveler's lodge. Misfortune indeed fell upon the wicked—the gray heaven was not in a drunken stupor after all.

The Six Counties of Taizhou

There are six counties in the Prefecture of Taizhou. The ones I did not

....

56 This is an allusion to the *Analects* 19.19. When someone consulted Zengzi about being a criminal judge, Zengzi said, "The authorities have lost their Way, and the people have been disorganized for a long time. Once you understand the motives behind any crime, you should feel grieved and compassionate for the accused instead of complacent and joyful [about your own ability]."

57 "Congenial, gentle, and easygoing" (*kaiti*) are the attributes of a "noble man" (*junzi*); this appears in several poems in the *Classic of Poetry*. For instance, a couplet in "Deep Ladling" (Jiong zhuo) reads, "The congenial, gentle, and easygoing noble man / Is the parent of the people."

58 The Chinese word for "turtle," *ao*, puns with the prefect's personal name.

have a chance to visit during this trip were Taiping and Ninghai, though I had been to Ninghai before. It is a wealthy area; its people are frugal, and its customs are decent. As for Taiping, judged from the behavior of Wu Molin, might it be a place with little sense of rites and shame? But be it so, one can always find a loyal and trustworthy man even in a small village with ten households, and we should not dismiss a place just because of one bad person.

Linhai's soil is poor, its customs are unkind, and its people harbor no far-reaching aspiration. Its mountains and rivers have a depressive aura. I once climbed onto a high place there and gazed into distance, and noticed a vaguely harsh atmosphere, which was quite strange.

Xianju's terrain is bare and craggy; in truth "there are few talented men but many rocks."[59] The local people are greedy and cruel, and I almost suspect that this is their inborn nature rather than something induced by circumstances. And yet, this is an impoverished county. How could any worthy magistrate, as the parent to the common folk, remain indifferent to this? If the right kind of crop were planted there, then some agricultural profit could still be reaped.

Huangyan has the Yandang Mountains to its left and the Tiantai Mountains to its right; in front of Huangyan there is Haimen, and behind it Square Hill serves as a screen. With fertile soil and deep sands, it is a well-to-do place. The locals had felt alienated since the "Incident of the Army of Huangyan Pacification," but after proper care and maintenance, the place has since recovered, and even its cultural ambience is being improved every day.

Tiantai is different from all of the other counties. It is the poorest, and yet it remains unshaken in its morals, and its people are ashamed of violating the law. Its only contemptible customs are the local gentry's love of lawsuit and the common folk's inclination to drown baby girls. Nevertheless, when we trace these customs to their roots, we realize that they are caused by nothing other than poverty. That the wise man takes delight in water while the benevolent man takes delight in hills is a statement made by the Sage.[60] When heaven produces myriad creatures, it

....

59   This quotation is from the Tang writer Liu Zongyuan's (773–819) famous landscape essay, "An Account of the Little Stone Wall Hill" (Xiaoshichengshan ji).
60   The quote is from the *Analects* 6.21.

always provides for them. I wonder if the poverty of Tiantai is due to the fact that people have not yet been able to make full use of the soil, or perhaps there is further work to be done about water conservancy and irrigation of the farming fields. I once went to the south city gate of Shaoxing, looked at the river there, and asked Ye Ahsheng about its source. Ahsheng said, "It comes from Great West Stream and Small West Stream, and flows into the sea. The water source is Blue Col." During my visit to the Correct and Extensive Temple, while watching the cascade at Stone Bridge, Qiutan told me that the water would flow through Xinchang to irrigate Cheng County. It dawned on me that the two waterways could certainly be put to good use. It is the nature of water to flow ceaselessly, and it is up to human planning and strategizing to guide its course and make it twist and turn. I regret that I did not stay long enough in Tiantai to talk to people who could show me the local terrain little by little, and this has been very much on my mind.

The city of Tiantai has eight gates, but there is no city wall. The gates never close at night, and so need not be reopened in the morning. From time to time there are petty thefts, but the thieves are good at stealing from their neighbors and do not aim for the faraway. They make off with no more than a thousand coins each time, and their moderation and honesty are quite respectable. Following the teachings of Master Zhizhe, the residents of Tiantai do not fish or hunt; it has been thus for almost three thousand years, from the seventh year of the Taijian era of the Chen dynasty until today.[61] The children of Tiantai are often very smart. I once saw a cute little boy at Flowing Light Pavilion. I asked about his age, and it turned out that he was only seven years old. I asked him if he had learned to read and write. He said, "'*You, you*, the deer cry.'"[62] I playfully tried to offer him some coins; he just smiled and ran away. People told me that he was going to be apprenticed to some businessman the following year.

If the spiritual energy of mountains and rivers is not expressed through human beings, it will be repressed and blocked. And yet, human

....

61   The Taijian era of the Chen dynasty lasted from 569 to 582. A mere 1,300 years, rather than three thousand, had elapsed between the Taijian era and the author's time.

62   This is a line from the *Classic of Poetry*, which was part of a child's education in premodern times.

beings themselves must also find a way to release such energy. If they do not cultivate their virtue and engage in studies, the ethereal numinousness of the human heart will be clogged, and it will be impossible to gradually draw out its pure concerns. If the Way of the Great Three [i.e., Heaven, Earth, and Man] is cut off, then the myriad principles will fall into disarray and the world will become lawless. Nowadays, talented people, like good timber, are numerous, but no great craftsman is in sight.[63] Is it really true that such an extraordinary region intends to conceal its treasure for self-amusement only? This is quite lamentable.

When the country is in good order, the Buddhists roam beyond the heavenly realm, the Daoists roam beyond the human realm, and the world is managed by the Confucians. At a time when the Buddhists and the Daoists hide their traces, the Confucians grow old and die at home, the common folk become increasingly impoverished and try to swindle one another, famines occur in succession, and brutal strongmen are ready to pounce on the weak, invasions and attacks from the enemy states are not far behind. Once I was visiting Jinhua, and my boat passed by the South River Temple of Lanxi. I went ashore to see sights, and noticed a couplet hanging on the two sides of a local theatre stage: "As tigers and leopards eat people, dragons and krakens arise into clouds; / when phoenixes and unicorns appear in the world, roosters and dogs will also ascend to heaven." I inquired about the author of the couplet, and someone told me it was written by a Buddhist monk. "Where is he now?" I asked. "He is long gone" was the answer I received. But how could such a couplet have been written by someone roaming beyond the heavenly realm? I composed a poem as a follow-up:

Leaping out of the ravine, rising to the clouds: a temper [—] virile;[64]
In those days, even Zhou Chu was like a dragon.[65]

....

63   The author is punning on *cai* (talent) and *cai* (timber).
64   One character in this line is illegible.
65   Zhou Chu (236–297) was a native of the Wu Kingdom in south China. In his youth he was notorious for being a local bully with great physical strength, and was considered by his fellow townsmen to be one of the "Three Scourges," along with a man-eating tiger and a water beast. After getting rid of the tiger and the "dragon," he realized that he was the third scourge and subsequently reformed his ways. He became a famous administer and general serving the Jin dynasty, and

Whether a man remains a recluse or comes out to serve:
    it matters for all time;
Deeds and fame in this world adrift:
    ten thousand bushels of grain for nothing.[66]
One should go to the falling flowers
    and seek a dreaming butterfly;[67]
The wandering honeybee should never bother
    with floating catkins.[68]
There are many understanding friends
    at the edge of the world—
Cherish your frosty blade,
    and wipe clean your sword's tip.

Fortunately, the country has been enjoying peace for a long time. Scholars are all studying the classics, and officials all obey the law. If we do not make plans and preparations for the future now, fostering true talents and fully utilizing the soil, but draining and exhausting them instead, then even a fool would feel apprehensive. Let me take Taizhou as an example: members of the gentry are smart, but receive no cultivation; the common folk are indigent, but get no help to become better off. Since the soil of Taizhou is poor, one must grow crops that are appropriate to it. Mulberry, hemp, cotton, catalpa, paulownia, and lacquer trees should be planted widely. Instead, the people of Taizhou use their most fertile fields for poppies nowadays. Some say that as long as it brings a handsome profit, what harm could there be in growing poppies? They little understand that poppies are poisonous, and that, after their juice saturates the soil for a long time, it is no longer possible to plant anything else there. This is much like eating arsenic to satisfy hunger, but the ignorant folk are uninformed and have no foresight. Besides, opium

....

     authored several works, including one about the local customs of the Wu region.

66   "Ten thousand bushels of grain" was the salary of a highly placed minister, and was used to refer to prominent official positions.

67   Zhuangzi dreamed of being a butterfly. Upon waking, he remarked that he did not know whether he was Zhuangzi dreaming of being a butterfly or a butterfly dreaming of being Zhuangzi. The story became a famous allegory of the illusoriness of human life.

68   That is, one should not be concerned with the affairs of the world.

destroys lives. How can we plant something that kills people in the soil that should nourish them? I hope that those who are bent on changing the ways of the world will give some thought to this matter.

In the art of war, grief leads to victory. In a person's life, grief is truly the major human emotion. Happiness may come from within, while joy and anger are caused by external stimuli; none of these emotions, however, forms the roots of human nature. In the old days, Mr. Bao Shenbo authored *The Twin Depths*.[69] His son-in-law read it and did not quite grasp its meaning. He questioned Mr. Bao, who said to him, "The key is to stay close to human feelings." What he means, I take it, is that we must get to the roots of human nature.

The "One-Headed Woman" at Huangyan

During my recent trip, I traveled to Huangyan by boat. On the boat there was a "one-headed woman" in her forties who was full of grief and good at wailing. The "one-headed woman" refers to a childless widow; when she weeps, those who listen to her are all deeply affected. Those ferry boats coming and going between Huangyan and Shaoxing always hire a woman like that, for if the boat is too crowded and passengers get into a brawl, she can restore peace with her tears. When I boarded the boat to Huangyan, it was packed. There were people from Hu'nan and from Anhui; most of them were conscripted soldiers, and the rest were farming hands and merchants. They were loud and boisterous, squabbling and bickering with one another ceaselessly. It was complete chaos. The woman walked into the cabin slowly, addressed all the passengers, and asked them to be quiet. In the meanwhile, her tears started to fall. Some of the passengers knew what she was up to, and questioned her on purpose, upon which she sobbed even more sadly. The passengers all burst into laughter. The woman began to relate all of the misfortunes she had suffered, but no one was moved. With tears streaming down her face, she proceeded to talk about how, in her remaining years, her sole livelihood depended upon these passengers, and so they were like nurturing parents to her.

....

69   Bao Shenbo was the courtesy name of Bao Shichen (1775–1855), scholar, writer, and calligrapher.

"But now that you are all fighting with one another," she said, "if something bad should happen to you, it would be my fault, and I would not be able to redeem myself even if I were to die ten thousand deaths. Wouldn't you feel sorry then? What's more, I can see that you are all traveling alone, but at home you may have a wife, you may have children, you may have parents and brothers. I imagine they are all relying on you. Now that you are away from home, your flesh and blood, near or far, must be thinking of you all the time. They worry about you traveling through wind and waves, fogs and dews. They may wake up from sleep because they have a dream about you, or they may be startled by a disquieting thought. Your children may pull their mother's clothes and ask about you; your wife may weep on her lonely pillow. They are all waiting for you to come home early and keep the household together. Now you bicker with one another like this—if you hurt yourself, how could you face your family?"

At this point she was so choked with tears that she collapsed on the ground with a sad cry. The passengers all looked at one another and were deeply touched. Some of them wept as well. They asked her to say no more, but she went on talking, sobbing and wiping away tears as if she were completely overwhelmed by her feelings. By the time she finally stopped, the boat was so quiet that it was as if nobody were there. . . .[70] Fortunately, the lotion for chapped hands is used only for washing silk,[71] and travelers all benefit from the practice. Otherwise, I do not know the limit of the application of such cunning. This is a good example of the Huangyan people's ingenuity.

. . . .

70 Two lines here were crossed out in the manuscript. A note, which was apparently meant to be the correct version, was written in the margin of the page right above the crossed-out lines, but the handwriting was too small and rough to be legible. The general sense of the note seems to be that the woman went on to rearrange the seating of the passengers, who all acquiesced meekly. The author then commented on how the woman's way of working the passengers was just like a military strategist.

71 This is a reference to a story in the first chapter of *Zhuangzi*. In the story, a family that made a living by washing silk had a secret recipe for a potent hand lotion. They sold the recipe to a traveler, who offered it to the King of Wu. The king's soldiers used the lotion on their hands during a winter water battle with the people of Yue and won a great victory, and the traveler was rewarded handsomely by the king.

Ten Poems on Xianju

The people of Xianju do not possess the Huangyan people's cleverness or the Tiantai people's benevolence; therefore, they constantly violate the law. And yet, what they gain by risking their lives is very little, not to mention that in many cases the accusation is simply false. This is truly lamentable.

I once composed ten poems about Xianju. They are as follows.[72]

(1)
Located in the human realm like all others,
This place alone is desolate, deplorable.

As autumn wind blows in the hills, ghosts cry;
> *There are many so-called phantom-coach birds in the local hills; they are also known as "goatsuckers."*
Pestilential vapors in spring fatten the pythons.
> *There is a mountain snake called Snow Python. It thrives in pestilential vapors and grows even fatter. Its meat is edible.*

Jade wrapped in stone: patterning exists in vain;
> *The hills produce a kind of patterned stone, which is often used for seals.*
Tide rises, washing metal sand on the cold shore.
> *The water of the rapids is extremely cold. Diviners who work by observing auras say that there is iron in it.*

A solitary town, overgrown in the wilderness,
Concealed by ten thousand layers of mountain azure.[73]

(2)
As the misty rain clears in the morning,
The mountains and groves reveal their natural charm.
> *In the mountains there are many pines, cedars, and other trees good for timber.*

....

72   Following traditional practice, the author appends many notes in prose to the poems. These notes appear in a smaller font in the manuscript, and I have preserved this feature in the translation and italicized the notes.

73   A note was crossed out here in the manuscript.

A fine breeze reverberates in crags and valleys;
Amid the tall trees, rosy vapors overflow.

A sweet aroma emits from the "cliff orchid" pendant;
  *"Cliff orchid" is no different from the ordinary kinds of orchid. Its root has
  sections like bamboo; its leaves also resemble bamboo leaves. It is a small
  plant, and can be planted in a pot. The local people like to wear it in their
  clothes, claiming that it can ward off heat and help women give birth to boys.*
Chuzhou's atractylodes bloom give off a pure aura.[74]
  *White atractylodes grow profusely in the mountains. They are cultivated
  by the locals. The kind from Chuzhou is the best, hence the name.*

Quiet, empty, distant from the dusty world:
Truly a suitable dwelling for immortals.
  *There was a local beggar, Old Chu Lai, who always wore a robe made of
  hemp cloth, in winter and summer. Even when he had nothing to eat,
  he did not appear hungry. He always looked to be in his forties. People
  thought he was an immortal.*

(3)
Cooking smoke at the tip of cold trees:
In the haze one makes out a few homes.

Roasting sweet potatoes—the mountain cogon grass is wet;
  *The locals are impoverished and cannot afford rice; they eat sweet pota-
  toes instead.*
Pounding clouds: the rice huller propelled by water tilts over.
  *This is the one device upon which the people of this county depend for
  their livelihood. They use waterwheels to irrigate their fields and pound
  rice. But when one family's land is watered, another family's land becomes
  dry. People often fight over the water supply and even file lawsuits
  against one another; some families went broke because of this.*

....

74   Atractylodes refers to *Atractylodes macrocephala*, known as *Bai zhu* in Chinese. It is
     a perennial herb that flowers from July to September and bears fruit from August
     to October; its root is used as a common ingredient in Chinese herbal medicine.

Flowing mist in the hills is suitable for bamboo;

> *The hills are good for growing bamboos. The locals, however, do not care*
> *about bamboos, and cut them off as soon as they sprout, because they*
> *believe bamboos attract ghosts and are inauspicious. Bamboos are grown*
> *by some people at Tiantai.*

Sand beach is warm, wonderful for tea plantation.

> *The soil is good for growing tea; but the locals do not know the right way*
> *of baking the tea leaves. As soon as they pick them, they boil them in*
> *a wok, and then they throw out the juice and dry them in the sun. The*
> *furled and unfurled tea leaves are all damaged, and their color and taste*
> *completely change. Since they make very little profit from their tea, even*
> *fewer people are willing to plant it.*

How regrettable, that in farm plot after farm plot,
Poppies bloom in the spring wind.

(4)
Singing of picking the "Blue Robe,"
The local folk brave danger, trudging in the craggy hills.

> *The "Blue Robe" is also called "Rock's Robe." It grows in deep ravines*
> *under shaded cliffs, where there is little human traffic. Produced by wet*
> *pestilential vapors, it is of a dark blue or cobalt color and as thick as*
> *coarse hemp cloth. It tastes like wood-ears but is not as smooth, and it*
> *has a very cold nature. Picking the "Blue Robe" is not an easy task: many*
> *people die of bites by poisonous snakes or tigers or by falling on jumbled*
> *rocks. Because of the difficulty of its acquisition, local officials think of it*
> *as a rare delicacy and demand it for their kitchens.*

The bones of rocks bring a hair-raising chill;
People risk their remaining years amid poisonous snakes.

Grand officials have a fastidious taste for delicacies;
The lives of the poor are thrown away to wind and dust.

At evening banquets, the government chef presents it to the guests—

Compared to it, the brasenia soup is not worth praising.[75]

(5)
The land takes pride in its perilous terrain;
The people are used to swindling and boasting.

Local music surprises the listener by its austerity;
> *The sound of local music is very sad and reduces one to tears. It is used for sacrifices, official business, weddings, and feasts. Those who understand music say that it is the sound of crying out to the heavens.*

The ritual of receiving guests showcases dance moves.
> *When the locals bow and kneel to greet or bid farewell, they make certain gestures like dancing.*

One may get in trouble over a peacemaking drink;
> *When there is a conflict between two families, their kinsfolk give a banquet to settle the dispute. However, as soon as the problem is solved, the kinsfolk give the two families a hard time by demanding money from them as a token of their gratitude. If they do not pay up, then the kinsfolk file a lawsuit. Some families consequently become bankrupt; occasionally people even lose their lives.*

Or become obsessed with the "flower gambling."
> *The "flower assembly" is very much in vogue. Numerous locals pursue the activity like ants, and many people have gone broke.[76]*

Late at night, the sound of sending off demons—
Gongs and drums regularly make an uproar.
> *The locals do not believe in medicine. If someone is ill, they say the patient is possessed by demons. They "send off" the demons to the wilderness by beating on gongs and drums; then they claim that the patient is cured.*

(6)
Down-and-out, cap and gown are lowly and humble;[77]

....

75 *Brasenia* is an aquatic plant in south China; its soup is considered a delicacy.
76 The "flower assembly" was a form of gambling that was particularly popular in the coastal area of southeastern China.
77 "Cap and gown" refers to the scholar elite.

Messy and confused, bandits and thieves raise a ruckus.

> *The county is famous for being the home of bandits in southeastern China, but in fact many "bandits" are falsely accused. The truth is that they are so destitute that they do not have anything to live on. The money they rob often amounts to no more than a few dozen coins, and for such a crime they receive capital punishment. They are led to the execution ground in a daze; some of them have no idea what they are going to be executed for.*[78]

Man and wife are separated like birds;

> *Many women cannot manage for themselves, and have to remarry three or four times, even if their husbands are alive and well.*

Struggling for food and clothes: crabs crawling on sand.

Their suffering: a hedgehog hiding its head;
Their sadness: a crow that loses its voice.

His Highness, who is the parent of the folk,
Might want to think of mulberry and hemp for their sake.

> *The soil there is good for growing mulberry and hemp. If the local people could plant and cultivate them and produce silk and hemp cloth, they might be relieved from their poverty somewhat; but somehow no one has considered this option.*

(7)

A lawsuit may drag on for years,
And involve dozens of families.

> *When one family becomes embroiled in a lawsuit, the neighbors are compelled to give financial assistance; otherwise, they would be implicated. Relatives and friends thus all get entangled in the mess; sometimes, even those who live tens and hundreds of leagues away are not spared.*

The common folk, so pathetic, are chased down like sparrows and rats;
Fanatic clerks act like krakens and snakes.

Copper, iron, gold, silver, and tin;

....

78   Two and a half lines were crossed out here in the manuscript.

Oil, salt, soy, vinegar, and tea—

Everything must be prepared in profusion,
In order to greet the officer's coach.

> *When someone gets killed in a fight, the officials arrive to conduct the*
> *examination of the body. The clerks take this opportunity to demand*
> *bribery, which they call the "fetching price." The bribery ranges from*
> *thousands of cash for a big case to hundreds for a small case, depending*
> *on the wealth of the village. But no village is exempt. If there is any lack*
> *at all in the food and drink and other provisions offered to the clerks,*
> *they take it from the local people like bandits and robbers. From pigs and*
> *chickens to wooden fences, nothing is left intact. The officials are unable*
> *to stop them. If they try to stop them, the clerks simply get up and leave,*
> *an action called "disbanding."*

(8)
Words are dangerous, capable of melting metal;
With outlandish accusation, imperfection can be found on white jade.

The official is surely a bright mirror illuminating everything:
How could an eminent clan harbor criminals?

> *Year after year the county is plagued by bandits. Some say that large local*
> *clans are in fact giving shelter to them. The clans are supposed to instigate*
> *the bandits to rob and steal, and afterward share the spoils; once the ban-*
> *dits are caught, the clans intervene on their behalf and once again make a*
> *profit. I wonder, however, if this could really be the case.*

Do not try to turn back the water flowing east;
Do not talk about the raft that goes against the currents.

Spring comes, autumn is gone:
One should just live one's life in silence.

(9)
I hear that there was a Magistrate Yu,

> *Lord Yu's name was Jieshi. He was a native of the Xi County of Anhui.*
> *He served as Magistrate of Xianju during the Xianfeng and Tongzhi eras*
> *[1851–74], and did many good things for the local people during his term.*

Who once upon a time rested his coach at this place.

Minister Du's heart was heavy with concerns;
Tears streamed down the face of Tutor Jia at Changsha.[79]

His character and deeds are nobler than anything else in all time;
He treated officials and the common folk as one family.

Even today, his gracious influence remains:
During the spring sacrifices, people weep over incense and flowers.
> The locals built a shrine to worship Magistrate Yu at Divine Tree Mountain. They make sacrifices to his spirit twice a year, once in spring and once in autumn. Those who suffer from injustice go there and pray to him in tears.

(10)
I, too, am a commoner in hard straits,
Not to mention wandering at the world's edge.

With hot tears, I lament the hill wraith,
And endeavor to continue the songs of Chu with odd writings.[80]

The fair one is on the other side of the autumn river;
Fragrant plants are equally distant in my dreams.

....

79   In this couplet the author compares Magistrate Yu to the Tang poet Du Fu, who expressed an intense concern about the troubled empire in his poetry, and to the Western Han political theorist and writer Jia Yi (200–168 bce), whose suggestions about state policy were not adopted, despite the emperor's sympathy, due to the opposition of his political enemies. In 177 bce, Jia Yi was exiled from the capital and appointed as tutor to the Prince of Changsha (in modern Hu'nan).

80   *The Songs of Chu* (*Chu ci*), also known as *The Songs of the South*, is an anthology of verse whose main texts were conventionally attributed to Qu Yuan (fl. 4th century bce) and his "disciple" Song Yu. Traditional interpreters read these works as an allegorical expression of Qu Yuan's lament over his political misfortune and his quest for a worthy ruler. "Fragrant plants" in these verses are taken to represent the poet's virtue, and "the fair one" (often a god or goddess) is supposed to be a reference to the worthy lord. "The Hill Wraith" is one of the "Nine Songs" from this corpus, in which the poet-shaman seeks an elusive mountain goddess.

The red "love bean" growing in the southland
Flowers in vain, year after year.[81]

I was traveling in the Wu region when I composed these poems, hence the mention of "wandering."[82] Ah, the "Turbulent Chu" is desolate and cold; I can hardly bear thinking of it further.[83]

The Birds of Xianju

There are two kinds of bird songs in the mountains of Xianju and both are very melancholy. One is known as "Poor Daddy." According to the local legend, once there was a girl who got up at midnight to feed silkworms but discovered that she had run out of mulberry leaves. Her father tried to steal some from someone else's mulberry tree, and was killed by the tree's owner. The girl cried sadly for three days and died of grief. Her spirit turned into a bird. The other bird song is known as "Big Sister, Go Pick Tea Leaves." It is said that there was a girl who was abused by her step-mother. Her little half sister, who was born to her stepmother, bullied her as well. Every day before dawn the half sister would urge her, "Big sister, it's time for you to go pick tea leaves now." The girl finally died of resentment and became a bird. I composed two poems to elaborate these tales.

(1)
Poor daddy! Poor daddy!
He does not have a son to support the household.
We suffer so much hardship tending the silkworms;
The leaves are all gone,
    the silkworms are hungry,
        and we are full of worries.
Poor daddy! He told me not to worry:

....

81   The "love bean" refers to the seeds of *abrus precatorius*, a symbol of love-longing.
82   The Wu region refers to the Yangzi River Delta, with Suzhou as the former capital of the ancient Kingdom of Wu.
83   The "Turbulent Chu" (Ji Chu) was the name of a musical piece that appears in *The Song of Chu*.

"Father's and daughter's lives depend on these silkworms;
I will steal some mulberry leaves, so you can feed them."
Poor daddy—he braved frost and dews
    on a cloudy night with no moon.
How pitiful that he never came home again—
With an ax our cruel enemy struck him down.
Poor daddy!
That I was unable to take revenge for you
    and report the crime to the officials!
The cold wind was howling,
    gods and ghosts were crying,
I wished to turn into a little bird
    and tell of my sorrow and pain.
Poor daddy!
In the spring months, the weather is fine;
The mulberry leaves are dense,
    the moon is mid-heaven.
I don't see my daddy anywhere,
I see only those mulberry trees in vain.
The earth below is thick, and the heaven above is high,
But my regret will never end.
Regret will never end,
Oh, poor daddy indeed!

(2)
"Big sister, go pick tea leaves!"
It is still dark outside—
Where do you want me to go?
Fog and rain in the hills: water flows on and on;
Abuse and injury in this world: suffering upon suffering.
Even though daddy says nothing at all,
He feels sad in his heart, his tears secretly fall.
Both are daddy's flesh and blood;
Why are they treated so differently?
We are not treated differently—
It is just that my little sister is spoiled.
Heaven above is high, the earth below is thick;
My father's and mother's kindness is infinite.

But truly my little sister is spoiled,
Truly my little sister is spoiled.
"Big sister, why don't you go pick tea leaves now?"

When those birds cried on a clear and quiet night, it nearly broke my heart.

PART TWO

TAIZHOU has been a desolate spot on the distant seashore ever since ancient times. Its people are probably what Ban Gu's work refers to as the "people of Eastern Ti."[1] During the Tang dynasty, Taizhou gradually became better known. And yet, when Zheng Qian was demoted to administrative aide of Taizhou, Du Fu wrote a poem to send him off, in which he regarded Taizhou as a foreign land, for it was a faraway border region with pestilential miasmas, not the kind of place that should be visited by a gentleman. Bo Daoyou claimed that it was the dwelling place of gods, and Sun Xinggong depicted it as an immortal isle.[2] This is just what an old saying describes: "Mountains and groves, bells and tripods—different people love different things."[3]

I have already turned forty, the age of "having no doubts," but I still live in shameful obscurity.[4] Rather than merely breathing in the world of men and being of no use for my home and country, I might as well seek out the mountain retreat and rest my spirit beyond the cloud vapors. If I

....

1   Ban Gu (32–92) was a historian and writer who authored *The History of Han* (*Han shu*).

2   Bo Daoyou, a native of Shaoxing, was a Buddhist monk who lived in the second half of the fourth century. Sun Xinggong was Sun Chuo (314–371), a prominent Eastern Jin poet who composed the famous "Poetic Exposition on Roaming Mount Tiantai" (*You Tiantai shan fu*).

3   "Mountains and groves" represent a reclusive life outside the public sphere, while "bells and tripods" refer to the lifestyle of an official.

4   Confucius remarked that he no longer had doubts when he became forty years old (*Analects* 2.4).

do that, then even with this heaven-forsaken body I might still manage to enjoy the blessings reserved for those with a fine reputation. I would be able to discuss poetry and classics as well as the principles of benevolence and righteousness with the young; I would also be able to chat about farming matters with old peasants. Not to mention there would be Daoist adepts and Buddhist monks who could entertain me; cranes in the autumn and gibbons in the spring to befriend me and quell my mundane thoughts. I would love to ride on the clouds and roam Heavenly Pillar Mountain. Therefore, on the day after I returned to Ningbo, I paid a visit to Chen Yuyu, who was a native of Tiantai. I expressed my admiration for him and asked him to help me find a small house there. Surely Yuyu would do something about this.

Birth and Early Childhood

I was born on the first day of the first month in the *jiayin* year of the Xianfeng era [January 29, 1854]. At the time, my late father was forty-six years old, so he nicknamed me "Four-six." I went to school at the age of four. My teacher was Mr. Zhang, whose personal name was De and courtesy name was Wangzong. He was an aging Licentiate Scholar. My classmate was our neighbor's son, Wang Kanghou, whose personal name was Jin. He was born one day before me, so I would address him as "Elder Brother Thirty," and he would call me "Little Brother First."[5]

As a child I did not like playing. I had a dozen cousins, who fooled around together and were sometimes as noisy as a boiling cauldron. I, on the other hand, just watched them with wide eyes. Occasionally, I would get into a fight with them, and none proved my match. I was fond of sweets, and would cry for sweets day and night. One day, I mistook alum for sugar and put it in my mouth. It tasted so horrible that I have stayed away from sugar ever since. My mother still teases me about it.

I was capricious by nature. My wet nurse would put dozens of toys in front of me to amuse me; but in the midst of pleasure, I would get up, toss them away, and leave them behind without ever glancing back, as if I had been suddenly seized by a deep sadness. Looking back now, I wonder

. . . .

5   Wang Kanghou was born on the thirtieth day of the twelfth month, hence "Elder Brother Thirty."

if that could have been an omen that I would suffer the early loss of my parents.[6]

Before I was born, my legal mother, Madame Chen, had prayed to the "Fretful Master" at Asoka Temple in Xiaoshan. That night, she dreamt that she had obtained a gigantic white conch, which was as bright and shiny as a mirror. That was how I got my baby name, "Treasure." I was, however, almost killed in the chaos caused by the Yue bandits.[7]

On the Run: 1861–1863

When the Yue bandits attacked Shaoxing, I was only seven. I was saved by our hired hand, Lu Sanyi, who was from Black Stone Village. Sanyi took me to his house. That was on the twenty-sixth day of the ninth month in the *gengshen* year [October 29, 1861].[8] At the time, the prefecture seat [i.e., Shaoxing] had not yet fallen to the bandits. Previously, when I was five and was living with my father at South Qinghe, where he was serving in public office,[9] I was sent home to Shaoxing in the chaos caused by the Nian rebels. Half a year later, my legal mother went back to South Qinghe before the appointed time, though she had promised to send someone to fetch me. But before she could do that, we were unexpectedly caught up in the Taiping Rebellion. At the time, there were only five of us at our Shaoxing home: myself, my grandfather's concubine Madame Li, my birth mother Madame Wang, my father's concubine Madame Lou, and my aunt, who is now married to Mr. Lu.[10] We were a helpless group. My paternal uncles and cousins did not have time to take care of us.

On the twenty-seventh day, the alarm was raised, and the danger

....

6   By the "early loss of his parents" the author refers to his father and his "legal mother" (i.e., his father's principal wife), not his birth mother, who seemed to be still alive when he was writing this book.

7   That is, the Taiping rebels.

8   A note, scribbled in the upper margin of the manuscript page, states, "It was the eleventh year [of the Xianfeng era], the year of *xinyou*; '*gengshen*' [the tenth year of the Xianfeng era] was an error."

9   South Qinghe was in Huai'an of Jiangsu, about three hundred miles to the north of Shaoxing.

10   "Lou" was crossed out in the manuscript and "Deng" (another surname) was added in the margin. The same happens later in part 2 when the woman's surname is mentioned again.

was pressing. On the twenty-eighth, the situation became a little better. Then there came news that the military forces organized by the magistrate had gotten into a fight with the civilians.[11] Many people died. Their bodies piled up inside the city gate, and nobody knew who they were. On the twenty-ninth, around midnight, one could see fires breaking out in the city in thirteen different places.[12] However, it was very quiet in the village. I suppose everyone was sitting behind closed doors and sighing with worries, just as we were. The bamboo leaves outside the house where we stayed made a rustling sound in the drizzling rain, from time to time arousing a bird from its sleep. Whenever that happened, we would be startled as well, and would look at one another in dejection. Sanyi's mother told us not to worry, and charged Sanyi with the task of taking care of me alone, saying, "Never mind the others." When he heard that, Sanyi burst into tears. As soon as first light appeared, we went into the mountains to hide from the bandits, but in the end nothing happened that day.

On the first and second of the tenth month, occasionally someone came from the direction of the city and said that the bandits had posted flyers to pacify the people. They asked the villages to give them what they could, and expected to cause no disturbance. People gradually calmed down upon hearing that.

At the time, some young people from the neighboring village were planning to form a "righteous militia" against the bandits. We speculated that once this happened, the bandits would suspect our village of being part of the conspiracy and descend upon us soon. One evening, there was a violent rainstorm. Sanyi, in the midst of drinking, suddenly leapt up and yelled, "Run! The bandits are here!" He scooped me up, carried me on his back, and fled into the mountains. The "bandits" indeed came. There were shouts all around, and the entire village clamored and took flight. Only in the morning did we find out that it was actually the "righteous militia" disguised as bandits. Thanks to Sanyi's mother, my mother, my aunt, and others were led to a hiding place in the graveyard and escaped harm. About ten villagers were killed or hanged themselves. Household

....

11   The Shaoxing magistrate was Liao Zongyuan (1810–1861), who died after the city was taken. The conflict between the civilians and the government troops on the eve of the fall of Shaoxing is well documented.

12   On this day, which was November 1, 1861, the Taiping army captured Shaoxing.

valuables, chickens, and dogs were all taken. That, gentle reader, was the doing of the so-called righteous militia.

Shortly afterward, the bandits really came. The "righteous militia" fought with them and lost. Everyone fled into the mountains, eating acorns during the day, and hiding among brambles at night. There was a Mr. Meng, who was a doctor from the city. He brought with him his wife and a three-year-old son. One day, as we were hiding together, it rained, and the boy started to cry. An old woman holding prayer beads and reciting the Buddha's name detested the boy, for she was convinced that his cries would lead the bandits to us. She kept muttering about it while reciting the Buddha's name. Thereupon Mr. Meng tore the boy apart and killed him with his own hands. My grandfather's concubine tried to snatch the boy from him but failed; she was so shocked and distressed that she burst into tears. I was still very young, and had no idea what it was all about; I remember only seeing guts spilling out and blood flowing all over the place, and I was trembling with fright. Alas, the love of father and son is human nature, and yet Mr. Meng cut it off just like that. There are truly all kinds of people in this world. As for that old woman, the saying "Even dogs and pigs would not want to eat such a person's remains" would quite appropriately apply to someone like her.

Danger soon became imminent, so we went to Tiaomachang. Tiaomachang was in the mountains, eight leagues from Black Stone Village. Both places were to the southwest of the prefecture. We took a shortcut by going through Cuangong. Cuangong was the site of the imperial mausoleums of the Southern Song emperors. Zhou Shengjie, my elder sister's husband, had sought refuge at Tiaomachang with his family, so we went to stay with them. Whenever an alarm was raised, Sanyi would inform us, and we would hide out in the mountains. This arrangement worked well for a while.

One day, however, the bandits suddenly came to Tiaomachang by way of Cuangong, which caught Sanyi by surprise. They burned the trees on the Song mausoleums; billowing smoke covered the sky. That was the twenty-seventh day of the eleventh month [December 28]. On that day, just at daybreak, there was a sudden thunderstorm, with violent wind and pouring rain. Hundreds of refugees were flushed down by the mountain flood and broke their limbs. Villagers fled in panic, and screams shook the sky. My mother and I stumbled into the woods, thinking we would surely die. But then Sanyi and his mother, both in tears, rushed there and found us, and we escaped together. Numerous people died during this attack. In some cases, entire families were killed. If not for Sanyi, how could I have made it? Now it has been twenty-three years since Sanyi passed away. One of his sons works hard in the field, and his family has gradually become well-off. I returned to Shaoxing in the *gengwu* year of the Tongzhi era [1870] and visited them. They took me to see Sanyi's grave. Surrounded by withered plants and some randomly strewn stones, it had a forlorn look to it. I offered food to Sanyi's spirit and burned some paper money. I called out to his soul, but there was no response. Looking at the last rays of the setting sun shining on the village houses, bamboos, and trees, I seemed to see his face and hear his voice just like in the old days. How could I not feel a pang in my heart!

At Tiaomachang there was an old woman neé Tang; hers was a well-to-do farming family. At the time, one bushel of rice cost 16,000 cash, and my brother-in-law's parents regarded us as a burden. Although it broke my sister's heart, she could not do anything about it. We wept together, and planned to go back to Black Stone Village and stay with Sanyi. And yet, Sanyi himself was impoverished. Old Woman Tang said, "It is true that rice is expensive at a chaotic time like this. But if the bandits come, our possessions will not be ours anymore. Why don't you all come and stay with me? Don't be so hard on yourselves." So she let us stay with her family and provided for us. It was also thanks to her that Shengjie's entire family, as well as my mother, myself, and others, came out alive from the calamity of the twenty-seventh. What she did was to demolish their house in advance and make it look like it had collapsed on its own; she bid us all hide inside, and then covered the entrance with mutilated corpses. After the rebellion, I saw her again—I was already eighteen years old, but she still called me by my baby name. She showed me around the mountain, pointing out to me places where we had taken cover, and having a good laugh about it. She also gave me a longevity tally, which she said she had received from a monk with supernatural powers at Xiansheng Temple. She was very happy to see me indeed. Now, shouldn't we consider someone like Old Woman Tang as both benevolent and wise? She is now in her eighties, and has as many as twenty-odd grandchildren. They are all hardworking, frugal farmers, well respected in the village. I pay them a visit every time I go back. My sister's family regularly socializes with them, as if they were their own kin.

Lu's Dyke was a river village in the southeastern part of the prefecture. It had several hundred families all surnamed Ni. My fourth sister lived there. When the prefecture seat was about to be captured, my fifth uncle's wife was rescued by their old servant, Ah Zhang, and fled to Houbao. When she heard that we were at Tiaomachang, she sent Ah Zhang to us for news. Only then did we learn that my second uncle's wife, my cousin Xinquan, Xinquan's wife neé Hu, my ninth sister, and my nephew Anxuan had all fled to West Port on the twenty-eighth [of the ninth month]. As for my sixth uncle, my seventh uncle, and my cousin Xiaoyun, their entire families, all living together, were trapped in Shaoxing. My seventh uncle's wife, Madame Yang, drowned herself. At this time, the alarm about the bandits was somewhat lifted. In addition, the bandits posted an announcement, declaring that all landowners were allowed to collect half a year's tax from their land. Lu's Dyke was close to our estate, so we sent Ah Zhang to take my fifth uncle's wife to Lu's Dyke, and we, too, all went there. The bandits stationed in the countryside would come to the village from time to time, but they were disciplined and did not disturb the locals. It seemed that their behavior depended on whether the leader directly supervising them was kind or cruel.

One day, the bandits entered into a battle with the local militia. I knew no fear then and went to watch. When I first got to the battleground, it was all quiet, with not a soul in sight. After a long time, there came the sound of a bugle and drums from behind the walls. A bandit rider galloped ahead and shouted, "Good brothers, charge, kill! Be careful! If we fail, we die. Charge, kill, good brothers!" His voice was drawn out and sad, as heart-rending as a breaking chime stone. At this, the drumbeat became faster and faster, and the soldiers all advanced with battle cries. A strong wind was blowing; guns and cannons went off like thunder. After a short while, smoke was everywhere, and again not a soul was in sight, as the bandits had already ridden away right after their victory.

During the battle the bandits had dragged their dead to an empty space and covered them with flags. At first, I was wondering why the bullets, as dense as flying locusts, never seemed to fall; but when I looked at the flags closely, I noticed that they all had tens of dozens of small round holes, because they were rolled up to wrap the bodies in several layers. There were some bandits who were not quite dead yet, and I kicked and trampled them to vent my loathing and resentment.

Weapons bode evil, and wars are dangerous. If one does not take caution, one will certainly lose. There is something about the bandit rider's battle cry that fits perfectly the principle of "proceeding to action with solicitude."[13] Otherwise how could they manage to unify thousands of people? Was not this the very reason that they could ravish a dozen provinces, and it took no less than the force of the entire country to destroy them in the end? They were truly both tough and cunning.

Shortly afterward, we again ran out of provisions. It so happened that we received an invitation from Diankou, so we went to Diankou.

Diankou belonged to the county of Zhuji, where my legal mother had come from. With mountains in the back and a river in the front, it was but a hundred leagues from Hangzhou. Yiqiao and Linpu were located upstream, and Fuchun was next to it. My maternal uncle and cousin had both passed away at a young age; my cousin's widowed wife neé Feng lived alone with her ten-year-old son, Youqiao. When she learned of our whereabouts, she invited us to join her. We were both sad and happy upon seeing each other. She had a place in a remote, isolated mountain village called Pig's Jaw, where she had stored up all her valuables. We all moved there.

By that time, Bao Village's resistance force had been formed, and the bandits who went to attack them at different times numbered tens of thousands altogether.[14] After each lost battle the bandits would vent their anger and frustration on the neighboring villages, burning and pillaging to their heart's content. Feng said, "We cannot afford to be careless about this." So she hired a dozen strong clansmen who earned their living by physical labor. One of the clansmen was named Wenjing; another was named Xiaofu. She placed me in their care.

We sought refuge at Ding's Port. But Ding's Port had too many petty thieves, so we came back to Diankou. Then I fell sick. I had come down with malaria at Ding's Port, which now turned into dysentery. Soon my head and face were swelling up, and my ten fingers were as thick as hammers. The elders were all shocked upon seeing me like this; they thought I had white jaundice, and nine out of ten with white jaundice would die.

....

13   This is an allusion to Confucius' remark in *Analects* 7.10.

14   The resistance force at Bao Village was led by a man named Bao Lishen (1838–1862). As the force repeatedly fended off the advances of the Taiping army, numerous wealthy families from various places in Zhejiang sought refuge in the village. After more than eight months of fighting, the village was eventually captured, and butchered, on July 27, 1862.

The bandit alarm was raised from time to time, and the cost of rice shot up. My cousin's wife was becoming destitute, for we had gone into the mountains to hide from the bandits and, upon coming home, discovered that the house had been robbed clean. We had bran and wild greens for food. My mother wept all day; even I myself thought I was dying. Fortunately, Xiaofu found a rare remedy and cured me.

I was, however, exceedingly weak and fragile, and was often half-starving. In the hills there was a spring as clear as a mirror. I would follow my mother to pick wild greens there. When we rested by the spring, I saw my reflection in it: I was emaciated and haggard like a ghost. When a chilly wind shook the trees, the cold would penetrate our very flesh and bones. At sunset, we would hold on to each other and walk home, and never failed to burst into tears.

As Bao Village's militia was growing increasingly powerful, many members of the Chen clan went to join them. My cousin's wife also wanted to go, but Wenjing convinced her not to. Soon afterward, Bao Village indeed fell. There was rumor that the bandits would kill everyone in Zhuji to vent their anger, so we again fled to Ding's Port, and Wenjing took me to Houbao.

Wenjing was a relative of my maternal grandfather's generation. My illness was most grave during the high summer, and every day Wenjing would carry me on his back, traveling back and forth in the mountains. As I was suffering from dysentery, stools mixed with blood would soil his back, which became festered. One of his associates regarded me as a burden, and urged him to dispose of me. Wenjing would not listen. He left after he took me to Houbao, and soon afterward died of illness. How painful! Though he was an elder, Wenjing had become a hired hand out of poverty, and had never assumed the authoritative attitude of a senior toward me. Instead, he loved me dearly and sincerely. My cousin's wife and her son thought that even they could not care about me more than he did. He died without a son, and, in the midst of the chaos, no one knew where he was buried, so I cannot even offer a cup of wine as a sacrifice to his spirit. As for me, I have been down-and-out all my useless life, and would probably have been better off dying early in childhood—but then, how could Wenjing have foreseen this? We parted hastily in war and turmoil, little knowing that the farewell would be our last. It is so very sad!

At that time, my cousin Xiaoyun and his wife, Madame Wang, had recently escaped from Shaoxing, and my fifth uncle's wife went to stay with them. They planned to go north by taking the sea route, and sent for me. This was why I went to Houbao. Houbao, however, was not far from Shaoxing, and bandit alarm was raised every day. We were just considering the possibility of moving elsewhere when the news of Zhou's death reached us.

Zhou was a native of Licheng from Shandong. He had followed his parents begging for food on the street in Yuanpu.[15] When his parents died, my father gave them a proper burial, and Zhou henceforth became a member of our household. He was eleven years older than I. In fact, I was born the year after he came, and because of that my father doted on him, and asked me to address him as "older brother" when I was learning to speak. Zhou was extremely naughty. He would run off in the middle of an errand, and pick a fight with other children. Once, when he was carrying me around and playing with me, he caused me to have such a bad fall that I bled profusely and passed out. He was so scared that he fled to Black Stone Village and stayed with Sanyi, and did not dare to come home for a long time. But after he returned, he remained just as wayward as before, and continued to enjoy pulling silly pranks on people. All of the servants and maidservants in the household disliked him and yet were afraid of him. He had, however, a very affectionate nature. Whenever there was any trouble or quarrel in the family, he would become upset and would not eat all day. During the Nian Rebellion he had come back to Shaoxing first, and then went north again with my legal mother. He was turning eighteen years old at the time. Later on, when my father heard of the siege of Shaoxing, he was very worried about us. Zhou said, "Sanyi is with them and can ensure their safety. But since Sanyi's family is poor, they might starve." He asked for permission to fetch us in person. My father thought he was too young to take the trip, and would not agree. He pled even more earnestly. My father finally gave in, and sent him off with a hundred taels of silver. He made it as far as Lianshupu, and died there.

Gu Baotang, a native of Shangyu, had been traveling with him. They parted ways at Lianshupu. Before he left, Gu Baotang said to him, "This is

....

15   Yuanpu was in Huai'an of Jiangsu. Subsequently it is also referred to as Yuanji-
      ang.

no more than a hundred leagues from Shaoxing. Once you find your master's family, let me know." As Gu did not hear from him for a long time, he began wondering. Then, upon learning of our whereabouts, he came to inquire after Zhou. We immediately asked my cousin Wuquan to go and look for him. Wuquan identified the boatman at Lianshupu, who told him that there had indeed been such a passenger: "But he had died of *sha* tympany."[16] Wuquan asked him about the money; the boatman replied that he knew nothing of it. Wuquan asked about Zhou's body; he pointed to a coffin and said, "That's it." Alas, I can well imagine the situation now.

I still remember that during the Nian Rebellion Zhou carried me on his back and fled in panic. I had no idea what was happening, and just wondered why men and women were all crying and running, cramming lanes and alleys. I asked Zhou; he replied, "Just eat your noodles, eat your noodles." This was because I had a particular weakness for noodles and any other flour-made food, and he was trying to divert me. After we returned home, I spent over a year with him every day. I can still picture to myself the way he laughed, and his voice is still ringing in my ears. Who could have known that our eternal parting would take place just before our reunion! I think on how he had hastily traveled a thousand leagues to be with us, completely disregarding his personal safety. Wasn't his single-minded perseverance enough to move heaven and earth and make gods and ghosts weep? And yet, he died alone, having suffered a grievance that would never be redressed, and we were even unable to recover his remains! As for me and my mother, we wandered and drifted amid the dangers of war, not knowing at dawn what might happen to us by dusk. Although I dearly wished to play and laugh with him again and together escape unharmed from the calamity just like in the old days, how could that be possible? Later on, after we finally made our way to Yuanpu, my father became tearful whenever we spoke of him. Therefore I have been making sure to personally offer a cup of wine to his spirit at the annual festivities throughout the years. You, my brother, have left for the world of shadows forever. Thinking back on the brotherly love we shared, how could I ever dispel this sadness over your loss!

As the threat became imminent, we again fled, this time to Temple's

....

16 "Sha tympany" (*sha zhang*) is a general premodern Chinese medical term for unknown disease.

East, and then from Temple's East to Tao's Weir and then to West Port. My cousin Xiaoyun's wife, Madame Wang, died in the tragic incident of West Port.

West Port, also known as Roosting Duck Village, was a water village outside of the western gate of Shaoxing. As Zuo Wenxiang's army was advancing, and the Shorthair forces were rising, the Taiping bandits grew increasingly desperate.[17] "Shorthairs" referred to local bandits, as distinguished from the Taiping bandits, who were dubbed "Longhairs." These local bandits would kill the Taiping rebels when they ran into Taiping rebels, and kill civilians when they ran into civilians; when they ran into the government's troops, they became the "righteous army." They moved around in tens of hundreds, and wherever they went, they cleared out everything like a violent storm. They left behind corpses piling up on the road and in the river, causing the water to stop flowing. After night descended, jackals and wolves roamed free and fed off the dead, and one could hear ghosts weeping in the wilderness. Disorder and turmoil prevailed. The situation was indeed so much worse than when the city of Shaoxing was first captured. We figured we could not stay put in the village, so we got ourselves a boat, and drifted in the winding tributaries and waterways every day. When hungry, we would pick water plants for food.

One day, we arrived at Xiju Nunnery. It was already twilight. Suddenly the Taiping soldiers came into view and tried to take our boat. The boat capsized, and we all waded to shore. Fortunately the soldiers had just suffered a setback in battle; retreating in blood and tears, they did not have time to kill us. After we entered the nunnery, the government's troops came. With brightly lit torches they pushed into the nunnery, making a great deal of noise. Frightened, we fled to the garden. As soon as we closed the garden gate, we heard a nun being pulled away. She cried and screamed, and then suddenly fell silent. We suspected that she died under the blade. Upon this my cousin's wife rushed to the river and threw herself into the water—the garden was located right next to the river, and there was no wall in between.

. . . .

17   Zuo Wenxiang was Zuo Zongtang (1812–1885), a statesman and general who
      served with distinction in the war against the Taiping Rebellion. His posthumous
      title was Duke Wenxiang.

When the bandits captured Shaoxing, she had tried to commit suicide by cutting her own throat, but the slash was not deep enough, and she was saved. By this time, her neck wound had healed, and we were all rejoicing in her narrow escape from death when things took such an unexpected, tragic turn. She had a baby son, Ren, who died as soon as he was deprived of his mother's milk. Later on, Xiaoyun went to Shaanxi and died there. Henceforth my grandfather's eldest son was left without a male heir to continue the family line. I cannot but feel pained in my heart. Even more lamentable is the fact that my cousin's wife did not die of the bandits but of the government's troops instead.

We fled from the nunnery while it was still dark. Ah Zhang, the old servant, escorted my mother and me to seek refuge at Dragon's Tail Mountain.

Dragon's Tail Mountain was thirty leagues from the south city gate of Shaoxing. My aunt, who had married into the Lu family, lived there. Earlier, my aunt had stayed on at Diankou with my grandfather's concubine and my fifth uncle's wife. Now she had been married to Mr. Lu for three months. My grandfather's concubine went with us, and we talked about going north to be reunited with my father. But my mother was suddenly taken ill, collapsing under the accumulated stress. She was very sick, and there was nothing to eat, so Ah Zhang collected and sold firewood to pay for our daily meals.

Ah Zhang was from Little Bitter Village, where his family had lived for generations. He was in his fifties, had no wife or children, and had been with my family for nearly twenty years. After Sanyi got me out on the verge of Shaoxing's fall, Ah Zhang figured that there was no one else whom he could consult, so he helped my fifth uncle's wife flee to Houbao. Sanyi was bold and uninhibited, while Ah Zhang was quick-witted and resourceful. He was particularly devoted to me, and often starved himself to make sure that I had enough food. I was very attached to him, and would become unhappy unless he was around. For this reason my fifth uncle's wife asked him to take care of me, and we lived together for six months. Fortunately my mother's health was restored, and soon afterward Shaoxing was recovered. Then, in another half a year, we went north. That was during the ninth month of the first year of the Tongzhi era.[18]

....

18 It should be the ninth month of the *second* year of the Tongzhi era, which is from

In those dangerous years, who could have protected us in the beginning if not for Sanyi? And if not for Ah Zhang, who could have seen to our safety in the end? And yet, I heard later that Ah Zhang had died of poverty and starvation. When I returned to Shaoxing in the *gengwu* year [1870], he was still there. I gave him some money, which displeased my cousins, and so Ah Zhang left in a fit of anger. That we should rely on him at a time of crisis and abandon him in years of peace! I truly do not see how Ah Zhang could ever forgive us. How very sad. A man braves hardship and risks his life, but once the crisis is over, those who have been sitting at ease get to offer their opinions on this matter and that: Ah Zhang was certainly not alone in encountering such a situation, for it has been like that since ancient times. In this sense, it was probably lucky for Sanyi, Wenjing, and Zhou to have died early; otherwise, even though I want to repay them for their loyalty, how can I avoid offending those who disagree with me? Being a servant in life and having no proper burial place in death—what good has their noble action brought them? Truly I do not see how Ah Zhang could ever forgive me.

After we made it to Yuanjiang, I again became gravely ill. My malady lingered for half a year before I was well enough to walk.

At the time when I went north, my cousin Xinquan was at Lihai;[19] my second uncle's wife died of fright when running into bandits; my ninth sister was married to a farmer; luckily, my cousin Xinquan's wife, Madame Hu, and my nephew Anxuan were all right. My fifth uncle had two daughters, i.e., my eighth sister and my "little sister," who both died in the turmoil. My sixth uncle and seventh uncle escaped from the fallen city and died not long afterward. My cousins—Jingquan, Wuquan, Xuequan, Puquan, Zi, You, and Liquan—were all my sixth uncle's sons. Now, thirty years later, only Liquan, Anxuan, and I are still alive. Wuquan has left behind a son. The thinness of our family has indeed reached the extreme. The sole comfort to be derived was that not one of the several hundred members of the Zhang clan had died by the blade. That was our only good fortune.

Because I was very young, I did not witness many mass murders committed by the bandits, but what I heard was enough to bring a chill to

....

October 13 through November 10, 1863.

19   Lihai was a town to the east of Shaoxing.

my heart. When Bao Village fell, since they could not easily kill off the thousands of men and women in the village, the bandits drove them into various houses; then they wrapped up cotton with bamboo mats, poured oil inside, erected the mats all around the houses, and set fire to them. The fire raged for eleven days and nights. Most of the people who died were from Hangzhou; next were the natives of Bao Village; people from Shaoxing took up about one-tenth. Afterward, corpses were scattered all over the place, maggots spread into the woods, and the horrible stench could be smelled from a dozen leagues away. How cruel! A maternal cousin of mine named Xiong and his wife were among the dead.

There were two brothers, Feng Zhiying and Feng Zhihua, whose family had lived at Temple's East for generations. Zhihua was kind, while Zhiying was reckless. When Shaoxing was captured, Zhiying joined the bandits. Later on, because of his merit in battle, he received a promotion to the office of "Xunfeng." Since then, he became even more uninhibited. His father was my family's tailor, and so when we were seeking refuge in Temple's East, we relied on them for protection. After a while, Zhiying was killed by the bandits for some offense. His head was hung on a pole, all bloody and terrifying. I was, however, extremely curious. So when I heard that Zhihua was going to steal his head, I went to ask him about it behind my mother's back. Zhihua said, "Yes, it's true." That night, he took me with him, and told me to wait for him while he climbed up the pole like a gibbon, holding a knife in his mouth. When he got the head, he kissed it and wept bitterly. I wept too, not quite understanding where *my* tears had come from. How poignant! It broke one's heart to see brothers separated by death like that. Sadly, because of Zhihua's physical contact with the unclean, he fell ill and died.

"Flames of War," Ghost Troops, and Other Strange Happenings

There were five sorts of "flames of war." The sort that had a sharp tip and flared up straight was beacon fire. The sort that had a diffused purplish light was the fire that burned possessions. The sort that was black in its upper part and red at base was the fire that burned houses. The sort that gave off a white smoke like clouds and drifted about below was the fire that burned grain. As for the sort with a congealed smoke and of a light green hue, that was the fire that burned corpses. I had tested this theory from the pinnacle of Snow Shadow Peak, and had never erred.

The sun also had five different colors. When it was reddish yellow and shone forth, everything was fine. When it was red like blood, then within three days a neighboring village would be slaughtered, for the sun was responding to the evil aura. When it was as yellow as sand, there must be a battle raging on within ten leagues or so, for the sun was covered by the dust stirred up in the battle. When it was as white as a sheet of paper, it was an omen that our own village would be invaded by soldiers. Occasionally, the sun would turn as black as ink, with a strong wind blowing. In that case, if one were to set out to battle, one would surely suffer defeat, overcome by the aura of the sun. If crumbling clouds were hanging low over the army formation, then the troops would lose the battle and the commander would be killed—there is some truth to such a saying. If I had not experienced this in person, I would never have known.

It seems that "ghost troops" also truly exist. Before Shaoxing was captured, my sixth uncle was a leader of the local militia. When he went out on patrol at night, he often heard the sound of hundreds of people clamoring ceaselessly in the east and west, and yet he could never locate their whereabouts. As the rebels were getting closer, the clamor became louder and louder. If, however, my uncle ever tried to follow the sound, a gust of wind would blow yellow dust right into his face. As the aura of decline and disorder prevailed, humans and ghosts became mixed up. I suppose all this was a consequence of the predestined disaster.

There was something else that was most strange. When I was with Sanyi at Black Stone Village, the "righteous militia" descended on us one night. There had been no warning whatsoever, and yet Sanyi abruptly leapt up, carried me on his back, and fled, and so we were able to escape alive. Afterward, we asked him how he could have known, and he did not understand it himself. All he could say was that somehow he was gripped by a sudden panic, and acted accordingly. In that case, it seemed that if one's sincerity touched heaven, heaven would send clear signs. Such happenings were certainly not limited to the resounding of the Luoyang bell in the east in response to the collapse of the bronze mountain in the west.[20] The manifestations might be different, but the principle of

....

20   This is a reference to the story that a bell sounded in the imperial palace at Luoyang during the Eastern Han in response to the collapse of a mountain in the Shu region (modern Sichuan). Another version of the story places the sounding of the bell in Chang'an (modern Xi'an) during the Western Han dynasty.

stimulus-response remains the same.

I have seen a will-o'-the-wisp three times. I first saw it from Mr. Sang's house at Ding's Port. It was hard to tell its color because the moon had just risen. It was floating and sinking like hundreds of thousands of stars. Later, I saw it again at Houbao—it was drifting slowly and leisurely in the remaining snow. The third time was at Tao's Weir. Some of its flames were as big as the moon, and had a dark green tint. Some people thought that many smaller ones had gathered together to make one large ball of flame; others believed that these large ones had a particularly strong aura.

My father's concubine, Madame Lou, was from Guangdong.[21] She said that when she was a child, she had seen a will-o'-the-wisp at the homes of the practitioners of the *gu* cult.[22] The glow of a man's soul fire was red, and that of a woman's soul fire was green. In this case, the light was supposedly emitted from one's soul. Perhaps there was indeed such a thing, though I have never seen a ghost. Nevertheless, I did have a remarkable experience. When my cousin's wife, Madame Wang, drowned herself at West Port, her body was washed away by the river. The next day, my cousin prayed by the river, and subsequently found her body. If the dead had no awareness, then her body should not have come to us; if the dead indeed had awareness, wouldn't she be just as good as alive? After this incident, one may understand a little bit more about the way of ghosts and spirits. Kinship touches one's deepest feelings, whether one is in the world of darkness or the world of light.

Human nature is such that it becomes good when accustomed to good, and turns evil when inured to evil. This is quite true. When the chaos first began, people all cared about and helped one another. Only after they were used to the ruthlessness of the bandits did they gradually change, even to the extent that they would no longer blink an eye at sharpening a blade and slaughtering fellow human beings like pigs and sheep. By the time the Shorthairs appeared, the state of things had gotten so bad that even pregnant women were not spared and their bellies were cut open. Dogs behaved the same way. As cooking smoke dwindled

....

21 "Lou" was crossed out in the manuscript and the surname "Deng" was scribbled in the margin.

22 The *gu* cult is a witchcraft practiced with venomous insects known as *gu* in the south.

and human traces vanished from the region, dogs had no home to return to and no food to eat, and so they would feed off the dead. They became fatter than usual, and their eyes turned glowing red. As fierce as tigers and wolves, they would pounce on people and try to bite them. People sometimes mistook them for bears, but they were just dogs. What madness!

Epidemic, Greed, and the Woman Dismembered at Lu's Dyke

Great turmoil like this is always followed by an epidemic. It is only natural that it should be so. In the worst-case scenario, the filthy air would congeal and rise up, and people would breathe it in and die. In less serious cases, when people drank contaminated water from a river with floating corpses, they became infected and had an outbreak of sores and ulcers. When the bandits cut off Bao Village's water supply, even half a cup of blood was sold for seven ounces of silver, which was something that had never been heard of since ancient times. Even if one had survived the war, one could hardly escape from the epidemic. But what I do not understand is this: money is for the living; at such a chaotic time, when one constantly feared for one's life, how could people still concern themselves with selling something for a high price? Refugees fleeing to Bao Village had brought with them several millions in cash. After the bandits went through the village, the Shorthairs went through it again; after the Shorthairs went through it, the locals came for a dig. In a world filled with dead bodies, the money was moved to the south in the morning, taken to the north in the evening, and then back to the south again. Those who fought over the money and got killed were numerous. Wasn't this the strangest thing?

The bandits did not always kill people because they found them detestable; sometimes killing was just a game for them. I once saw a woman at Lu's Dike who came with several bandits from the east. They were laughing and joking with one another, and seemed quite jolly. Then suddenly she said, "Dong Er, you heartless man!" One bandit asked, "What do you mean?" The woman laughingly dumped on him. In a fit of anger, the bandit drew out his sword. The woman said with a chortle, "Why, just try and kill me!" Even before she finished her words, he cut off her arm. The bandits were still laughing as the arm was severed. Then they took off her clothes, exposed her breasts, cut them off, and threw them away. Still laughing aloud, they left. I went over to look at the breasts: they were covered with blood, and inside they were filled with something of a pale red color like pomegranate seeds. I picked one up to take a closer look, and it seemed to be quivering in my hand. I was seized with a great terror and went home.

Abruptly getting angry in the midst of laughter, and then in the midst of anger bursting into laughter again—this was the temperament of a bandit. That woman grew too familiar and playful with them, and subsequently got herself killed. There was a reason why this happened.

The Occupation of Shaoxing and Its Aftermath

When Shaoxing was first recovered from the bandits, the southeastern section of the city was still intact. During the occupation, my family's old house at Xianhuanhe had been inhabited by Qitianyan.[23] Qitianyan was the name of an official rank of the Taiping bandits, which was about one grade lower than their "king." Consequently, on the four walls of our house colorful murals had been painted, such as a lion, a elephant, a tiger, and a dragon, just like in a temple. The bandits fled Shaoxing on the twenty-eighth of the first month [March 17, 1863]; then, on the twenty-ninth, my cousin Xiaoyun went back first to take a look. There was more furniture in our house than before the occupation, and our calligraphy and painting collection, spread throughout thirteen rooms, was untouched. At that time, government officials were urging people to donate money to reward the foreign troops, and it was impossible to stay in the house, so Xiaoyun left. Seven days later, another cousin of mine, Xinquan, went back, and there was nothing left in the house anymore. He asked people in the neighborhood about it, but those people turned out to be none other than the Shorthairs. They had cleared out our house and combed through everything. This, however, was bound to happen under the circumstances, and was hardly any surprise.

While fighting with the government troops, the bandits at Shaoxing took hundreds of thousands of coffins and put dirt in them. If a section of the city wall collapsed under cannon fire, they would fill the gap with

....

23   Qitianyan was named Yu Guangqian, who was promoted to the rank of Qitianyan shortly after the occupation of Shaoxing.

those coffins. In the section near the west city gate, there was no intact body in those coffins, and the coffins were left there even after the city was recovered. I could not immediately return to the city because my mother was too ill, but one day I had to travel to Houbao for something, and on my way there I looked at the city from afar. I saw coffins piling up like clouds, and there was no telling whether the dead were soldiers of the imperial army or bandits. People I ran into were all dark and emaciated like ghosts. Some had "Heavenly Kingdom of Peace" tattooed on their faces; they were the ones who had escaped from the bandits. Some bandits had hidden among the civilians. They were tortured and extorted for bribery, and some were killed. Occasionally, however, there were people who were wrongly executed as bandits. As for those who had joined the bandits and bullied their fellow townsfolk, six to seven out of ten had died. In general, the ones who were having the best time were the Shorthairs. They assumed the name of "righteous militia" and became filthy rich. Government officials simply left them alone.

When I went to Houbao from Ding's Port, my cousin's wife, Madame Feng, and her son Youqiao returned to Pig's Jaw, and my father's concubine was with them. Half a year after Shaoxing's recovery, I went north to join my father, but she stayed behind. According to her, the situation at Pig's Jaw was worse than anything I had seen. People were cooking their leather trunks and even cut up dead bodies for food. Nothing was left of plant roots and tree bark. By that time, my cousin's wife had used up her savings. Fortunately, Youqiao has established himself in the world today. He has four sons and two daughters, and his family grows more affluent every day. My cousin's wife passes her time playing with her grandchildren. I visit them every time I go back, and she still teasingly calls me "yellow fatso"—the nickname I got when I was sick and swollen with white jaundice. As we become tipsy with a few cups of wine and reminisce about the old days, when death was lurking everywhere, we still feel chills down our backs.

Edible Flora and Fauna

There is an animal in the hills whose popular name is "root-digging mountain beaver." It is about the size of a cat, and belongs to the fox family. It loves to eat tree roots. Pig's Jaw has a lot of them. It makes a whining sound like a strange ghost. It often holds a twig in its mouth and uses its front paws to steady it, like a human being playing flute, which looks rather comic. During the daytime they hide away, nobody knows where; at night they come out in flocks. I once caught one; we skinned it and ate it. It was delicious. Its fur was of a dark red hue and unusually smooth and soft, good for making a coat. In those turbulent years, people vied with one another to catch these animals for food, so the species almost became extinct in the region.

There is also a sort of mountain cat known as the "hawk-capturing beaver." Its claws are extremely sharp. When a hawk goes after it, it turns over on its back and claws at the hawk's belly, and the bird of prey often gets killed instead. It would bite people and feed off the dead, thus being of the same kind as the Shorthairs. Its meat is smelly and inedible. Only after one treats it with vinegar does it become delicious and crunchy. There are also pangolins and hedgehogs in the mountains. Both being edible, people would hunt them down, and few could get away. From this I have learned that in a chaotic age, even birds and animals cannot live in peace.

Of edible seeds and fruits, the mountain chestnut is the best. There are also "black rice" and "bitter nut," which are wonderful for satisfying hunger. The "black rice" resembles the fruit of the common nandina but is black, and grows particularly abundantly in the hills around Black Stone Village. Once, as I was following my mother to collect them, it rained, so I started running home. After a while, I realized I had lost my mother, so I rushed back to look for her. After I found her, I again started running, all the while wondering to myself why my mother was so slow, little knowing that it was not my mother being slow but me being too fast. In those days, I would go up and down those hills as swiftly and nimbly as a bird. I was nine years old then, which was exactly the age when a child could, as the poet Du Fu said, "climb the tree a thousand times a day."

After we came home, we would make a solid meal out of the nuts we had collected. Sometimes we saved them in a bag made by my mother. One day, the bandits suddenly descended on us. We fled in a panic and forgot to take the bag with us, and became famished. Spotting a tree laden with red persimmons, I climbed up to pick them and fell off the branch. I almost died from the fall. Thinking back, I find it all very funny now.

The juice of the "bitter nut" can be used to make bean curd. It has a slightly astringent taste. When steamed, it is very filling. I regretted that there were not a lot of them. There are many kinds of medicinal herbs in the mountains and forests, too numerous to enumerate. I used to recognize them all, but now I have gradually forgotten what I once knew.

The loveliest herb is the "domino plant." It looks like shepherd's purse but is much larger, and each of its leaves resembles a Chinese domino piece. It has everything from "heaven," "earth," "man," and "harmony" to "stool," "one," "five," "two," "four," and "three."[24] But it is rare to find a domino plant complete with all the pieces, which has an amazing effect in treating physical injuries. Youqiao's servant, He Xi, was once wounded by a bandit. We found thirty domino plants, pounded them into pulp, and applied this to his wound. He was healed in no time. "Faded early bamboo" was what we called the new shoot of early bamboo that has withered; it cures swelling. When I suffered from white jaundice, they boiled it and made me drink the broth, as well as bathed me with it. The effect was miraculous.

The Pleasures and Horrors of Childhood

The mountains at Zhuji are close to Kuocang Mountain. If one sets out from Diankou and travels by way of Wuxie, it is no more than half a day's trip. Regrettably, I was too young back then, not to mention that it was in the midst of great turmoil, so I did not get to explore the secluded beauty of the landscape. Nevertheless, there were a few things I greatly enjoyed. I had thought to myself that not having to study was the most marvelous thing in the whole world—that was the first of my joys. The second was that everyone who was older than me cared about me and doted on me. My third joy was to be able to go up and down the cloudy peaks and climb the treetops, as agile and fast as a monkey. A number of scenic places I visited are worth recording here. They are Underworld Path, Bronze Dyke Hollow, Old Man's Nest, Snow Shadow Peak, Sweetness Range, Shared Joy Peak, Deer Horns Mountain, and Bodhisattva Grotto. All of these places are absolutely captivating.

Underworld Path is ten leagues long and constitutes the main road from Diankou to Pig's Jaw. At the end of it there is a temple called Ten Gods, built for the Ten Kings of Hell. Towering pines and cypresses shade

....

24   All of these are the names of Chinese domino pieces.

the temple grounds from the sun, so that even during the daytime it seems to be twilight there. A footpath that is as winding as an autumn snake zigzags through scattered rocks and steep, craggy cliffs. Even when someone is coming face-to-face with you, in an instant you can lose him in the shrouding mist. It is truly an extraordinary place. The bandits disliked it because of its perils, so they set fire to it.

I remember the statues and colored murals in the temple as being stunningly beautiful. There was a statue of a Wuchang demon that held an iron shackle to put around a person's neck.[25] I was scared at first, but eventually got used to it. One day, I went there with some other children, and we saw the body of someone killed by the bandits. Together we lifted the dead man up and tried to get his neck through the shackle. The corpse was heavy, and fell flat on its back; the demon statue fell with it. We all laughed aloud, and then we started beating its legs. How naughty we were! I have no idea why I was not frightened.

Bronze Dyke Hollow has a cascade falling over sixty meters. The mountains around are of a moist green. The trees never turn yellow, and all year the climate remains as mild as in late spring. Some people believe that there is sulfur under its waters. I suspect that this is true. It is about thirty leagues from Pig's Jaw. In those days, I would go there in the morning and come home in the evening, as if it were an easy trip. I was clearly very good at walking long distances back then.

Old Man's Nest has hundreds of winding stone caves concealed by trees; the large ones have room for more than ten people. They look over deep ravines, a wonderful Peach Blossom Spring for taking cover from the bandits.[26] One day, when we were hiding there, the bandits came and set fire to the trees. People rushed out and raised a huge ruckus. The bandits were taken by surprise and ran away, and a dozen of them fell into the ravine. From then on, we did not dare to go to those caves anymore, although the bandits never came back.

Snow Shadow Peak is the pinnacle of the mountains. If one looks down from it, one can see into the distance several tens of leagues. When the bandits attacked Bao Village, they had to take the road under the

. . . .

25   The Wuchang demon is the Chinese Grim Reaper that takes a person's soul to hell.
26   Peach Blossom Spring is a utopian community far away from human society depicted in the poet Tao Yuanming's (365–427) famous "Account of Peach Blossom Spring" (Taohuayuan ji).

peak. They held on to vines to ascend, advancing on the winding mountain path like ants. Seen from the distance, Bao Village was only about
as big as a dinner plate; when it was taken, cannons were blasting off,
but one could hear only a vague sound and see a thin strand of dark
smoke. Tens of thousands of people sank into oblivion in an instant. I
suppose Snow Shadow Peak is no more than two thousand meters high
and about twenty leagues from Bao Village. If it had been higher, one
would not have been able to see even the dark smoke. In one tiny speck,
numerous tiny specks vanish; in numerous tiny specks, one tiny speck
disappears. And yet, human beings continue to dream their great dream,
and none wakes up from it. From past to present they have always been
busy distinguishing favor from disfavor and gains from losses, harming and murdering one another. What ignorance! I turn around and see
the mountain flowers in bright red blossoms as if they were smiling; the
realm of happiness in nature and that of suffering in the human world
are as far apart as clouds and ravines. As I look up at the blue sky, the
white sun is shining forth with a dazzling light. It is all very sad.

The Sweetness Range is just over twenty leagues from Pig's Jaw. My
fifth maternal uncle, Mr. Yiting (his personal name is Jing), used to
have a villa there. Its flower and herb garden followed the contour of
the mountain. There was also a pond of about half an acre. All around
were fruit trees in red and yellow colors. With new bamboo shoots and
delectable fish, it was truly a happy land. In the years of the turmoil, my
uncle's entire family moved there. My uncle had a run-in with the bandits; he fell off a cliff and almost died. The estate has not only been laid
waste but belongs to someone else now.

Shared Joy Peak is to the left of the Sweetness Range. Standing on
top of it, one sees cloud and mist underneath. When the setting sun casts
back its last light, the cloud vapors take on many different colors. That
used to be my favorite sight. Even when the bandits came, I sometimes
would not leave, and by a stroke of luck managed to stay unharmed.

Deer Horns Mountain is so named because it has two facing peaks.
Situated between the Sweetness Range and Shared Joy Peak, it has layers upon layers of strangely shaped rocks as sharp as halberds. There was
no soil or plant whatsoever on that mountain. Once the bandits drove
people up there and forced them to jump off the cliffs. Those people broke
their heads or limbs, and their painful cries pierced the sky. The bandits thought it was great fun. Later, some clever folks prepared dry wood

and gunpowder and scattered them in the cracks of the rocks. They lured more than a hundred bandits there by telling them that there was hidden gold. Once the bandits were on the mountain, they lit the fuse, and the bandits were all blown up in one huge explosion. After the blast the rocks took on even more distinct colors, so the mountain is also known as Colorful Brocade Peak today.

Bodhisattva Grotto is eight leagues from Pig's Jaw. Within a two-league radius of the cave, there are many strange-looking rocks as well as dark green pines that grow tall and lush. The cave is spacious and can easily accommodate a hundred people. It branches into dozens of smaller caves like a winding alley. There used to be snakes, but they were exterminated by refugees. Some of the bandits were enticed into the cave and got killed. In a fit of anger they sealed the cave up, but people always found their way out from another cave and took down the blockage when they got out. The bandits could do nothing about it.

As for Pig's Jaw, its scenery is beyond description. For seven months I roamed there day in, day out, from morning to dusk. Even though it was a time of great chaos, I thought my life was like that of gods. Every spring, every rock, has a numinous charm. Simply because it is deep in the mountains, people rarely come to visit, and so it is not adequately appreciated. But then, divine things hardly need the admiration of men.

Narrow Escapes on Water

Shaoxing has always been a water town. With its big rivers and small streams, one can go everywhere by boat, and it was possible to get away from the bandits that way. Nevertheless, boat prices had gone sky-high in those years; and if one ran into the bandits on water, one could do nothing but accept death without being able to put up a fight. I had encountered life-threatening danger on the water five times altogether. Then again, I had also learned everything about the strange beauty of the misty rivers of the southland.

When we went from Tao's Weir to West Port, we had to cross Hujia Pond.[27] In the midst of our crossing, a gusty wind suddenly arose, and

....

27 "Hujia" was changed to "Hejia" in the manuscript. The same happens later in this paragraph when "Hujia" occurs again.

our boat was blown about like a tumbleweed. Our boatman jumped into the lake and swam away. Stranded and helpless, we found ourselves in a terrible predicament. Just then a large boat approached, and it turned out to be the bandits. The boat was coming closer and closer, when, all of a sudden, it capsized, and the dozen bandits in the boat were all washed away by the waves. That was quite a relief. Soon afterward, the sun went down, and the wind grew stronger. Our boat drifted in the dark, and finally came to an abrupt stop. When the moon was out, we took a good look around, and discovered that we were already near the shore. All around us, however, were floating corpses, and that was why our boat had stopped. My mother prayed in tears while I collapsed and passed out. We were saved by some villager only after daybreak. We went on by way of Dog Neck Pond. The pond is so named because Hujia Pond, which is over ten leagues wide, becomes as narrow as a dog's neck in this section, and only one boat can sail through it. Our clothes and shoes were all soaked, and we stayed with a farmer for a day. Fortunately Ah Zhang tracked us down, and we were reunited with Xiaoyun and others.

One evening, when we were at Temple's East, we got news that the bandits were going to "clean the village" because they thought some villagers were planning to form a militia against them. To "clean the village" meant killing everyone. We hired a boat in a panic and tried to get away. However, the boatman turned out to be a Shorthair. In the middle of the river, he suddenly took out a knife. Fortunately a village woman who was with us pushed him into the water, snatched the knife from his hand, and killed him with it. We then fled to Cypress Lodge.

My family's ancestral shrine was at Cypress Lodge. The head of our clan prepared a separate boat for my mother and me, which took us to the deep recesses of the village. It was early autumn. As the sky was clearing up after a rain shower, there was a refreshing coolness in the air. Although there were not many villagers left, some bean and melon trellises still remained. In the setting sun we heard fishermen singing in the distance. One could well imagine what it was like during a time of peace.

At Dragon's Tail Mountain, my mother fell ill. One day, the bandit alarm was raised all of a sudden. We learned that some Shorthair bandits had fought with the Taiping army and lost miserably, and that the Taiping soldiers on their trail were about to reach Dragon's Tail Mountain. We hurriedly boarded our boat. But the locals all competed with one another to get into the boat, which became too heavy and capsized. We managed to avoid drowning by holding on to drooping willow branches and climbing back to the river bank. After we fled on foot for three or four leagues, Ah Zhang seized a boat transporting human waste and found us. We quickly rowed into a branching stream and hid among the reeds.

A strong wind started blowing. At dusk, we looked in the direction of the village from afar: it seemed to be in great turmoil. The sound of crying and shooting, like water noisily boiling in a cauldron, continued all night. As the moon was about to go down, the morning wind blew on our wet clothes, and the cold penetrated our flesh and entered our bones. My mother and I faced each other and both burst into tears. Ah Zhang opened up his jacket and wrapped me in it. The next day, it was already noon when a villager informed us that the bandits had finally left. We went back, and found that the house we rented from a Mr. Tai was luckily still intact. However, there were flames and smoke throughout the village; broken body parts were strewn about, and blood was everywhere. I cannot bear to describe the awful smell of burnt flesh. Oh the cruelty of it all!

After Shaoxing was recovered, we received no definite news in the village. Some said that the government's troops had been defeated and that the bandits were going to kill everyone in the region; some said that the city had been recaptured but that the bandits were going to send in reinforcements to take it back; some said that the Shorthairs were going to grow their hair long and help the Taiping bandits fight the foreign troops; some said that the foreign troops coveted our land and were going to attack the imperial army. There were several scares in one evening. In the meanwhile, my mother's illness was getting worse and worse. Ah Zhang said, "Everything is fate. If heaven wants to destroy us, we will die whether we run away or not. In that case, it would be far better to die in the house than in the wilderness." One day, the Shorthairs suddenly descended upon us. Ah Zhang carried me off in a hurry and boarded a boat. Then he went back to fetch my mother and my grandfather's concubine. During the interval, our boat was snatched by two strong village women, who threw me into the river. By the time Ah Zhang returned and helped me out of water, I was already half gone. Fortunately the villagers beat the Shorthairs, and we went home.

Two days after we went home, the Taiping bandits came. We got into a boat and fled by way of a small stream branching off from the river. We were caught in the rain, and drifted for three days and nights. After the boat was shattered by a rock, we were stranded on the shore in the wilderness, having no shelter, and picking duckweeds for food. After three days, we finally located another boat, and set out for Houbao. The waterway to Houbao was, however, blocked by dead bodies. There was an accumulation of white "corpse wax" that was several inches thick. Maggots crawled into our boat and in an instant were everywhere. The stinky smell made us so sick that we thought we were about to die. We had to turn back, and ran into the bandits on the way. We thought there was no escape this time, but it so happened that a fight broke out among them, and we slipped away during the riot.

We went back to Dragon's Tail Mountain. After that, things gradually improved. My cousin Xinquan came to visit us; my mother was also on the mend, although she had been reduced to skin and bones, and did not even have the strength to weep anymore.

Generally speaking, during a time of chaos it is better to seek refuge in the mountains than on water. One can fend for oneself in the mountains, but on water one must rely on boats. Nevertheless, if there had been no Shorthairs, the situation would not have been nearly as bad. Even though the Taiping bandits were ruthless, their intention was to conquer and occupy a region, and they wanted peace. The Shorthairs, on the other hand, straddled the two sides. When they could have their way, they would slaughter and pillage the entire village. It was lamentable.

Reunion with Father and Father's Death

It has been thirty years since the civil war caused by the Yue bandits. I still remember that when I first made it to the north and was reunited with my father, he held me in his arms and wept. He said, "I am an old man now. Our property is all gone. I suppose for your sake I will have to work for another ten years." My father enjoyed fishing and roaming. He had always wanted to take a small boat, put on a fisherman's hat, and wander to his heart's desire on the misty waves; but by this point, he lost all hope of realizing his dream. He passed away six years later at the age of sixty-three. I turned seventeen that year.

I applied myself to study for no more than five years, that is, between the time I was twelve and sixteen, before beginning to travel for my livelihood. How dare I aspire to be a Jiang Kui or a Liu Guo?[28] My only wish is not to completely abandon my ancestors' enterprise, and that is all.

> Riding on horseback is certainly not as good as riding a buffalo;
> A short jacket, setting sun, the empty hills.
> One should just return to Winding Valley—
> There is no point in spreading one's fame throughout the world.[29]

Vast are the mountains shrouded in clouds. They have been there from ancient times until the present day. In a mood of leisure and detachment, I will disappear into them. Who, I wonder, would hold on to me and not let me go?

....

28 Jiang Kui (1154–1221) and Liu Guo (1154–1206) were both well-known Southern Song poets who never served public office.

29 Winding Valley is in He'nan. The Tang poet Han Yu (768–824) wrote a well-known essay seeing off his friend Li Yuan, who was going to live at Winding Valley as a recluse; henceforth Winding Valley became a figure of withdrawal from public life.

PART THREE

The Nian Uprising

I have given a full account of my experience during the chaos caused by the Yue bandits. As for Yuanjiang's sufferings during the Nian Uprising, there are things I cannot bear speaking of. When the Nian bandits were advancing toward Yuanjiang, the director-general of the Grand Canal, whose name will not be mentioned here, was giving drinking parties, complete with musical performances, to entertain himself and his staff.[1] Although the alarm had been raised and was in fact growing more and more urgent with every passing day, he paid no heed to it. Only when the bandits reached Wang's Camp, which was no more than ten leagues from Yuanjiang, did he begin to panic. He tried to commit suicide, but was stopped by his concubines and servants. So he threw his snuff bottle on the floor and said, "It is all over!" By that he meant he was going to give up on his reputation and flee. He escaped by taking to the Huai River. That was on the twenty-ninth day of the first month in the —— year of the Xianfeng era [February 20, 1860].[2]

I escaped from Yuanjiang unharmed thanks to young Zhou, who carried me on his back and saved my life. My three mothers went south,

....

1   This was the Manchu official Gengchang. Later he was sent into exile at Xinjiang as punishment for his negligence.
2   The year was left blank in the manuscript. It should be the tenth year of the Xianfeng era.

and our old house at Dusi Lane was burned to the ground.[3] The bandits pillaged the city for eleven days, and over two hundred thousand people died. How lamentable. This might have been destined to be; nevertheless, if preparations had been made earlier, or if afterward the government troops could have driven the bandits away from the city sooner, it would not have come to that.

The Nian's strength was their cavalry. They used long spears and halberds as weapons. Fast and vigorous, they could easily traverse a thousand leagues. They valued money and material goods but cared little for land, a characteristic that was quite different from the Longhairs. To entrap the Longhairs, it was appropriate to surround them on all sides, but to crush the Nian bandits, it was best to fortify the defense works and clear the fields of supplies, as these were the only proper methods to subdue them. Because of this I have come to realize that the most important thing in fighting is to identify the effective strategy, not to rely on strength and numbers alone. Creatures such as whales, salamanders, sharks, and crocodiles are so mighty that they can swallow a boat, but when they are deprived of water, they die. If one knows the correct way of overpowering them, what is the point of risking one's life to battle them among crushing waves, and shaking up heaven and earth during the process? Reflect on this well, and one may be able to communicate with gods and spirits. As long as one learns how to take advantage of the enemy's shortcomings, it is not so difficult to clear the air breathed out by the giant clam.[4]

Chen Laomo was a native of Zichuan County of Shandong. After a famine caused by a poor harvest, he and his wife became our household servants. When the Nian came, they stayed behind and would not leave the house. The bandits set fire to the house, and people dragged them out. A cat died in the fire. Laomo and his wife wept bitterly over the cat, and thought that they were not as good and honorable as it had been. At the time, my father was under orders to guard Chengzihe. After the bandits were gone, he went home to inspect the situation. Laomo suffered seven wounds, and his wife almost died from burns. My father admired their loyalty, and provided for them for the rest of their lives.

....

3   That is, his legal mother, his birth mother, and his concubine mother.
4   Mirages were believed to be produced by a gigantic clam breathing out air.

Among our servants Laomo was rather slow on the uptake, and yet, when calamity befell, he did not betray us. If the director-general of the Grand Canal had been like him, then even though he lost the opportunity to defeat the bandits, wouldn't he have been able to absolve himself? Even if he had suffered the fate of our family cat, he would have been honored by later generations. How terrible that he should have taken flight in a panic! Nevertheless, one can very well predict how things will turn out in certain situations, for even before disaster struck, his governance was in disorder, and he was notorious for his corruption. Ding Mu'an (named Qu), a student of Shanyang, composed a poem about him, which reads as follows:

> After amassing a mountain of copper
>   right on the main route,
> He went on to build a golden mansion,
>   having calculated the government tax.
> His favorite concubine faced the candle
>   and became even more depressed—
> There was no need to laugh at the poor husband
>   who had become so obsessed.

It seems that the director-general's only difference from the Nian bandits was that he did not hold a spear or halberd in his hands. One simply cannot expect someone like him to die for his country, for that will never happen.

Yuanjiang used to be the wealthiest city in the Huai-Yang region. It was situated on the grain transportation route from the southeast to the capital; moreover, every year the Yellow River had to be worked on, for which the state treasury always gave tens of millions of taels of silver. Haizhou was where the organization of salt transportation was located. For these reasons, cap and coach gathered at Yuanjiang like clouds, and merchants and traders vied with one another to go there. In terms of the exquisiteness of workmanship in one hundred arts and crafts as well as the magnificence of music performances and parties, Yuanjiang was always far superior to other places. I have heard from the elders that, during the peaceful and prosperous reign of the Qianlong and Jiaqing emperors, the sound of carriage wheels and horse hooves was ceaseless all night long, and the wax tears of candles piled up in the city's ten thousand households.[5] That was truly a fine scene in an orderly world! Later on, the course of the Yellow River shifted to the north, the rules of the salt business changed, and grain transportation was carried out via sea route after the civil war. Therefore all the glory and opulence of Yuanjiang, like embroidered brocade, were completely gone. Nowadays, there are but a few bends of the canal, with two lines of sparse willows along its banks looking rather desolate in the sunset. Whenever something reaches its zenith, it will decline: this is a natural principle, so there is perhaps no need to feel surprised. It is just that the remaining panache of the place is still capable of stirring melancholy, for although the coaches of the eminent have largely vanished, the merchant's wife is still playing the tune of the "Golden Silk Thread" of the old days on her *pipa* flute.[6]

The city wall of Yuanjiang was built by Lord Wu Qinhui of Xuchi in the early years of the Tongzhi era when he was the director-general of the Grand Canal.[7] The square stones were all taken from Lord Fan's Dyke. Though small, they were quite solid. I fear only that, with Lord Fan's Dyke gone, if one day the Yellow River should return to its former course, the common folk may all turn into fish.

When the bandit Lai Wenguang was in desperate straits and fled east, the construction of the city wall of Yuanjiang was not yet completed. As Lai was approaching, civil and martial officials all hurriedly climbed up onto the wall. I, too, went up there to take a look. The commander-general, Mr. Zhang Conglong, was a tremendously brave and resourceful man. His assistant commander so-and-so was a big fellow with a striking appearance; in truth he looked like those majestic door-gods, Shentu and Yulei. He and Mr. Zhang were sworn brothers. However, he

....

5   Emperor Qianlong reigned from 1735 to 1795; his son, Emperor Jiaqing, reigned from 1795 to 1820.

6   "The Robe of Golden Silk Thread" (Jinlü yi) was a carpe diem song from the eighth century sung by a famous singing girl, Du Qiu. The "merchant's wife" playing her *pipa* flute is an allusion to a long poem by the Tang poet Bai Juyi (772–846), "The Ballad of *Pipa*" (Pipa xing). The poem describes a woman who had been a glamorous courtesan when she was young, and was married to a merchant in middle age; the merchant constantly traveled for business and left her alone with melancholy memories of her carefree youth.

7   Lord Wu Qinhui was Wu Tang (1813–1876), who was famous for his administrative competence. He was director-general of the Grand Canal from 1863 to 1866. Qinhui was Wu Tang's posthumous title.

was extremely cowardly. He rode beside Mr. Zhang, who led the cavalry out of the city. In ten paces he fell off of his horse five times. Mr. Zhang laughed heartily and urged him to go back. Then Mr. Zhang rode ahead and engaged in fighting, and in a little while slew dozens of bandits. The bandits collapsed and ran away. Later on, Lai Wenguang was captured at Pingqiao, and was subsequently sent to Yangzhou to be executed.[8] During the battle at Yuanjiang, there were no more than five hundred soldiers in the city. Fortunately the bandits were hungry and tired, and Mr. Zhang was good at combat. Otherwise it would have all come to a very bad end. Afterward, that assistant commander so-and-so was also rewarded for his "first-class merit." That was an auspicious affair indeed.

Numerous happenings in human life are all predestined. It is said that bullets and cannonballs have eyes and go only for those who are doomed to die. I believe it. When I followed the crowd and went up on the city wall, bullets and cannonballs were falling from the sky as densely as locusts and raindrops. Lord Wu's headpiece was shaken loose by cannon fire, flew off of his head, and knocked down one of his personal guards, who died on spot. Lord Wu was unharmed. Isn't this a piece of clear evidence of the above saying?

I was thirteen years old at the time. I knew no fear coming and going in the midst of mountains of swords and trees of daggers. My legal mother was very concerned, but my father let me be, observing that if I had not died earlier at Yue, how could I die here at Yuanjiang? When I think about it now, I feel it was truly a rare stroke of luck. Mr. Chen Guorui, the Imperial Guardsman, once said, "One must be tough in battle and forget one's body is made of blood and flesh. One often wins that way. As soon as one feels attached to something, one cannot but lose." This is certainly true. Nevertheless, Lord Wu's steadfastness also came from years of experience, and ordinary people have no way of comparing with him.

The Nian rebels were even more ferocious than the Taiping bandits. Lai Wenguang was both Taiping and Nian, so he was particularly cunning and fierce. When he was on the run, he had no more than three hundred cavalry with him, but they were more competent than a thousand men. There were over a hundred women riding with them, and they were as fast as lightning. They could hold the reins in their hands and stand

....

8   Lai Wenguang (1827–1868) was captured on January 5, 1868.

up in their saddles. Even when the horse's belly touched the ground, they could still shoot left and right. Their skills were superb. One of them was captured and sliced alive. She never stopped cursing and swearing until she died.

According to her, the bandits had all gone through a sort of ritual known as "beating up the tough good guys." That is, before the civil war, there were often a dozen young men hanging out in the marketplace. Holding iron rulers and bronze sticks, they would set up a curtained enclosure in an empty space and beat a gong and drum, inviting people to come and wrestle. Those who wanted to join their organization would step forward with bare hands and allow himself to be beaten by the crowd until he was on the verge of dying. If he never uttered a cry of pain throughout the process, he would be regarded as a "tough good guy" and offered money and medical care. After being beaten three times, his reputation as a "tough good guy" was established, and he would become a sworn brother of the other young men. If one died from the beatings, then he would be provided with a coffin and a proper burial. If one frowned ever so slightly during the beating, the young men would smile and dismiss him politely, considering him unworthy of being one of them. At first, no one knew exactly how such a phenomenon had come about; then people gradually realized that the Nian bandits had started colluding and instigating rebellion a number of years earlier, and that their rebellion did not appear out of the blue one morning. As the saying goes, "The frost one treads on turns into solid ice."[9] When those who are responsible for defending the country encounter such people, how can they afford not to be vigilant and take preventive measures?

The Assassination of Governor Ma Xinyi

The safety of the state lies with its ministers. This is certainly because they possess prestige and power, but also because of the positions they occupy. I was sightseeing at Coiled Incense Tower when Lord Ma Duanmin was assassinated.[10] I remember hearing a sudden clamor outside,

....

9   This is a quotation from the section on the Kun hexagram in the *Classic of Changes*, indicating cumulative effect.
10 Lord Ma was Ma Xinyi (1821–1870), the governor-general of Jiangxi, Jiangsu, and Anhui. Duanmin was his posthumous title.

and people were all saying that Nanjing had been seized by the remaining Taiping bandits and that the governor had been killed. There was a great disturbance in the streets, so I hurriedly hired a boat and returned home. Not until the next day did we receive definite news, but some people had already fled the city. Even at a distance of a thousand leagues, people could be shaken up like that—isn't this clear evidence of the great importance of ministers?

At that time, the prime minister from Nanpi was on an inspection tour in Jiangsu, and the court ordered him to investigate.[11] He had the assassin, Zhang Wenxiang, executed in the marketplace. The official who tried the case was Mr. Wan Qingxuan from Nanchang, the magistrate of Qinghe.[12] He was my father's best friend, which was why I was able to learn about this case in great detail. Lord Zeng Wenzheng wrote an elegiac couplet for Lord Ma: "Fan Xiwen, who worried about the country before everyone else, had never enjoyed a single moment of leisure; / Who had slain Lai Junshu? His death was to sadden a hundred generations."[13] The couplet showed concern for the country and commended loyalty, and its phrasing was grand and appropriate. From it one could well imagine Lord Zeng's magnanimity.[14]

When the assassin Zhang Wenxiang was executed in the marketplace, a man named Li Zhaoshou wept for him bitterly, calling him a "righteous friend," and planning to give him a proper funeral. This almost led to disaster, and for this reason Lord Zeng detested him. Li had been a Nian

....

11   The Prime Minister from Nanpi was Zhang Zhidong (1837–1909), a native of Nanpi, Hebei.

12   Wan Qingxuan was a late Qing official well-known for his administrative competence, and the maternal grandfather of Zhou Enlai, the premier of the People's Republic of China.

13   Lord Zeng Wenzheng was Zeng Guofan (1811–1872), an important late Qing statesman and military general. Xiwen was the courtesy name of Fan Zhongyan (989–1052), a Northern Song statesman and writer. His essay, "The Account of Yueyang Tower" (Yueyang lou ji), famously states that a benevolent man should "worry [about the country] before everyone else and enjoy oneself after everyone else." Lai Junshu was the courtesy name of Lai Xi (d. 35), an Eastern Han general. He was assassinated on the eve of a military campaign.

14   It was speculated that Ma Xinyi's death had to do with the conflict between the imperial army and the fierce Xiang (Hu'nan) militia that played a key role in suppressing the Taiping Rebellion. Zeng Guofan was the leader of the Xiang militia.

bandit; he surrendered and was made a provincial military commander because of his merit in battle. Later, it so happened that he had a conflict with Mr. Chen Guorui, and the two got into a brawl on the Yangzi River. Lord Zeng enumerated his misdeeds and dismissed him from office. He was eventually executed for breaking the law.

Fierce and aggressive fellows like Li took advantage of war and chaos; as soon as they made a name for themselves, they became fearless and threw caution to the wind. Greedy and cunning, bent on indulging their desires, they could not escape from punishment in the end. Some people said that it was like "putting away the bow after the birds were killed," but little did they know that those men had done it to themselves. Therefore Lord Zeng immediately disbanded the Chu army after he vanquished the bandits, and replaced it with the Huai troops, in the hope that through such a transformation they could gradually be tamed.[15] He preserved many people's lives this way.

Coiled Incense Tower was particularly scenic among Buddhist monasteries. It was located in a place known as Hexia, which was none other than Mei Gao's hometown, about a dozen leagues from Yuanjiang.[16] There was a magnolia tree there that was so big that its shade spread over an acre. In springtime, its blossoms were as brilliant as a sea of silver, illuminating everything around. I had visited the monastery a number of times. To the west of Yuanjiang was Flower Field; there were numerous roses there, stretching as far as the eyes can see, and one could smell their sweet scent ten leagues away. It was also quite a remarkable sight.

Remembering Cousin Xuequan

At that time, my cousin Xuequan had come to Yuanjiang from our hometown, and we studied together. During our time off, we would go and appreciate the flowers. I have not been to these places for almost thirty years now, and it has been nineteen years since my cousin passed away. Time went by slowly but surely, and all too soon everything is like a dream. How can one bear the small fascinations of the living, consider-

....

15   The Chu army refers to the Xiang militia, which was broken up by Zeng Guofan after the Taiping Rebellion was suppressed. Afterward Zeng mainly relied on the Huai militia from Anhui, developed and organized by Li Hongzhang (1823–1901).

16   Mei Gao (b. 153 bce) was a Western Han writer.

ing all that has happened?

My cousin's name was Wentao, and Xuequan was his courtesy name. He was the fourth son of my late sixth uncle Kuisheng, who was a "Filial and Incorrupt" graduate.[17] My cousin had been sickly since he was born, so he did not begin his studies until he reached seventeen years of age. But he was smart, and within two years he had finished all of the *Classics*. When he took up a brush and composed an essay, he was able to stand out among his peers. He went back to our hometown to take the civil service examination, but failed twice. He gave up after the second attempt, and went to live with my eighth uncle Shaozhu in the northwest.

At that time, Lord Zuo Wenxiang was leading an army to suppress the Dungan Revolt.[18] My eighth uncle, as vice prefect, was in charge of military supplies, and my cousin assisted him in his responsibilities. Afterward, just as my uncle was going to purchase an office for him so that he could directly contribute to the country, my cousin Wenzhi, whose courtesy name was Qinquan, was killed in battle as an expectant appointee for a ninth-rank office under the leadership of Lord Zuo. My eighth uncle died of grief. I received a letter from Xuequan, who told me that even though he was in a difficult situation, he would do everything he could to take my uncle's coffin back home; and that he hoped he could also be buried in the hills of our hometown one day. It was very sad, for who would have thought that his remark about his own burial would come true [prematurely]?

My cousin emulated the styles of Wang Wei and Meng Haoran in writing poetry, and that of Zhao Wenmin in practicing calligraphy.[19] He had loved traveling all his life. Whenever he encountered a beautiful landscape, he would linger all day along. His manner was natural and relaxed, and people described him as "a person from the Jin and Song

....

17 "Filial and Incorrupt" (*xiaolian*) was an unofficial reference to graduates in the civil service examination on the prefectual or provincial level in the Qing dynasty.

18 The "Dungans" are now called the Hui people or the Chinese Muslims. The Hui uprising broke out in the northwestern provinces of Shannxi, Gansu, and Ningxia, as well as in Xinjiang, and lasted from 1862 to 1877.

19 Wang Wei and Meng Haoran (689–740) were both prominent Tang poets. Zhao Wenmin was Zhao Mengfu (1254–1322), whose posthumous title was Wenmin. He was a famous painter and calligrapher.

dynasties."[20] He was only twenty-eight at the time of his death, which happened on the seventeenth day of the third month in the *yihai* year of the Tongzhi era [April 22, 1875].[21] How sad. My cousin did not want to end up being an average person; and yet, he never had a chance to demonstrate his talent. Isn't that so-called fate?

> The cold tide of the river
>> washes over white sand;
> I leisurely set sail
>> to roam at the edge of the sky.
> As long as I can keep my traces
>> distant from worldly feelings,
> I will play with rosy mist and vapors
>> in great spirits, day after day.

This is my cousin's poem. Although it is but a small example, one can get a rough idea of how he regarded himself.

When my cousin was in the northwest, from time to time he would write me about the Dungan Revolt. At that time, Miao Peilin was the only Nian bandit who had been captured and executed; the other major troops led by Zhang Lexing and Ren Zhu'er had all fled to the northwest and combined forces with the Hui rebels. Therefore the Hui rebels were particularly formidable. Their cruelty was something I could not bear to listen to. It was said that when they captured an enemy, they would often hang him upside down between two trees, draw blood from his thighs, and drink it, for they believed that if they did not drink their enemy's blood, they would not possess courage. They would also gut a person's belly and fill it up with straw and beans to feed their horses, calling it a "trough of flesh." This was the old practice of the bandits of the late Ming dynasty. How brutal! At first I thought that my cousin must have learned this from hearsay, and did not quite believe it. Later on, when I was touring Songjiang, I visited Mr. Yao Gusheng. He said that he had once been to Gansu, and that what he witnessed there was even worse.

....

20   The Jin (265–420) and Song (420–479) are known for their admiration of the discourses of Laozi and Zhuangzi, which emphasize the value of naturalness.

21   The *yihai* year was in fact the first year of the Guangxu era.

I also knew a man named Fang Hao, who was a former soldier in Lord Zuo Wenxiang's army. I met him at Jinhua, and he told me the same thing. According to Fang, the Hui rebels always wrapped their heads in white cloth when they fought; when they raised their arms and called for action, they were as swift and ferocious as a strong gale and as fierce as thunder, and would crush everyone in their way. If Lord Zuo had not been so good at disciplining his army, it would not have been so easy to think of destroying them.

Fang showed me "The Essentials of Military Operations," which he said Lord Zuo instructed the soldiers to recite and learn well. I read it and found it similar to the "Song of Battle Training" composed by Lord Zeng, but more concise and to the point. So I made a copy of it. Its table of contents is as follows:

Recognize true personal integrity. Respect the disposition of the troops. Make your mouth and ear trustworthy. Take caution about leaking information. Obey orders. Establish military regulations. Promote courage. Exercise caution in time of peace. Exercise restraint. Work on self-cultivation. Urge tolerance. Clarify military discipline. Forbid in-fighting. Refrain from making noise. Assess martial arts. Train spiritual strength. Train hands. Train feet. Train body strength. Inspect battle formation. Exercise in battle formation. Understand marching regulations. Issue orders. Guard against losing things during marches. Cross rivers. March through mountain forests. Set up strict patrol rules. Regularize inspection. Punish commercial activities. Safeguard camp gates. Watch over coming and going. Inspect weapons. Be prepared for fire. Forbid harassment of civilians. Report secrets. Punish instigators of commotion and disturbance. Train for real battles. Cultivate battle wrath. Be of one mind. Be careful about night patrol passwords. Caution marksmen. Avoid shooting blanks. Keep weapons in good order. Care for the wounded. Deal with being trapped on rivers. Deal with losing banners and drums. March through valleys. Regulate pursuing troops. Execute captives and traitors. Be fearful about killing innocents.

There were altogether fifty sections, with an appendix of various battle formations. How sad! Soldiers, bandits—they were all just farmers' sons in the beginning. Who had sown the seeds of discord and caused them to hate and kill one another? How pitiful!

I did not start writing poetry until I was fourteen years old. My teacher was none other than my cousin Xuequan. After that, not a single day went by that I did not compose poetry. Upon seeing that, my father handed me a collection of memorials by Lord Lu as well as the "Five Sets of Bequeathed Guidelines" by Lord Chen Wengong of Guilin.[22] He said to me, "Son, remember this: you must pursue what's useful in your studies. Chanting lines about the wind and moon is a waste of your time." I respectfully retired and read them, and henceforth my actions went against the times, until I find myself in serious straits today. Although I am despised by the world, I suppose I will be able to face my father in the underworld one day and tell him that I have not greatly disobeyed him.

Travels for Livelihood after Father's Death

After my father passed away, my family's financial situation became increasingly stressed, so I began to travel for my livelihood. My first trip was to Jinsha.

Jinsha was a town on the eastern seashore. To get there, I went to Yangzhou via Gaoyou, and passed through Hailing on my way. Hailing, also known as Guoxiahe, was eight hundred leagues from Yuanjiang. After I set out from Yuanjiang, I first made a stop at Huaicheng. That was during the ninth month of the *jiaxu* year [October 10–November 8, 1874]. The frosty wind was chilly, and falling leaves made a rustling sound, which intensified my melancholy. I climbed onto the Fishing Terrace of Marquis Han. Reflecting on how the marquis's transformation into a tiger did not last long before the "meritorious dog" was boiled alive, I could not help shedding tears over his fate.[23]

....

22 Lord Lu was Lu Zhi (754–805), a famous Tang statesman and writer. Lord Chen Wengong was Chen Hongmou (1696–1771), widely regarded as a model minister of the Qing dynasty.

23 Marquis Han was Han Xin (d. 196 bce), a military commander who had started out as an impoverished young man but eventually played a crucial role in the founding of the Western Han dynasty. After the Han was established, Emperor Gaozu began to eliminate his generals. Han Xin plotted rebellion and was subsequently executed. Emperor Gaozu had once compared his generals to "meritorious dogs" on a hunt, and his prime minister strategizing behind the scene to the hunter. The author combines this remark with another old saying: "Once the rabbit is captured, the hunting dog is boiled alive."

After that I went into the city and boated on Spoon Lake. The lake encircled the city like a green jade ring, and there were still some fading lotus flowers and sparse willow trees left. My friend, Yu Lang of Shanyin, whose courtesy name was Xingru, once composed the following lines, which furnish a fitting description of my experience:

Comes autumn—
what a fine road in the Southland!
The only thing missing
is the soft water chestnut in the western wind.

At Huaicheng, I stayed with Mr. Zha Changqing of Haining in the northern part of the city. Mr. Zha's name was Youchun, and he was a descendant of Zha Chubai.[24] He and my late father were good friends, and the two of them had much in common. After lingering there for several months, I went on to Baoying. Baoying had a famous local drink called Buddha's Mash. It was quite a brew.

Then I went to Gaoyou. Between Baoying and Gaoyou there was a village called Jieshou right by the lake. A filial son lived there, and I paid my respects to him. The filial son, Zhu Changchun, worked as a barber. He was a man of integrity. At first he was not particularly known for his filial piety. Then, one day, it rained very hard, and the lake water kept rising. If the dyke were to break, the tomb of Zhu's mother would be right in the path of the lake water, so he stayed beside the tomb in a temporary hut, crying day and night. The dyke indeed broke, but his mother's tomb was preserved intact. The field around the tomb, which spanned several acres, remained intact as well. It was as if heaven had guarded it against the flood. All of the villagers were amazed. They believed that heaven could indeed be moved, and spread the story far and wide. The prime minister from Hefei reported the happening to the court, and the filial son was officially recognized according to conventions.[25] They subsequently asked him to change his profession. The filial son refused, saying, "This line of work is what my parents had me take up." His behavior was truly commendable.

....

24   Zha Chubai was Zha Shenxing (1650–1727), a prominent Qing poet.
25   The prime minister from Hefei was Li Hongzhang.

Gaoyou was the hometown of Master Qin Huaihai.[26] When I passed the city, I sang his song lyric, "A wisp of cloud is smeared on the hills," and his panache seemed to be still present in the place. My boat zigzagged from Clear Water Pool. The hanging willows on the shores were reflected in Pearl Lake, and fishing boats emerged and vanished among the misty waves. It was quite a scenic outing that expanded my spirit. That evening, we moored by Lujin Goddess Shrine. Wang Yuyang once wrote a poem about it:

> Kingfisher feathers, bright pearl studs:
>> still as vivid as ever;
> Clouds over the lake, trees around the shrine
>> of a darker emerald color than the sky.
> As the traveler ties the hawser,
>> the moon is just beginning to sink:
> In the wild breeze outside,
>> blooms a white lotus.[27]

It is a lovely poem, quite worthy of its reputation as a masterpiece.

When I reached Shaobo, I visited Yang Chunhua and had a drink with him. Then he took me to Yangzhou in his boat. Yangzhou had always been a city of pleasure; but since the civil war, its vitality had not yet recovered. Already tipsy, Chunhua tapped on the side of the boat and sang the song lyric "Famed metropolis east of the Huai."[28] When he got to the lines "its ruined pools and towering trees, / seem weary of telling of war," his hair bristled with rage, and his voice was like the cracking of metal and stone. Truly, Jiang Shoumin's flesh was not even worthy of

....

26   Qin Huaihai was Qin Guan (1049–1100), a renowned Northern Song poet best known for his song lyrics.

27   Wang Yuyang was Wang Shizhen (1634–1711), a famous early Qing poet. His poem is titled "Passing by the Lujin Shrine Again" (Zai guo Lujin si).

28   This is a song lyric to the tune of "Yangzhou Ardante," composed by the Southern Song poet Jiang Kui in 1176. It laments the devastation of Yangzhou during attacks by the Jin people, who were in control of north China. The translation is by Stephen Owen, in *An Anthology of Chinese Literature* (New York: W.W. Norton, 1996), 632–33.

being devoured by the people of Yangzhou.[29]

After we entered the city, I first went to see Viburnum Flower Temple, but the temple was already gone, and there was only an empty site. I also visited the Tower of Ten Thousand Buddhas. It was magnificent. Many of the baldies at the monastery were, however, involved in unlawful activities.[30] I hear it has been burned down since. On the next day I ascended Shu Hill, and paid respects to the statue of Lord Shi Zhongzheng at Plum Blossom Ridge.[31] I set out after spending two nights at Tailai Guest Lodge, and passed by the Temple of the Goddess on the way.

When I reached Tai Zhou, I heard that my old friend Qian Jufu, whose personal name was Qixin, was gravely ill, so I went to see him. A native of Xiushui, Jufu was an informal and unrestrained person by nature. I had first met him at Huai'an, and we got along well with each other. He was cracking down on salt smuggling at Yangzhou in the capacity of the head of the Salt Registry when he became unwell. Prior to this, I heard that Jufu had taken a concubine at Yangzhou and was quite obsessed with her. I did not quite believe the story, so when I saw him, I asked him about it. With a smile he said, "Haven't I come to this precisely because of her? Even so, she is not going to betray me." He showed me his spittoon, and I was shocked to see blood in it. He just smiled. He died two days later. That evening, his concubine hanged herself. How extraordinary! Indeed, she did not betray him in life or death. The woman's surname was Hu, and she was rather ordinary in physical appearance. She was married to Jufu for no more than a year. Jufu had always been sickly, so his death should not be blamed on her. Today's world does not lack people who, though full of passion in life, turn away from their beloved in death, but

....

29   Jiang Shoumin was a merchant. In 1842, a group of wealthy Yangzhou merchants amassed a huge sum of money and offered it to the British army to avoid an invasion (even though the British did not plan to take Yangzhou, but went on to Nanjing instead), and Jiang Shoumin was the chief negotiator. In 1853, when the Taiping army came to Yangzhou, he tried to play the same role, with the promise that no Qing troops would defend Yangzhou; but the scheme was botched, and he lost his life in the process.

30   "Baldies" is a pejorative reference to Buddhist monks. The Tower of Ten Thousand Buddhas was located in Tianning Monastery.

31   Lord Shi Zhongzheng was the Ming minister Shi Kefa (1601–1645), best remembered for his defense of Yangzhou against the Manchu army. After being captured, he refused to surrender, and was executed.

she actually put a noose around her neck and followed her lover underground. The girl of the Swallow Tower who had to be motivated by Tutor Bai's poem was nothing when compared to her.[32] Jufu must have done something right to deserve someone like her. I stayed at Tai Zhou for three days to help manage his funeral, and then left for Rugao.

After I arrived at Rugao, I looked for the old site of the Mao family's Shuihui Garden, but could not find it.[33] Instead, I chanced upon a fragmented scroll in the marketplace, which turned out to be a list of the names of the Restoration Society members. I found it strange that so many people were involved in this "Restoration Society" business. They interfered in state affairs, and yet had never accomplished anything or made any useful suggestion. All they did was talk—why did they bother? I once remarked that ever since the case of Xiong and Yang, there were no more gentlemen left in the Donglin Party—those who joined later might very well be regarded as evildoers.[34] I threw away the name list, and left for Xiting.

From Xiting onward, the land was mostly constituted of saline-alkaline soils, and there was nothing worth seeing. I reached Jinsha, and stayed there for half a year before returning home.

....

32   The girl of the Swallow Tower was Guan Panpan, a famous courtesan who became the concubine of Zhang Yin, a military governor in the Tang dynasty. After Zhang died, Guan lived alone in the Swallow Tower, which Zhang had built for her. The poet Bai Juyi wrote a set of quatrains about her, one of which alludes to a famed ancient beauty who killed herself upon the imminent death of her lover. As the story goes, Guan Panpan committed suicide after she read the poem.

33   The Mao family's Shuihui Garden at Rugao became well-known because of Mao Xiang (1611–1693) and his celebrated love affair with Dong Xiaowan (1624–1651), a famous courtesan who became Mao's concubine. Mao Xiang was an eminent poet, writer, calligrapher, and painter, as well as an important member of the Restoration Society, a reformist group of literati members associated with the Donglin Party (see the note below) and deeply involved in late-Ming political faction struggles.

34   The Donglin Party was a political faction formed in the last years of the Ming dynasty, so-named because of its association with the Donglin ("Eastern Grove") Academy. Xiong Tingbi (1569–1625) was a general supported by the Donglin Party. He was involved in the loss of territory to the Manchus in the northeast, and was executed by the Ming court. Yang Lian (1572–1625), a member of the Donglin faction, made an appeal for him as well as sent a memorial to the throne accusing the powerful eunuch Wei Zhongxian (1568–1627), and was also executed.

On my way home I stopped at Tai Zhou to see the pine trees at Pine Grove Nunnery that were said to have been planted during the Jin dynasty. The pines, though not very tall, were twisted and sprightly; every branch stretched out and touched the ground, like the extended claws of a dragon, covering well over half an acre. Of a dark green color, they were luxuriant, deep, and ancient, truly a marvelous sight. After that, I went back to Yuanjiang.

Trip to Shaoxing for Father's Burial

In the following year, I was going to find a burial ground for my late father in our hometown, Shaoxing, so I crossed the Yangzi River again.[35] By now I had crossed the Yangzi three times.[36] Each time the vast wind from heaven blowing on the river eased one's concerns. In the past, someone had said that the words from Chen Jialing's song lyric, "The waves washed away the previous dynasties," were those of a heroic man; that the words from Gong Zhilu's poem, "Flowing water and green hills send off the Six Dynasties," were those of a talented man. To me, however, neither is as good as Junior Tutor Yao's couplet: "The River has tides that reach the Iron Jar, / but there is no footpath in the wild fields taking me to the Gold Altar."[37] Its depiction of this beautiful landscape seems as intimate as one's own palm.

After I crossed the Yangzi, I visited Jiao Hill. Jiao Hill was not very big, but quite remarkable, and its numinous beauty and secluded wonder were of a different order altogether. Ascending Buddha's Pavilion and looking out into the distance, from time to time I could see sails going

....

35 The author refers to the year following the *jiaxu* year, in which he set out for Jinsha, not the year after he returned from Jinsha.

36 The first time was when he left South Qinghe/Yuanjiang to seek refuge at Shaoxing from the Nian rebels in 1860. The second time was when he and his mother went back to South Qinghe to join his father in 1863. The third time was when he escorted his father's coffin back to Shaoxing in 1870.

37 Chen Jialing was Chen Weisong (1625–1682); Gong Zhilu was Gong Dingzi (1615–1673). Both were prominent poets. Junior Tutor Yao was Yao Guangxiao (1335–1418), an early Ming cultural and political figure. He was appointed junior tutor to the crown prince, a title of prestige. "Iron Jar" was an ancient fortress by the Yangzi River. Golden Altar (Jintan) was the name of a town to the south of Danyang.

swiftly across at the treetops. It was such an enjoyable view that it put me in the mood of an immortal roaming at the edge of the sky.

Then I went to Danyang, and moored my boat outside the city wall. The boatman pointed to a bridge and told me that it was where Mr. Zhang Guoliang, the former Longhair, had died in battle.[38] In the middle of the night, I got up alone, pushed open the awning, and looked outside. A crescent moon was on the rise, and a cold wind penetrated to the bone. The water under the bridge made a sobbing sound, as if the spirits of the dead were still lingering there. Ah, the Longhair rebels have all been terminated. Mr. Zhang, a remarkable man, pulled himself out of the bandits and pledged allegiance to the state. While he was alive, he was honored; after he died, he was lamented. Wise and worthy, he was worlds apart from rebels like Wei and Shi, who were killed off like isolated boars and rotten rats.[39] Although he did not live to see peace restored, his accomplishments were great, and his reputation was distinguished. As long as people remember him in their hearts, his spirit lives on. May his soul take comfort in this.

I arrived at Changzhou the next day. In the entire Wu region, Changzhou was particularly rich in literary culture; it also received the heaviest blow during the civil war. In the past, the shores of the river were lined with row upon row of houses, which were as dense as fish scales or the teeth of a comb; today, however, there is only misty desolation that fills one's sight. It is quite lamentable. As for Wuxi, the light and color of its hills and waters are just like in a painting; with its famous brew and delicious fish, it is still a land of joy, as it has gradually regained its former glory after years of recuperation.

When I reached Suzhou, I temporarily moored my boat at the Terrace of the Filial Marquis. Then, with a good wind, we crossed the Wusong River and entered Pingwang. Going east from Pingwang onward, one was in the province of Zhejiang. Frosty leaves were sparse there, and misty waves vast: it seemed that even the energy of heaven and earth had shifted with the change in the provincial territory, which was quite amazing.

....

38 Zhang Guoliang (d. 1860) was a general who served with distinction in the suppression of the Taiping Rebellion. He was buried by Yin's Bridge at Danyang.

39 Wei was Wei Changhui (d. 1856), and Shi was Shi Dakai (1831–1863). Both were major leaders of the Taiping Rebellion.

Jiaxing was called Zuili in ancient times. Together with Huzhou, it forms the gateway of western Zhejiang. Therefore the Longhair bandits assigned a large body of troops to Jiaxing, and ordered their "Eastern King" to stay there in charge of defense. As they built particularly high city walls, the imperial troops attacked Jiaxing for a long time without being able to take it, and Lord Cheng Zhonglie died in battle.[40] The customs of Jiaxing are pure and honest. The locals engage in sericulture and make a good profit. Although it has declined after the war, the city is relatively intact compared with other places. When I was there, a relative of mine also happened to be visiting, so we went boating together on Mandarin Duck Lake. We ascended Misty Rain Tower and looked out into the distance: the sun was shining, a warm breeze blew in our faces, and we felt our concerns lighten. In the evening we turned back in moonlight. As we toasted each other in our boat and recited Chen Jialing's song lyric opening with the line "Spending the night on water, by the cracking maple roots," the elders' pleasure in feasting and versifying at the beginning of our dynasty seemed to come alive before our eyes.

I went to Shimen the next day, and on the following day got to Hangzhou. I entered Hangzhou from Wulin Gate, and spent the night at a Buddhist monastery. The next day I crossed the Qiantang River and arrived at Xixing. First going against the currents on the Little Western River, I then took a boat south, and reached the western part of the city of Shaoxing.

This was the second time I returned to Shaoxing after the civil war. The first time was in the *gengwu* year [1870], when I escorted my father's coffin back home and interred him temporarily at the foot of Lower North Hill outside the south gate of Shaoxing. This time I chose a burial site for him at a place called Houting, which was on the south side of Yaomen Hill outside the south gate of the Eastern Outer City. Near Houting there was a rest stop for travelers, which was known as Guangfu Pavilion. It had three rooms for people to burn incense and make offerings to the Buddha. I borrowed the rooms to put up the workers, and I stayed there as well. That was in the eleventh month of the *yihai* year of the Tongzhi era [November 28–December 27, 1875].[41]

....

40   Lord Cheng Zhonglie was Cheng Xueqi (d. 1864), a Qing general.
41   It should be the first year of the Guangxu era.

About four or five leagues to the west of Houting there was a shrine called Si River Pavilion. Shaoxing was another four or five leagues to the west of the shrine. During my stay at Houting I would go to Shaoxing every day, because my legal mother had already returned to the city. When tired, I would rest at the shrine. The shrine faced a river flowing toward the Eastern Pass, which one had to go through in order to cross Cao'e River. There was a huge tree by the shrine. The local people set up a tea house under the tree and provided drinks for travelers. Oftentimes, when the sun was about to set, I would sit there with farmers and rustic elders and chat and laugh with them, and enjoyed it immensely. Occasionally we would watch an opera performance together. The plays themselves were not really worth seeing, but it was worth seeing what made a play a play. Rise and fall as well as successes and failures that took place in the course of hundreds of years were shown in an instant, and one would do well to ponder the reasons behind them. Master Quan Xieshan once said that watching a play was tantamount to reading the *Classics* and histories, which is quite true.[42]

Fishing was something I had not known much about before this trip. About ten paces from Guangfu Pavilion there was a pond as clear as a mirror. I tried my hand at fishing there, but did not catch a single fish all day. A peasant woman passing by chuckled and said, "Eh, what a pity!" I asked her, "What do you mean by that?" "Well," she replied, "you obviously don't know anything about fishing. When fishing, you must focus your thoughts, calm your passions, and let your mind and hand both get so used to it that they become subtle. When they become subtle, then you are all set." I listened to her advice, and it worked. I was so happy that I would go fishing every day. Indeed, I became so obsessed that I forgot to eat and sleep. After a while, I said to myself with a sigh, "One can never catch all the fish in the world. Getting too greedy and not knowing when to stop—this is no good." Thereupon I gave up fishing altogether.

The harvest of new grain is a farmer's supreme joy. There are, however, things related to it that one cannot bear mentioning. During my stay in the countryside, besides supervising the workers in the construction of my late father's burial site, I had nothing else to do, so I began to explore various nearby villages. By custom a tenant farmer had to pay rent to the

....

42   Master Quan Xie Shan was Quan Zuwang (1705–1755), a Qing scholar and writer.

landowner. If the landowner was a kind man, then after the tenant farmers turned in what they owed him, they still had some remaining grain to themselves for survival: this was the best-case scenario. If the landowner was unkind, then hunger and cold immediately struck the tenant farmers. When they could hardly make a living, they began to resort to all sorts of deceptions. Some mixed mud and sand with the grain they turned in to the landowner; some gave short measure; some sprinkled water on the grain to make it swell; some steamed it to make it look like more than there was. Even worse, men would act tough and refuse to pay, and women would stand around and weep and beg for reduction in what they owed. The landowner hated such behavior, and would either report them to the local officials or bully them. The weak ones could not escape from harm; even the strong ones were broken in the end. This was the situation in a year of good harvest. With a poor harvest, they would become destitute and homeless. It was very sad.

The common folk are the foundation of a country; for them food is heaven, and farming is the origin of food. Their sufferings have been intensified in recent years, and yet they have nobody to turn to. To make things worse, those who put the trivial before the important are always showing off their wealth.[43] It is human nature to feel attached to one's parents and love one's wife and children. If a man works hard all year and yet does not have enough to provide for his parents, wife, and children, it is quite understandable that he becomes envious and reckless. As I was reflecting on all this, I felt dejected for months. It might seem appropriate that those who sit around enjoying the rent they have collected do not care about the farmers, but those who manage the state should certainly be more circumspect in their planning and strategizing.

Rich families own many acres of land. They sit around enjoying the rent they have collected from their tenant farmers. If they receive a little more or a little less, it does not matter much to them, and it is truly shameful that they haggle over everything with those who have calluses on their hands and feet. They love to say "Those tenant farmers are crafty and obstinate" over and over again, but how exactly are they being "crafty and obstinate"? I once saw a rent collector come to a village in a big boat, and all the villagers received him with the utmost respect. They

. . . .

43   This refers to merchants.

said, "How late you are, dear mister, in coming to our village this year!" The tenant farmer was an old man. He came forward with a hunched back, and the rent collector regarded him with contempt. The old man offered chicken and ale to the rent collector, who merely nodded, but would not eat or drink. Shortly after, the rent collector went over the payment he received, and found it inadequate. He glared at the old man, who knelt down and begged for mercy, but the rent collector completely ignored this. He directed his servants to search the old man's house and found some grain. The old man started weeping. The rent collector again ignored this, saying, "What a cunning fellow you are!" He seized a pig from the old man, and told him that this was his punishment. At that the old man could not stop his tears from flowing. This, gentle reader, represents a general picture of rent collectors. I cannot bear speaking of it any further.

After the war, many people lost their homes. When I was traveling from the south, I saw nothing but acre after acre of wasteland. In some places, the government would hire people to cultivate the fields, and so outsiders lived together with the locals. They often engaged in lawsuits that lasted years, or got in armed fights. People had a hard time because of this, and would leave their hometown at the drop of a hat. Wandering from place to place, they were destitute and desperate, and had no one to talk to. As fathers and elder brothers passed away, sons and younger brothers became increasingly impoverished. They had little means of making a living, so they sought illegal profit. Decent people detested them, and deception and fraud were being practiced every day. Lord Zeng Wenzheng once said that after a period of chaos, public morality deteriorates even more. If we trace the origin of the problem, we find it is all due to poverty. From the past to the present, there has never been a time when people could give up the essentials to pursue the trivial and yet obtain prolonged peace and stability. Human beings by nature hate making an effort and love being at ease. When people try to devour one another after having lost their sense of ease, it is like wrapping up flames with a piece of paper. No wonder mature and experienced people are deeply worried about it. What, then, should be done about it? I suppose we should all cherish what we have and be prudent.

About twenty leagues from Houting was a village called Fanjiang. Fanjiang had a Laoyue Temple, which was the most popular temple in the prefecture. As the work on my father's burial site was about to be completed, someone urged me to consult the gods for the date of interment, so I paid a visit to Laoyue Temple. I found the temple packed with villagers who came to offer their prayers. There were more than a hundred elderly women sitting on the ground and mumbling something. I listened to them and realized that they were reciting the Buddha's name. Thereupon I left with a chuckle. I went to Shaoxing instead, and sought out a diviner there to help me make a decision.

The Buddha and the gods have little to do with one another. What sort of foolishness is it to mumble the Buddha's name at a temple built for the Daoist gods? And yet, if one were not foolish, why would one mumble the Buddha's name in the first place? In the foolishness of human beings we also find the goodness and tolerance of human beings. Who does not know that the Buddha and the gods are mere statues made of mud? People nevertheless hope that they will confer blessings, repeat what all the others say, and seek good fortune from sheer emptiness. This is truly pitiful. Then again, if people all had adequate clothing and food and did not suffer from any want, why would they still do this? Those who detest the common folk for worshipping the gods and the Buddha would do well to take this into consideration. But, of course, if one gathers together with shamans and witches, carries on criminal activities and breaks the law, then our sagely ruler will have to mete out punishment.

After the interment date was chosen, I went to Lower North Hill to bring my father's coffin.

Lower North Hill was about ten leagues from the south gate of Shaoxing. I left at noon, and it was already twilight when I got there. My little boat zigzagged on the winding tributaries; there were mountains on both sides all the way. Trees had become bare, and plants had withered. A frosty moon appeared in the clear sky. It had been five years since my father died; during these five years I had been wandering all over the world to make ends meet, and yet had been growing more destitute day by day. If I had engaged in scholarship, it would have been difficult to make a living; and yet, to go along with the times was not something I was happy doing. As I reflected on these things during my boat trip, I could not help shedding tears.

Elder Zhang, the man who watched over my father's temporary grave, came to greet me, and took me home for a rest. Elder Zhang was in his fifties; he had a wife and a son. They were gentle and respectful folks who remained content with their lot of plowing and weaving. Their house faced the river, with mountains in the background; it was surrounded by bamboos and trees. On the porch there were a few dozen rows of bee-hives. The bees made honey in late spring, which they used for brewing mead, something they enjoyed greatly.

When my father's coffin arrived at Houting, all of my relatives gathered together. After interment we paid off the grave neighbor. "Grave neighbor" was a local term for the grave keeper. My father's grave neighbor was Zhao the Six, who was from Tangxia Village. He was a farmer who lived just across the river from the burial site.

Afterward I returned to the city and thanked all of my relatives. One of them invited me to go on an outing to the Song imperial mausoleums. When I was seeking refuge from the Taiping bandits at Tiaomachang, I had been a mere dozen leagues away from the mausoleums. At that time, however, I never had a chance to go there, and found it quite regrettable. So I happily accepted the invitation. We went by way of Fusheng Village. When we first got there, there was a drizzling rain. We sat for a little while in a farmer's house before we visited the shrine built in honor of the chivalrous Mr. Tang.[44] The shrine was in ruins. Only at Emperor Gaozong's mausoleum were there still a few rooms left, although they were so dilapidated that they could hardly provide shelter from wind and rain. In one of the rooms, we saw a stone table and an incense burner chiseled out of stone. It was very quiet, with not a single soul around, and the rest were just desolate mist and overgrown weeds. Nothing but a broken stele marked the mausoleum of Emperor Lizong. Seas changed into farming fields and farming fields again changed into seas, leaving bleakness to fill one's sight. I sought for the famed evergreens, but could find none. It was all very sad. At dusk, dark clouds began to close in, and the mountains around us were growing heavy with shadows and silence. A fast rain chased us, and I seemed to hear ghosts weep. We boarded a boat and went back.

....

44 The chivalrous Mr. Tang was Tang Jue (b. 1247). After the Southern Song was conquered by the Mongols, Yang Lian Zhen Jia, a Tibetan monk, was put in charge of religious affairs in the south. He ordered the Southern Song imperial mausoleums dug up, rifled through the treasures, and scattered the remains of the Southern Song emperors. Tang Jue, a commoner from Shaoxing, collected the bones of the emperors, gave them a proper burial, and planted evergreens to mark the burial sites.

The next day we visited the Orchid Pavilion.[45] The Orchid Pavilion had recently been renovated, and turned out to be extremely splendid. The Goose Pool and Ink Pool were both in a neatly square shape. Outside the pavilion was a winding stream in a tiled channel. We tried to put a wine cup in, which barely flowed on the current. Thereupon we left with a chuckle.[46] But we did spend some time strolling in the midst of "dense trees and tall bamboos" and taking in the clarity of the scene, and that was a rather memorable experience.[47]

I fell ill after the trip and did not recover until a full month later. Then I went on an outing to the South Town.

The South Town was where Yu's Mausoleum was located.[48] People always visited it in the third month of the year, because there was an "incense market" on Incense Burner Peak at that time. Since I did not like the crowds, I went before the third month. Yu's Mausoleum was surrounded by mountains; its structure was grand and magnificent. The road to the mausoleum was lined with lofty steles rising high above trees. I composed a poem during my visit, which is as follows:

The dwelling place of the divine spirit for all eternity—
I look up to its somber and harmonious edifice.
At ritual sacrifice His Imperial Majesty makes offerings;

....

45 "Lanting," commonly rendered as the Orchid Pavilion, is located to the southwest of Shaoxing. It became famous after the celebrated calligrapher Wang Xizhi (303–361) gathered with a group of friends there in the spring of 353, in observance of the Lustration Festival. Everyone present was asked to compose poetry, and those who failed to produce a poem had to drink three goblets of ale as a penalty. Wang Xizhi wrote a preface to the collection of the poems, which remains one of the best-known landscape essays and calligraphy pieces in Chinese history. Wang Xizhi was said to have a particular fascination with geese; he had also supposedly washed his writing brush in a pool when practicing calligraphy in his youth, and turned the pool black. Goose Pool and Ink Pool have become an obligatory part of the scene at Lanting, and it is still true today.

46 "Floating a wine cup on a winding stream" was an ancient custom observed at the Lustration Festival. People would float a wine cup in a winding stream; whenever the cup stopped in front of a person, the person would drink from it. Wang Xizhi's preface makes mention of the practice.

47 "Dense trees and tall bamboos" are a phrase in Wang Xizhi's preface.

48 Yu, or Yu the Great (Da Yu), was a legendary ruler in antiquity famed for his flood-control method.

The Yangzi and Han Rivers pay their tribute.
With a lush color, trees tower toward heaven;
Around the palace: mountain flowers in bloom.
Had the book collection been preserved intact,[49]
Its aura would have grown finer every day.

This poem was meant to convey my impression of the truly unique scenery of this place.

As I looked toward Incense Burner Peak from Yu's Mausoleum, I found it was still higher up in the clouds. To get to it one must go through the "Lean Buffalo's Back." Lean Buffalo's Back was a ridge of mountain as thin as a thread; it acquired such a nickname because it was both steep and slippery. Since I had just recovered from my illness, I felt apprehensive, and did not want to take the risk. I asked the people living in the mountains about it, and they told me that at the time of the "incense market," even a young woman would mince her way up there, and that, thanks to the Buddha's blessing, nobody had ever been injured. Nevertheless, I did not feel like trying it.

Instead, I left for Lion Hill, also known as Hou Hill. I took a boat to penetrate into the belly of the mountain and meandered forward. Strange rocks were hanging down and cast reflections in a clear pool. As slanting sunlight streamed in, gold and emerald colors were shining forth brilliantly upon each other. It was remarkable. After a couple of hours, suddenly the vista opened up. Precipitous cliffs of motley colors rose up on all sides; in the midst there was a pool, its water sometimes appearing dark green and sometimes clear and shallow. It was very quiet there. Indeed the silence was so profound that I felt the place did not belong to the dusty human world. Even if I had died there instantly, I would have been perfectly happy.

The Academy of Master Stone Case had once been located on the mountain, but had since become deserted.[50] An itinerant monk built a small monastery on its old site, and I went there to have a meal. Then I returned via the Woodcutter's Wind Canal. Speaking of enjoyable trips

....

49   According to legend, this was where the Yellow Emperor kept his book collection.
50   Master Stone Case was Zhang Dai (1597–1679), a late Ming writer and scholar. He
      was a native of Shaoxing.

in my hometown region, I have to say this was the best.

After I came back from Lion Hill, someone told me about the scenic landscape at Seven Stars Crag, so I gave it a try. It was about the same as Lion Hill; only the caves were deeper, the rocks were all black, and it was freezing cold. On the crag there was a Bodhisattva shrine that looked toward the pool. It was solitary and tranquil, and I spent the night there. Sitting in front of a lamp emitting a greenish light and facing the ancient statue of the Bodhisattva, I felt at peace. The poem I wrote that night contains the following couplet: "Into a clear dream enters the intermittent chimes; / a subtle incense gives expression to the heart in meditation." It has been almost twenty years since my visit, but I still think back on it, and have never forgotten the scene.

After returning from Lion Hill, I planned to go on an outing to Plum Mountain, but was not able to. So I went to Zhuangxie at a relative's invitation instead.

Zhuangxie, also called Zhongxie or Grave Mound Slope, was in the Wan Mountains. People said that many palace ladies of the Song dynasty were buried there, but the cemetery ground had long become a farming field. My host was very hospitable. Nevertheless, the place was desolate and lonely; moreover, there were tigers in the mountains, and even in the daytime people carried guns. So every day I spent my time upstairs looking at the books and paintings collected by the host's forefathers, which were half eaten through by insects. Only a painted screen in colors by Yun Nantian was still intact.[51] Its brushwork was full of vitality, doubtless an authentic piece. My host treasured and protected it like his own life, considering it more valuable than yellow gold.

I had, however, once heard from Mr. Yang Peiyuan (whose personal name was Baoyi) of Yanghu that in his old age, Yun Nantian would paint a fan for seventy copper coins, and often suffered from want of food and clothing.[52] Is it true that prominence and obscurity each has its time, but that those who have made it find it hard to earn recompense in the end? Tang Yin once wrote the following couplet: "The paddy field by the lake—nobody wants it; / who, I wonder, will buy the mountain in my

....

51   Yun Nantian was Yun Shouping (1633–1690), a major early Qing artist best known
      for his flower paintings.
52   Yang Peiyuan (1835–1907) was a painter and calligrapher from Jiangsu.

paintings?"[53] It makes one sad to recite it even after many generations. People in this world all grieve at the Xiang River and mourn Jia Yi, but if the man they lament were alive, they would most likely think nothing of him.[54] "With a reputation that lasts ten thousand years, / all that happens after one's life is silence." Du Fu had thus expressed his sentiment. Isn't it because such a man has nowhere to try out his talent? Yet, even in deep mountains and hidden valleys, there must be someone who appreciates him. Comparing him with those who leave no name behind or those who do leave a name behind only to be scorned and detested—there certainly is a difference. Therefore a gentleman should learn from this where to place himself.

Among the many snakes in the Wan Mountains, there were the so-called King Python, Huipai, Litoupo, and Bamboo Leaf Green. King Python was the most poisonous. Short but stout, it was of a golden color, and its eyes gleamed like lightning. Huipai was only the size of a lizard; it made a sound like a frog, and was of a slightly dark color. Wherever it slithered, the plants in its path would wither. Resembling a wilting tree branch with dead leaves, Litoupo was hard to distinguish in the bushes; as soon as one touched it, one would die on the spot. Bamboo Leaf Green was no more than a foot long, as slender as a chopstick, and of a dark green color throughout its body. Occasionally it might have black spots. Its head had a crimson dot, and its tongue was as bright red as a peach blossom. It would not bite people lightly, but once it did, there was no cure. There were many other kinds, but they were not as poisonous, and there was an antidote for their poison.

A most remarkable thing once happened to my host's cousin at many removes, who was a woodcutter. One day, when he was climbing the mountain, his hand was bitten by a snake. He struck the snake and killed it, and cut off his own arm. Then he chopped the dead snake into a farina and applied it, along with some medicine and water, to his severed arm, put it back, and wrapped it up with cloth. He was healed overnight. Nobody understood how this was possible. Was it because the mountain folk were so used to the mountain that they even knew the nature of

....

53   Tang Yin (1470–1523) was a Ming painter and poet.
54   For Jia Yi, see note 79 of part 1. When Jia Yi was crossing the Xiang River in exile, he composed a famous "Lament for Qu Yuan;" Qu had committed suicide in his exile (see note 80 of part 1).

alien species there? Nowadays, stratagem meets stratagem and gives rise to deception; when country people encounter such wiles, eight or nine out of ten would die, but city people deal with the situation as casually and easily as taking off their shoes. I suppose it is also a matter of habit. How strange!

I heard of the *chang* ghost when I was seeking refuge from the Taiping bandits at Pig's Jaw.[55] During my stay in my relative's mountain residence, I went through his book collection and would often read until midnight. One evening, just as a drizzling rain was sprinkling the windows, suddenly a strange sound, shrill and sad, came out right behind the house. Even the candlelight became dimmed, and it sent shivers down my spine. I closed the book and quickly rose to my feet. At that moment my host silently entered the room and motioned to me to be quiet. Taking a musket in hand, he fired a shot through the crack of the window. With a loud bang, a flurry of leaves fell from the trees. When that strange sound was heard again, it was already several layers of the hills away.

At the time, the warning about tigers was quite serious. At night one could hear gongs and drums reverberating throughout the neighborhood. Sometimes villagers set fire to the forest, and I would gaze at it. The flames were like startled snakes or flashes of lightning, raging and surging forth freely. In a little while, they became mixed with the white clouds in the sky. Suddenly emerging and then just as suddenly vanishing, they twisted and coiled in a marvelous manner, and the transformation was impossible to predict. That was quite a spectacle.

Return to Yuanjiang

After several days, I took my leave, and returned to Yuanjiang, as my whole family was still living in the north. I once again went by way of the Little Western River. Along the river there were mountains on both sides. They were extraordinary and majestic, casting their reflections in the clear water unruffled by wind. The peaks competed with one another in beauty and charm, and just as on the Shanyin road, they came in such

----

55 The *chang* ghost was believed to be the spirit of a person who had been killed by a tiger and was subsequently controlled by the tiger.

a rapid succession that my eyes could hardly take them all in.[56] I moored my boat at Coin Islet. This was where the Eastern Han magistrate Liu Chong accepted the one coin.[57]

The next day I passed Xiaoshan. Xiaoshan had a Xiang Lake. I heard it was very scenic. Regrettably I was in a hurry and did not have time to visit it. Upon reaching Xixing, I spent the night at Wang Xianghe's Transit Office. The next morning I crossed the Qiantang River. The Qiantang River was as big as the Yangzi, but not as grand or as magnificent. On the river, I saw the hills of Fuyang in the distance. They loomed and disappeared in the morning fog, as pretty as in a painting; it was quite impressive. I arrived at Hangzhou and entered the city through Wangjiang Gate. I rented a boat at Jian Bridge and set out from there.

At dusk I passed Banshan. It was late spring, and the peach blossoms were in bloom. In the past, the peach blossoms of Banshan were described as "scarlet snow." Unfortunately it was already dark, so I could not see them, and have regretted it until this day. Arriving at Shimen, we moored at the bend of the river. A newly planted willow tree by the river danced in the breeze. The sky had just cleared up after a drizzle, and a light chill was upon us. I asked the boatman to buy some ale and gut a fish, and we had a few drinks together. I got happily drunk. By the time I woke up the next morning, I had no idea that the boat had passed Jiaxing.

We again went via the Woodcutter's Wind Canal and reached Pingwang. In a couple of days we passed Suzhou and arrived at Wuxi. I drank from the "Second Spring of the World."[58] Then I hurried toward Changzhou and passed through Benniu. Benniu's ale was rather poor and undeserving of its reputation, which was a pity. I paid a visit to my old friend Yan Chiya (whose personal name was An), but he was not at home.

I went on to Zhenjiang, and ascended Miaogao Terrace of Jinshan Temple. A couplet was hanging on the Terrace: "We wish the Buddha

....

56   This is a well-known remark of Wang Xianzhi (344–386), Wang Xizhi's son (see note 45). Shanyin County was in Shaoxing.
57   Liu Chong served as prefect of Kuaiji (the prefecture seat was Shanyin) and was much loved by the local people. When his term was over, several elders of Kuaiji each presented him with a hundred coins. Unable to decline and yet unwilling to accept, he took only one coin.
58   This is the spring at the Hui Mountain to the west of Wuxi.

could lower his two hands / And deprive all human hearts of their unevenness." This couplet was preaching the dharma on behalf of the ancient masters. In the past, the Zen master Foyin regarded the universe as a folding chair, and Master Dongpo left his jade-decorated belt as a treasure to "stabilize the temple."[59] With such a majestic mountain and river like a writhing dragon and leaping tiger right in front of them, the two elders treated them as if they were nothing. What kind of visionary mind they must have had! Compared with them, those who put a false gloss on the Kaiyuan and Tianbao eras were not worth speaking of.[60]

Seen from afar, Guazhou was as small as one's palm; at Liuhao and Qihao, masts stood in great numbers like trees in a forest—in fact they looked like bitter fleabanes and brambles in the distance. Jiao Hill and Suan Hill were two spots of misty hair coils. Light dancing on water and shadows cast by clouds reflected each other and sparkled. The battlements on the city wall were irregular, and the red banners fluttered in the wind. The mountains surrounded the boulevards and marketplaces, and sailboats crossed the dark blue waters. Such a sight was truly able to give a traveler the feeling of exhilaration, and I hailed the scene as the acme of perfection.

I reached Yangzhou, and looked for the site where Grand Tutor Xie played chess and wagered his nephew's villa, but could not find it.[61] Some

....

59   Master Dongpo was the poet Su Shi (see note 42 of part 1). Foyin (1032–1098) was
      an eminent monk of the Northern Song and a good friend of Su Shi. When Foyin
      was the abbot of Jinshan Temple, Su Shi reportedly donated his jade-decorated
      belt to the temple.

60   The Kaiyuan and Tianbao eras lasted from 713 to 756 under the reign of Emperor
      Xuanzong of Tang. It was a time when the Tang reached its zenith of power and
      prosperity. The eras were followed by the An Lushan Rebellion in 755 and the
      devastation of the Tang empire.

61   Grand Tutor Xie was Xie An (320–385), an eminent statesman of the Eastern Jin
      dynasty and a chess lover. In the year 383, on the eve of a massive military attack
      from the northern ruler Fu Jian, Xie An played a game of chess with his nephew
      Xie Xuan (343–388), who was in charge of a much smaller defense army. They
      made a bet on Xie Xuan's villa. Xie Xuan had always been a much better chess
      player than his uncle, but on that day, he was too nervous to concentrate and lost
      both the game and his villa to an unruffled Xie An. Turning to another nephew,
      Yang Tan, Xie An said, "The villa now is all yours." He then went to the villa and
      held a big party. Only after midnight did he return home and deal with all of the
      military matters awaiting his decisions. The Eastern Jin army won a great victory

fellow traveler invited me to visit the pleasure quarters, and I went along. I could not help becoming intoxicated, but without the talent of a Du Mu, what would I do with the reputation of a heartless lover?[62] The next day I boarded a boat and went to Shaobo to see Yang Chunhua. Chunhua had just left with a friend for Nanjing; his two sons prepared a meal for me, and I stayed overnight.

Then I hurried toward Gaoyou. Our boat encountered a strong wind at Mapeng and almost capsized. In another two days I arrived at Huaicheng. The guards at Huai Pass gave me a hard time. Reciting the poem on passing Lugou Bridge by Master Shu Tieyun, I could not help chuckling.[63]

After I returned home, I devoted myself to reading and waiting on my aging mother every day. Although our circumstances were strained, I did not care. As the proverb says, "One does not stop unless one reaches the Yellow River." I did not seek other means of livelihood because we had not run out of rice or firewood yet. My procrastination had caused me to lose many opportunities. Nevertheless, I have never regretted my choice.

Out of the eastern gate of Yuanjiang there was a bridge called Mr. Zhu's Bridge. Going through the bridge and walking further east, one would see a temple, which was known as Compassionate Cloud. There was water on all sides of the temple, and on all sides of the water were willow trees. Although it was not far from the city, its scenery was lovely. Every day I would linger there in the company of Lan Youzhi (whose personal name was Yan) to while away the time. Youzhi was a native of Hunyuan of Shanxi, the grandson of Mr. Suting, the former director-general of the Grand Canal.[64] His family was caught up in the civil war and became impoverished. He was, however, honest and upright, and considered it beneath his dignity to do anything about it. People

. . . .

over Fu Jian's invading troops.

62   Du Mu (803–852) was a Tang poet, well known for his many celebrated poems about Yangzhou. His most famous poem contains this couplet: "After ten long years I woke at last from a Yangzhou dream— / I had only won the fame for careless love in its blue mansions" (Stephen Owen's translation, in *An Anthology of Chinese Literature*, 631). The "blue mansions" refer to the entertainment quarters.

63   Shu Tieyun was the studio name of Shu Wei (1765–1816), a poet. He wrote a poem on passing over Lugou Bridge outside Beijing and being harassed by the illiterate guard at the bridge pass.

64   Lan Suting was Lan Dixi (1736–1797), whose biography appears in *The Draft of Qing History* (*Qing shi gao*), 325.

regarded him as a strange bird. The two of us would sometimes take pleasure in walking around in the wilderness and laughing like madmen, or discussing poetry until dawn. One day, right by the temple, we heard a child sing: "Willow catkins bloom, on the third day of the third month; / Spring wind blows the clothes thin." Youzhi was quite taken aback and remarked that it was the "piping of heaven." I playfully added a couplet to those lines: "I am a poor girl who alone feels sad on the tower— / My lover is traveling at the edge of the world; when will he return?" Youzhi was even more enthralled, and thought that it far surpassed the ballads of the Qi and Liang dynasties.[65] Soon afterward, Youzhi went to Wuhu, and we were henceforth separated. I got a letter from him when I was visiting Songjiang, but I have no idea where he is now.

Another friend I had at Yuanjiang was Yu Mosheng (whose personal name was Zhixiang). Mosheng was from Zichuan of Shandong. He was poor, and did secretarial work to provide for his mother. He also loved poetry. When we became tipsy from drinking, his extraordinary energy would burst forth. One day he wrote the following couplet on his door: "In life, I lodge myself on Botong's veranda; / in death, I shall rest next to Yao Li's tomb."[66] Then he left for Chizhou and never came back. I composed a song lyric on boating in the West Lake with the following lines:

> In recent years, the hair on my temples has turned white;
> In loneliness I think of my talented friends—
> From them I have not heard anything.
> A felt cap, a silk whip;
> Traveler's wheels, way station horses;
> Floating duckweeds, broken stalks—
> > adrift in several different places.

I wrote these lines with those two friends of mine in mind. I suppose

65   Qi (479–502) and Liang (502–557) were two short-lived dynasties in southern China. There is a corpus of ballads from this period, most of which are quatrains in five-syllable lines and sing of romantic love.

66   Botong was Gao Botong, a wealthy man of the Wu region. Liang Hong (fl. 1st century), a scholar and recluse, once worked for him as a hired hand and lived on his veranda. Yao Li (fl. 550 bce) was a swordsman and assassin, whose tomb was in Suzhou. After Liang Hong died, Gao Botong had him buried by Yao Li's tomb.

they are both aging now from having been beaten down by life. It is really sad.

Cloud Terrace Mountain of Haizhou was no more than two hundred leagues from Yuanjiang. I had always wanted to go there, but was not able to, which was regrettable. I heard that the mountain was verdant and majestic, with many layers on all sides, and its depth was inexhaustible. The mountaintop was always sealed by clouds. When the sun first rose, it was splendid in cinnabar and emerald colors, so fresh and moist that it seemed to be dripping with water. On the mountain grew immortal vines and ancient trees that lasted for hundreds of years. Some of them were concealed by flying cascades, and some were hidden in the deep grottos. The tracks of numinous spirits emerged and then vanished—no one could trace their origin. Buddhist monks and feathered folks cultivated themselves on the mountain, and often accomplished miracles. It was truly the place where gods would come and go, the residence of divine beings.

Someone had once presented my father with a gift of two jars of white clouds from the mountain. The jars were sealed with layers of cotton paper. We put them in a quiet room, and pierced a tiny hole with a needle. A gossamer thread rose slowly from the hole, and then it would coil and curl and finally fill the space like misty silk or foggy gauze, hanging still in the air. I would face it in silent meditation, as its soft scent made one feel slightly drunk. That was quite pleasurable.

We also acquired a fleeceflower tuber from the mountain, which was twisted and gnarled like a melon. We opened it up with a bamboo knife: its texture was of a pale red, with a very fine grain and slightly wrinkled. My father and legal mother ate it, and felt it contributed to their well-being. But it was nothing extraordinary on the mountain, and the locals sometimes regarded it as a regular foodstuff. Was this why many people there lived well over a hundred years? Or might it be because the soil to the north of the Huai River, from Yuanjiang on to Taoyuan and Suqian, and then to Feng, Pei, Xiao, and Dang, became gradually rich? Feng, Pei, Xiao, and Dang were where the Exalted Emperor of the Han and Xiang Yu had risen to prominence.[67] The people there were talented

....

67   All of these places are in modern-day Jiangsu. The Exalted Emperor (i.e., Emperor
       Gaozu) was Liu Bang (d. 195 bce), the founding emperor of the Western Han

and loyal. However, they would kill a man for the slightest grievance, which gave the four counties a reputation of being difficult to govern. I have heard, however, that nowadays they plant poppies everywhere, and many people have become opium addicts. Though they have land, they cannot enjoy the use of land; though they have people, they cannot enjoy the use of people. As a result, their strength has weakened little by little.

In general, local customs change from the north to the south of the Huai River, and then change again from the north to the south of the Yangzi River. When change reaches its extreme at Suzhou and Songjiang, where the three rivers and five lakes converge, then the way of life becomes increasingly soft and brittle, which gives rise to cunning and cleverness.[68] Master Wu Meicun once said, "When mountains and rivers are charming and delicate, they produce Ji and Yun."[69] This is quite true. From Suzhou and Songjiang to the western part of Zhejiang, the terrain rises higher and the soil becomes richer; then a numinous energy gathers in Hangzhou. . . .[70]

Trip to Hangzhou

Two years later, my family circumstances deteriorated, so I went to Hangzhou on the thirteenth day of the seventh month in the *wuyin* year of the Guangxu era [August 11, 1878]. I had passed through the same places several times by then, and the landscape was pretty much the same every time. Going in circles thus, like a donkey round and round a millstone, I could not help laughing at myself. . . .[71]

....

dynasty. Xiang Yu (232–202 bce) was his major rival in the contention for throne.

68   Songjiang is in modern Shanghai.

69   Wu Meicun was Wu Weiye (1609–1671), a renowned poet. Ji and Yun refer to the brothers Lu Ji (261–303) and Lu Yun (262–303), scions of a prominent southern family and talented writers. They lived in Huating (modern Shanghai) before they served the Western Jin dynasty.

70   A sentence was crossed out here and an illegible line was scribbled in the margin.

71   A sentence, "This was on the thirteenth day of the seventh month in the *wuyin* year of the Guangxu era," was crossed out here, and the date was inserted into an earlier sentence in the margin. A blank page follows this passage in the manuscript. The next section begins in sheets of paper with a different layout: they are larger than the previous sheets, and have thirteen lines instead of ten.

Sojourn at Songjiang

In a declining age, the ruler does not act like a ruler, a minister does not act like a minister, a father does not act like a father, and a son does not act like a son—not to mention husband and wife, brothers and friends. When ethical principles are destroyed, then humankind will come to an end. Heaven and earth will close up once every one hundred and twenty thousand years—does this refer to just such a phenomenon? When one tries to trace to the root cause of the problem, there is but one word: greed. So I say that the fall of a country is brought about by the greed of officials. The greedier the superiors are, the more stricken the common folk are. When the common folk are stricken, then cunning and deception arise, and the public morals are more and more corrupted every day. When cunning and deception arise, and public morals are more and more corrupted every day, the orders from superiors are increasingly urgent and strict, and the common folk are increasingly ill at ease and perturbed, until the situation finally becomes uncontainable. Although occasionally there are superiors who are not greedy, those under them attend to them with humble words and ingratiating expressions and do not dare to act otherwise, and after a while, the superiors grow so comfortable with this that they take it for granted. The common folk are distrustful, which gives rise to impious thoughts; the superiors are used to the status quo, hence full of lethargy. This is how things are.

At the end of the Ming dynasty, when the southern capital was captured, Qian Qianyi was the first to surrender. He spoke to Prince Yu, who had a proclamation circulated in the southeastern provinces. At that time, the situation was about to be settled. Then suddenly there was the incident of Jiaxing, and the troops of Wu, known as the "righteous troops," rose in arms.[72] As their dynasty fell and their emperor died, they exerted themselves to seek revenge. Who could blame them? However, when I read Xia Wanchun's poem "The Lord's Feast in the Army," I encountered the following couplet: "I have exhausted my family fortune

....

72   Qian Qianyi (1582–1664) was a noted Ming official, poet, and scholar. In 1645, when the Manchu army led by Prince Yu (1614–1649) reached Nanjing, the capital of the Southern Ming regime (see note 48 of part 1), Qian Qianyi submitted and went on to serve the Qing dynasty. In July 1645, the people of Jiaxing in northern Zhejiang rose up against the Qing forces, but the resistance was soon crushed.

to provide for the great military governor; / upon meeting one another, we look at our swords, and brush their frosty tips."[73] I really could not understand it. Were they "greedy like a wolf and recalcitrant like a ram," enjoying drinking parties like Song Yi?[74] What sort of time was it that they would carry on in such a way, and cause loyal and righteous orphans to beat their chests and weep tears of blood? I suppose the way in which they behaved came from an entrenched habit, but it was also a matter of fate. Now, after the weeping in the wilderness at Xilin, who would lament the lone spirit of the loyal Wozi? And after Wozi followed his friend to sink in the Xiang River, who would mourn the unyielding soul of Kaogong?[75] Greedy men and degenerates destroyed the prosperous Ming empire; majestic phoenix and auspicious dragon tried in vain to save the world from the last *kalpa* fire.[76] I lingered at the place and was choked with tears.

Sojourn at Suzhou

After staying at Songjiang for seven months, I went to Suzhou. Suzhou had gradually recovered its former prosperity. Gentry members, officials, worthies, and men of outstanding talent were like flowing water and piled hills there, which made an ordinary fellow quite lose his color.

....

73   Xia Wanchun (1631–1647) was a literary prodigy. He was actively engaged in the anti-Manchu campaign and used all of his family assets to fund the cause until he was captured and executed.

74   Song Yi (d. 207 bce) was a military leader in the rebellion against the Qin dynasty (221–201 bce), and Xiang Yu (see note 67) was once his deputy. Instead of advancing his army against the Qin forces, Song Yi feasted and drank while his soldiers suffered from cold and hunger, and issued an order that anyone who was "greedy like a wolf and recalcitrant like a ram" should be beheaded. He was killed by Xiang Yu, who was angered by Song Yi's approach.

75   Wozi was Chen Zilong (1608–1647), a Ming official and noted poet who was a native of Songjiang. Xilin was the name of a hill at Songjiang. Kaogong was Xia Yunyi (1596–1645), Xia Wanchun's father, and a good friend of Chen Zilong. They both chose to drown themselves rather than submit to the Qing forces. After Xia Wanchun was captured, he was taken to Nanjing; as he passed by Xilin Hill, he wrote a famous poem, "Weeping in the Wilderness at Xilin," in remembrance of Chen Zilong.

76   *Kalpa*, or *jie*, refers to an eon in the Indian cosmology, and "*kalpa* fire" is the conflagration that ends a *kalpa*.

I went to Shantang, and first visited the Tombs of the Five Heroes.[77] The site was in the midst of a flower market, with a towering stone stele standing erect. I reverentially paid my respects. In the middle was the tomb of Yan Peiwei; on the left was Shen Yang, and on the right was Yang Nianru; Ma Jie was further to the left, and Zhou Wenyuan was further to the right. Beside the tombs there were several pine trees and junipers, which were twisting and writhing, coiling and dense. The ground underneath was embroidered with dark green moss, with emerald green vines curling upward like smoke. The environment had no gloomy aura, which was remarkable. Eunuch Wei was powerful enough to lead the Son of Heaven astray, and enslave the great ministers; only these five people he could not deprive of their will, even if he had them killed. If not because Heaven wanted to maintain moral principles through them, how could they behave like this? I had nothing but the deepest respect for them.

I ascended Tiger Hill. After the civil war, all man-made structures on Tiger Hill were ruined. Walking up the steps, I went to sit at "the Seating Place for a Thousand People." Master Daosheng's Lecture Terrace used to have the seal script calligraphy of Li Yangbing, but the present inscription was no longer the same.[78] Only the four huge characters carved on the cliff over the Sword Pond—"Wind Ravine, Cloud Spring"—were written in vigorous brushwork. I went over and rubbed them lovingly for a long time. Alongside was an inscription by Tang Liuru.[79] To the left there were some vague marks on the rock, which looked like writing, but they were covered by kingfisher-green vines, and I could not see clearly. Looking down into the pond, my reflection took on an emerald color. With cupped hands I scooped up some water and drank it—its refreshing coolness seeped into my heart, both calming and uplifting my spirit.

....

77   The Five Heroes were five citizens of Suzhou who were executed for their opposition to the powerful eunuch Wei Zhongxian (see note 34).
78   Daosheng (d. 434) was Zhu Daosheng, an eminent monk most famous for his advocacy of the belief that all sentient beings possessed "Buddha nature." His belief caused controversy at first, and he was expelled from the monastic community in Jiankang (Nanjing), so he went to Suzhou and resided at Tiger Hill. As one local legend goes, the Seating Place for a Thousand People was where people gathered to listen to his lectures. Li Yangbing (fl. the 8th century) was a celebrated calligrapher of the Tang dynasty.
79   "Liuru" was the studio name of Tang Yin (see note 53).

Going east from the cliff, I climbed the stairs of the "Fifty-three Wise Ones." Then, after turning westward and passing the Double Wells Bridge, I was at the summit. I once read Lord Sun Wending's "Account of My Southern Journey."[80] It contains such a description: "I looked into the distance on Tiger Hill, and saw bamboos and trees embrace the villages on all sides, and water chestnut and lotus cover the waters. With dense shades and deep green, even heaven and earth turn emerald." But now it was not like that at all, and I wondered why. Was it due to life's vicissitudes, or was it because of the laziness of the local people? I felt a pang about the change.

I had climbed Tiger Hill more than once. This was because I stayed at Suzhou for several years, and whenever I had some spare time, I would go to Tiger Hill, and whenever I went there, I would linger all day. I composed a quatrain about it:

Floating dust on half the bed: Scholar Liang's veranda;[81]
A branch of spring dream: Wu Yun's flute.[82]
The road of east wind by the Tiger Hill bridge:
Once again in the year's splendor, every step has its charms.

There was nothing worth seeing in the city. Only the Lions' Grove was not bad.[83] I once spent a night in there. In the moonlight, I noticed that those exquisite layered rocks seemed to be moving on the ground. When I looked closely, I saw some standing, some sitting, some lying, and some dancing or playing with one another—crisscross, here and there, they truly were all lions; it was just that the similitude was found in the shadows, not in the shapes of the rocks themselves. The garden was said to

....

80   Lord Sun was Sun Jiagan (1683–1753), a prominent Qing official.
81   Scholar Liang refers to Liang Hong, the Eastern Han scholar and recluse who once worked as a hired hand and lived on the veranda of the man who hired him. See note 66.
82   Wu Yun (d. 484 bce) was better known as Wu Zixu, a famous cultural figure from ancient China. After his father and elder brother were wrongly executed by the King of Chu, Wu Zixu escaped to Wu and finally enlisted the help of the Wu king to take revenge on Chu for his father and brother. As legend goes, he played the flute in the Wu marketplace and begged for food for years before he rose to eminence.
83   The Lions' Grove is a famous garden in Suzhou.

be the handiwork of the Lofty Recluse Ni.[84] That should not be far from the truth.

The Garden of Gray Waves was in the southern part of the city. Its deep pool of autumn water made one have faraway thoughts. In the garden there was a shrine built to the Three Hundred Worthies.[85] A couplet hanging in the shrine read:

> Those whose names were known in the world for five hundred years
> share the same hall, the aroma of the food offering emitting
> from the sacrificial vessels: the karmic law of cause and
> effect in this case was not actualized by the Arhats;
> In twenty-four histories, worthy men of former times were always
> recorded in group biographies, their writings and their ability in
> governing equally outstanding: the tradition had been truly
> started by the one who gave away the throne.[86]

I read it several times and felt a solemn admiration.

Mu's Garden was the former residence of Mu Tianyan.[87] With "its ruined pools and towering trees," it was overgrown and melancholy. In the northern corner of the garden there was a small mound, and the locals told me that it was the grave of the beloved concubine of Li Xiucheng, the Longhair bandit known as the "Loyal Prince."[88] When the city was captured by the imperial troops, she hanged herself, and was buried there by the locals. Was this really true? The "Loyal Prince" feigned benevolence and righteousness to please people with personal favors. It was not that

....

84 Lofty Recluse Ni was Ni Zan (1301–1374), a celebrated Yuan dynasty painter and poet.

85 The shrine was first built in the 1820s with the portraits of over three hundred noted people of the Wu region carved on stone. Later the number was increased to over five hundred.

86 The couplet was composed by Xue Shiyu (1818–1885), a Qing official and calligrapher. The one who gave away the throne refers to Taibo, the eldest son of the Zhou king Gugong Danfu, who yielded the throne to his younger brother and went to live in Wu (the Yangzi Delta region). The people of Wu claimed descent from Taibo.

87 Mu Tianyan (d. 1696) was a prominent early Qing official.

88 Li Xiucheng (1823–1864), the "Loyal Prince," was a major leader in the Taiping Rebellion.

people did not know that he was trying to fool them; nevertheless, they thought of him with some affection, and still do in the present day. Was this because people loved chaos by nature? How could that be? It was in fact all because He Guiqing's troops, defeated, fleeing east, raped and pillaged so much more dreadfully than the bandits that the common folk could not even preserve their families.[89] Then the bandits came and saved their lives. Thereupon the common folk could not but be moved and feel grateful to the bandits. This being the case, could those officials solemnly lording over the common folk aspire to not be second to bandits?

On the city wall at Xu Gate there was a broken stele. It was so damaged by the elements that the writing was almost illegible. I made out a few lines as follows: "The hegemonic enterprise have been extinguished; the luxury and prosperity completely melt away. Deer roam on the Gusu Terrace, and flowers fall into the waters of Brocade Sails." The language was poignant and charming, and I wondered who had composed it.

There was another stele there, on whose top were carved the words "Tablet of Faith." It turned out that a local resident of Wu County, surnamed Guan, who lived during the Daoguang era [1821–51], owned a hundred acres of land in the mountain. He had four sons, who were not equal in merit. He was afraid that they might start fighting over the estate after his death, so he divided the land in advance, put it in writing, and asked for the local government's permission to carve it on a stele as evidence. He also stated in the inscription that he was willing to pay back all the debts he owed in money and grain, so as not to burden his children. The father's love was so deep and sincere that it pained one's heart. But how much time had elapsed before the stele was already abandoned to ruin? One did not even know whether he had any offspring left. The affairs of this world are vast, and human life is as dim as a dream. It was more than I could bear. I composed a song lyric to the tune of "Paradise in a Jug":

Alone I go up the city gate tower,
Brushing aside the moss covering the broken steles,
    I read carefully, one line after another.

....

89   He Guiqing (d. 1862) had been the governor-general of Jiangxi, Jiangsu and
      Anhui. He was defeated by the Taiping army, escaped to Shanghai, and was even-
      tually executed by the Qing court for cowardice and mishandling affairs.

The regrets over splendor and decline for a thousand years,
    so piteous, each one written brings tears.
I think of how, in this world,
    people manage their households and their country
        with the same obsession and affection;
And how, in both cases, the only thing that remains—
    the pattern of the moss, in a mournful green.

I am a wild fellow at the edge of the sky, adrift
    upon lakes and seas, a solitary body
        in ten thousand miles.
Having seen the vicissitudes of the world,
    this pair of dark eyes strained, tearing.
Dancing in drunkenness, singing madly,
    tossed by wind, driven crazy by the rain—
        in this life of one hundred years, sorrow
            follows upon sorrow.
As I wake from the dream of yellow millet,
    the blue robe is soaked with tears,
        as if washed through.[90]

The last lines allude to how, every time I thought of the steles, I would sigh for days.

The landscape of the Lake Tai region was particularly remarkable in the southeastern provinces. Living in the city day after day, I felt cooped up and unhappy, so I would go on outings all the time. I first went to Western Hill of Dongting. The hill was merely ninety leagues from the city by water, and could be reached overnight. Upon entering the Bay of Avoiding Summer Heat, I found it to be picturesque and quiet. With its bends and turns, it offered too many things for my eyes to take in. After

....

90   "The dream of yellow millet" refers to a famous story from the Tang dynasty, in which a man dreams that he experiences the rise and fall of fortunes and lives a whole lifetime, but upon waking, the yellow millet being cooked on the stove is not done yet. The blue robe soaked with tears is a phrase taken from "The Ballad of Pipa" by Bai Juyi (see note 6), in which the poet-narrator is deeply moved by the *pipa*-playing woman as he reflects on his own similar down-and-out circumstances.

I climbed onto the top of the hill, I stayed in a room of the little storied house of the Qin family. Looking over the lake, with mountains in the background, I saw sails traversing the distant sky, and clouds stretching across tall trees. The scene was expansive and had a spiritual beauty; even paintings could not surpass it.

After several days, I climbed Flying Cloud Peak, and gazed afar from the summit. It was late autumn, and oranges were ripening. The orange groves formed a hazy expanse of embroidered brocade, opening up a completely different world. I had heard from people that the scenery was particularly marvelous when the loquat fruit were turning yellow. I did not agree. Vigorous and yet charming, deep and luxuriant—the landscape was always the best at the time of fallen leaves and clear frost. There were many gardens in the mountain, which were built by grand officials upon retirement. It was a pity that most of them were in ruins after the civil war. However, when a drizzling rain first stopped, or the sinking sun had just set, the gardens took on a lovely freshness, which was quite nice.

After I left Western Hill, I went to Mudu. Of the various scenic spots, Mudu was the closest to the city of Suzhou. I went there by way of Hengtang. The water nearby was rippling; the mountains in the distance were full of charms. Famous gardens were adjacent; bamboos and trees were verdant. In the early morning one might look for couplets; on a cool evening the scene warmed up one's dreams—it all brought ample pleasure to a person. In addition, paying a visit to the plum blossoms at Dengwei was an enchanting affair for all time. It was just that, at the time of flowering, there were always large crowds of men and women who set out all sorts of food and drink for picnic. It was redolent and tumultuous, and I found it unbearable.

When I first arrived at Guangfu, I had a vegetarian meal at a Buddhist monastery. Then I took advantage of the perfect autumn weather and explored the surroundings on foot. Following a stream and going deep into the mountain, I felt as if a wafting aroma and sparse shadows were leading me along. Then, between Bamboo Col and Copper Grotto, I found a dilapidated temple and stayed there overnight. At the time, a frosty moon was clear and bright, and the mountains were quiet on all sides. Taking a stroll on the temple grounds, I looked at my shadow, and felt I was no longer in the mortal world. The mountain god was generous to me indeed.

I went up the Cloud Range the next day and looked at Lake Tai. Lake Tai was of eight hundred square leagues, and its watery expanse had millions of acres of misty waves. The seventy-two peaks were a floating azure and dripping emerald. It was one of the grandest views of the world.

Then I left for Fan's Mound. Fan's Mound was the burial place of Lord Fan Wenzheng.[91] The rocks there were jutting out like spears or banners. They were all over the mountain, soaring into clouds and leaning against the sun, forming a view of the "ten thousand tablets paying homage to heaven."[92] The Fan clan has remained prosperous to this day. Did this, then, mean that geomancy was something to be believed? People who thought so did not understand that, if someone possessed Lord Fan's virtue, even if he were not buried in a place like this, his offspring would prosper; if he did not possess Lord Fan's virtue, even if he were indeed buried in a place like this, it would be to no avail. Master Zhu's theory of the principles of heaven and earth was a credible one.[93] What, then, did this have to do with geomancy? As for the magnificent aura and majestic structure of the grave site, as far as I knew, there was nothing comparable except for Yu's Mound. Only Lord Fan's integrity and kindness made him worthy of such grandeur.

In general, not a single mountain in the Wu region was unattractive, and every body of water there had beautiful ripple patterns. The energy of nature was concentrated in human beings, so the Wu folk were all pleasant and charming. As for Heavenly Aroma Mountain's precipitous appeal, Xuan's Tumulus's fine panache, the Cloud Range's cold, lofty height, and Western Hill's luxuriant verdure: these were all unique wonders and the epitome of perfection.

There was indeed something about the local flavor of the Wu region that could captivate one's heart. There is no need for me to mention piping and singing in the painted boat and lingering over its gorgeous landscapes, for even its mountain songs, village ballads, and boat ditties had the manner of the soft waters and gentle hills. Once, as I was traveling by boat between Lotus Pond and Li's Market, the boatmen sang a song that went like this:

....

91 Lord Fan was Fan Zhongyan. See note 13.
92 "Tablet" refers to the tablet held in the hand by court officials when having an audience with the emperor.
93 Master Zhu refers to Zhu Xi (1130–1200), Southern Song neo-Confucian thinker.

An eighty-year-old grandma instructs the young girl:
If a man fondles your titties, *that is, breasts,*
    don't make a peep! *That is, keep quiet about it.*[94]
The osmanthus flowers smell sweet—
    but for how long?

As a breeze blew ripples on the water, the voice and sentiments were both drawn out, and stirred up the thoughts of loyalty and love as in the *Li sao*.[95] How charming! There were other songs such as this one: "In the seventh month, touch-me-nots are purplish red; / Lovers meet each other in the bedchamber." A poet could rack his brain but would never be able to reproduce even one ten-thousandth of it. Nevertheless, from these songs one could also see the frivolity and decadence of the local customs.

During my prolonged stay at Suzhou, I often felt lonely and had few joys. I had met Yu Simeng (whose personal name was Long), a student from Wucheng, at Songjiang, and formed an intense friendship with him. He also came to Suzhou, and the two of us would from time to time get drunk in taverns, singing and weeping together. I presented the following poem to him:

One handshake brings us so much happiness
    that ten thousand things are all set right;
Between ocean and sky, roaming carefree,
    two leisurely gulls.
The clear frost is slowly aging,
    a sparse forest has its charms;
Together we walk into the tavern
    in the west of the city.

I also befriended Lü Xiuliang (whose personal name was Jinshou) of the Wu County, who was a carpenter. I wrote the following poem for him:

....

94   The author appends notes, italicized here, to the song in a smaller font.
95   *Li sao* is part of *The Songs of Chu*, believed to be authored by Qu Yuan. According to traditional interpretation, the romantic pursuit of goddesses portrayed therein is a figure of the poet's quest for a worthy lord.

In friendship I expect a blandness
　　that endures recollection;
Always sharing a goblet of ale
　　in the spring breeze.
Who truly appreciates
　　this wild fellow Zhang Daye?
In the whole wide world,
　　there is only Mr. Lü the Woodworker.

Being poor and humble, we felt compassion for each other, and furthermore enjoyed a spiritual affinity. I had never imagined I would be able to find such an appreciative friend in this life. Now Simeng had left, and Xiuliang had been dead for almost ten years. Xiuliang never read a single book in his life, but he treasured writing.[96] Once he saved from the ashes a scroll of poetry, which was copied out in the hand of Lord Gao Zhongxian (i.e., Gao Panlong), as well as a volume of *Illustrated Biographies of Chivalrous Swordsmen* drawn and printed by Ren Weichang (i.e., Ren Xiong).[97] He cherished them for over a decade. Because I loved collecting books, he gave them to me. Later on, while I was staying at Wulin, I inscribed a song lyric on each.[98]

(1)
The disaster befalling the Donglin clique;
the arresting officers from the Northern Court:
　　these vicissitudes are already long gone.
Words written out in a small hand, messy, fragmented;
An old man's sentiments, all stirred up:
　　The poetry scroll of those sad times remains.
The master of the Studio of Piled Tiles—
　　how many times he must have rubbed it
　　　　and regarded it with admiration. . . .
On the scroll there was the following seal inscription: "The Cherished

....

96　Lü Xiuliang was likely to be illiterate or near-illiterate.
97　Gao Panlong (1562–1626) was a political figure and writer of the late Ming dynasty who belonged to the Donglin Party. Ren Xiong (1823–1857) was a painter from Zhejiang, known for his bold and innovative style.
98　Wulin was Hangzhou.

*Collection of the Studio of Piled Tiles." I had no idea who the Master of
the Studio of Piled Tiles was, and did not have the time to do research and
find out. . . .*[99]

(2)

Who had portrayed
    in such an impassioned and free manner
        these extraordinary men, open and upright,
            entangled in the wind and dust?
Hazy and elusive, most of them having no names,
    their stories are said to come from
        the scattered unofficial history of the Tang dynasty.
Poor fellows—I suppose none of them had had a chance to wear
    jade pendants and the purple silk ribbon of official seals.
Their hearts were in turmoil;
    though silent, they clutched their fists,
        and their eyes glared in anger, even in death.

I cannot bear thinking back on the day
    when we ran into each other at the Wu marketplace;
        you held a scroll in your hand, and showed it to me.
In life and death we will help each other out:
    the way of the chivalrous men
        must be like this.
We had once sworn
    that in a tavern we would die
        dancing wildly in drunkenness.
Now in an instant
    only this solitary creature is still here,
        carrying the damaged scroll, weeping,
            facing the dusty world alone.
    The above lyric on the illustration of the Chivalrous Swordsmen *was
    written to the tune of "Catching Fish."*

....

99   After the explanatory note, there are two empty lines in the manuscript before
    the next song lyric begins. This seems to indicate that the first lyric has been
    deliberately left incomplete.

Xiuliang also gave me an ancient mirror, which had a kraken carved on its back, and a painting of "Drunken Zhong Kui."[100] My song lyrics on these two objects are as follows:

(1)

The rivers and seas are clear,
    illuminating the sleep of the kraken.
After many times of rubbing and cleaning, it was
    buried and hidden, sunken and dimmed.
An aging hero, a tired traveler adrift,
    are worn and haggard in the same way.
Tipsy with wine, face flushed;
But when all the singing is done,
    who can bring consolation
        for all the things one has witnessed?

At the end of the road, how much repressed resentment?
In this drifting life, how many dusty burdens?
Everything is murky and gloomy,
    bright only for a moment,
        and dim again.
I do remember in those bygone years
    we entrusted each other with our lives—
        and my heart was intoxicated.
All it is worth today,
    in this traveler's lodge,
        as the candle is burning out:
            a few clear teardrops.
The above was written to the tune of "Ancient Mirror."

(2)

A fine festival was Duanwu—[101]

....

100   Zhong Kui is a figure in Chinese folklore who is supposed to be in charge of ghosts and demons.

101   Duanwu is a traditional festival celebrated on the fifth day of the fifth month according to the Chinese lunar calendar. On this festival it is customary to drink

the time when
  dense clusters of redbud bloom,
    and pomegranates spit scarlet.
With a beaming smile we went into the hall
  to offer festive greetings,
    sing and play the pottery and bamboo ocarinas in turn;[102]
And what was more, drank numerous cups
  of calamus wine.
Carrying this paining scroll in my hand, I hung it
  on the whitewashed wall,
    pointing to the crazy posture of Zhong Kui,
      and getting a smile from my dear mother.
Together we admired his drunken demeanor
  and wild dancing.

This scene is still fresh in my eyes,
  but time is different now,
    and I wonder how everything has turned
      into bleak wind and rain.
I am at the edge of the sky,
  always in hard straits,
    with no one to talk to.
Don't even bother, at this twilight hour,
  to ask about my youthful aspirations.
In this mortal world I share with others
  the same months and years,
    but I am no longer in the mood
      to spend them in the mortal world.
I want to go home now, and weep
  in front of that deserted tomb.
  On the Painting of Zhong Kui, to the tune of "Celebrating the Newly Cool Weather."

I find the thought that Xiuliang is no more too much to bear. "'A peer-

---

calamus wine and hang a portrait of Zhong Kui on the wall to ward off evil spirits.
102   A phrase that indicates the harmony of brothers.

less gentleman of the domain' was Prime Minister Xiao himself; / with regard to being an understanding friend, Marquis Han was in fact a secondary person."[103] Not to mention that I have never received any recognition—so what am I doing here, living this down-and-out life?

> Tossed in wind and rain, a little boat,
>   the traveler's far-flung dream;
> A candle burning out, with its ashes
>   the dejected soul melts away.
> This lonely life—who would feel with me
>   about parting,
> And snap a willow branch for my sake
>   at the waystation?[104]

I composed the above poem when I went to Jingkou in the third month of the *yiyou* year [April 15–May 13, 1885]. It expressed my resentment that Xiuliang did not come and see me off at the river. I had asked so much of him in life; how can I bear forsaking him in death? As I recall our friendship, my pain is endless.

Xiuliang died on the last day of the third month of the *bingxu* year [May 3, 1886]. I took care of his funeral and buried him on the plain of Zhu Village outside Xu Gate. After that, my situation worsened. On New Year's Eve my debtors crowded the door, and I almost did not survive that one. With a jug of ale, I looked at my shadow in despondence. That was when I composed a song lyric with the following lines:

> Where are my old friends now?
> Let this life drift in blood and tears,
>   from now on,
>   year after year,
>   like a blown catkin and floating duckweed.

....

103 Marquis Han was Han Xin, the Western Han general and military genius (see note 23). Xiao He (d. 193 bce) recognized his talent when he was still down-and-out, and recommended him to Emperor Gaozu, calling him a "peerless gentleman of the domain."

104 "Willow" (*liu*) puns with "detain" (*liu*); hence the custom, upon parting, of snapping a willow branch and presenting it to the person who is going away.

Trips to Hangzhou, Shaoxing, and Xianju

I again left where I was staying, and went to Hangzhou in the first month of the *dinghai* year [January 24–February 22, 1887].

At that time I had only about a thousand cash in my wallet. Thinking that Simeng was in Huzhou and might be able to help me out, I took a detour to visit him on my way to Hangzhou. When I arrived, Simeng was depressed because his house had been burglarized on New Year's Day. We had a good laugh about it. Simeng said, "Let's just go and get drunk." So every day we went to drink at the tavern run by Brother Li under Grandma Jin's Bridge. Brother Li was from Shaoxing. As he considered me his fellow townsman, he was particularly hospitable to me. Thereupon I composed a quatrain:

> In recent years my great mood has all but frittered away;
> So I get drunk and sing a song at the edge of sky.
> The man who is most affectionate and most memorable:
> Brother Li, who lives under Grandma Jin's Bridge.

Simeng loved that poem.

I realized I could not stay long, so I took my leave, and went by river through Xinshi, Lianshi, Shuanglin, and Nanxun. Drifting on the misty waves, I befriended water birds and had my fill of perch sashimi, thoroughly enjoying the pleasure of travel.

I regretted that I had not been able to exhaust the views of the West Lake and the surrounding hills during my previous visits, so once I got to Hangzhou, I pawned my clothes and went on West Lake every day. Commissioner Xu of Panyu, feeling for my circumstances, wrote a letter to the magistrate of Xianju on my behalf, and advised me to try my luck there.[105] Thereupon I made haste to cross the Yangzi River and return to Shaoxing to pack for my upcoming trip. I also took the opportunity to pay my respects to my father's tomb.[106] After ten days, I embarked on my journey to Xianju.

....

105　Panyu is in Guangdong. Commissioner Xu of Panyu might be Xu Yingheng (1820–1891), a prominent late Qing official from Guangdong who served as provincial administration commissioner of Zhejiang.

106　"Father's" was crossed out here in the manuscript, and "ancestors' [tombs]" was scribbled in the margin.

My first stop was Eastern Pass. Eastern Pass was an important town in the vicinity of Shaoxing. I had a relative there, who invited me to stay with him overnight. He showed me a painting by Lord Wang Wencheng (i.e., Wang Shouren) in his art collection.[107] The painting is titled "Soldiers Crossing a River." The scroll was merely a foot long. In the painting, layers of waves were running high, and snow was falling over a thousand leagues. Withered, broken reeds made a mess. Two old soldiers were walking along, shivering in the cold, and apparently full of misery. Their expressions and demeanors were so vivid that they seemed to have come to life. How remarkable! His Lordship had never been known as a painter. Were his painting skills eclipsed by his other achievements? On the painting there was a long colophon, of which I regret I did not have time to make a copy. Its gist was as follows: the ruler, living deep inside the nine-tiered palace, loved to aim high and pursue what was far beyond him, so he engaged in opening up the frontier territories every day, and little did he know about the suffering brought about by military campaigns; even during the recent inland wars, there were already soldiers whose fingers had fallen off in the freezing cold and whose skin was chapped, just like in this painting; therefore Lord Wang had produced this painting in order to give warning to future generations. I suspect that this painting was created while His Lordship was suppressing the rebellion of Chenhao.[108] His intention and the way in which he articulated it were both profound and magnanimous.

I once saw a painting at Suzhou. In the painting there were several crumbling old rooms; two widows, emaciated and of a dark complexion like ghosts, were weaving on the looms. A cold crescent moon hardly shed enough light to penetrate the dark. The desolate and melancholy atmosphere was something I could scarcely bear looking at. The inscription on the painting read, "'Wine and meat go bad and give off stench within the vermillion gate; / in the wilderness are the corpses of people who have died of exposure.'[109] The dead can no longer come back to life; the living are about to lose their lives. After I paint this, I chant slowly; a chilly

....

107 Wang Shouren (1472–1529), a native of Zhejiang, was a prominent Ming official, military leader, Confucian thinker, and writer.
108 Zhu Chenhao (d. 1521) was a member of the Ming imperial family. He rebelled in 1519 and his army was crushed by Wang Shouren in just over one month.
109 This is a couplet by Du Fu.

wind stirs grief." Underneath was signed "Xiangnan." I had no idea who it might be. That painting also possessed a power to move the viewers.

After I left Eastern Pass, I crossed Wormwood Dam, and changed my boat for a raft. Then I arrived at Painting Mountain. With its ten thousand layers of cloud screen, and thousand piles of snow waves, it was truly a rare sight.

Painting Mountain marked the boundary of Sheng County. After Painting Mountain we came upon Immortals Peak. Immortals Peak was verdant and lofty, even more so than Painting Mountain. Streams flowed over the rocks into the springtime pool; the sound of a bell was concealed behind the towering trees. When a clear breeze was blowing, white clouds surged forward. It was an extraordinary scene. I did my best to persuade the boatman to stay there overnight. However, after dusk we were suddenly caught in a thunderstorm; my luggage was soaked, and I found myself in an awful predicament. The boatman wrapped me up with a mat, tied me with ropes to stabilize the bundle, and set me under a cliff. Ha, I had never imagined I would come to this! Song Wan was bound in rhinoceros hide because of his crimes; in the case of Deng Ai, he was enfolded by a felt rug for the sake of accomplishing something.[110] What was *I* doing rolled up in a mat?! After a while, the rain gradually came to a stop, and moonlight was shining through the crack in the mat. I got a hand out to unfasten the rope, and rose to my feet with a chuckle. I felt like a newly ordained Buddhist monk entering his very first temple. I was starving, but the boatman was sound asleep and I did not have the heart to wake him up, so I waited until dawn. At breakfast I had five bowls of rice and still could not stop eating. The boatman glanced at me askance, as if wondering how this passenger could be so hungry. The Way of "eating one's fill" was not something easy to impart!

After I left Immortals Peak, I reached Female Alligator Mountain. Female Alligator Mountain was massive: its immensely tall cliffs soared

....

110   Song Wan (d. 682 bce) was a general of the Domain of Song who killed his ruler in
       a fit of rage and sought refuge in the state of Chen. People in Chen got him drunk,
       tied him up in an ox hide, and sent him back to Song, where he was executed.
       Deng Ai (d. 264) was a general from the Three Kingdoms period who played a
       key role in Wei's conquest of Shu. In his campaign against Shu, he once wrapped
       himself up in a felt blanket and rolled down a precipitous mountain where there
       was no footpath.

into the clouds. The rocks were as black as lacquer, and there was not a single blade of grass growing on the mountain. I congratulated myself on not having spent the previous night there; otherwise I feared that some demon might have snatched us.

As we moved eastward, the mountain range became less precipitous, and the currents of the mountain streams also slowed down. When I arrived at Sheng County, it was in the fourth month, and people were reeling new silk. The sound of the loom came from under the trees everywhere. Village girls were baking tea leaves, and children were digging up bamboo shoots. It was all very pleasant. From Sheng County onward I traveled by land. The porter who carried my luggage was called Yatou. Yatou was a seventeen-year-old native of Tiantai. He was spontaneous and easygoing, and knew how to read and write. Traveling through the spring mountains with him as my companion was a great pleasure.

Between Sheng County and Xinchang, for dozens of leagues the fields were laid out densely and draped in various shades of green. A couplet from my poem, "Slender bamboos divided the footpath overgrown with moss; / spring currents lightly brushing past the spreading fields," might help one visualize the scene. After I got to Xinchang, I had a meal in a mountain tavern, and composed the following quatrain:

> Spring mountains, spring scene:
>   the time of flowers in bloom;
> Willow catkins, paulownia fuzz:
>   they are flying together.
> The hospitable host of the mountain tavern
>   urges the guest to stay—
> A pot of spring bamboo shoots
>   makes a thick soup.

This was a factual record.

That night I stayed at Banzhu. The next morning I crossed the Huishu Range for the first time. Afterward, Yatou said he would really like to see Mount Tianmu, so we went out of our way to fulfill his wish. As we meandered through the cloudy forest, the sight we encountered was both secluded and remarkable. When we finally reached Tianmu, we saw a huge rock with a large inscription saying, "The Site Visited by Li Bai in

His Dream."[111] I could not help chuckling. This, I suppose, was the so-called insight of a frog at the bottom of a well. The monastery there was deserted and not worth viewing; moreover, the local government had just stationed soldiers at the place to guard against mountain bandits. So we sat only for a little while before we were on our way again.

We crossed the Range of Soaring into Clouds. The morning rain had just stopped; water drops were still dripping from pines and firs. There was a White Cloud Monastery on the range, and we took a break there. A monk received us respectfully, and made us some new tea, for which I was very grateful.

In the afternoon we crossed the Guan Range and were in the territory of Tiantai.[112] After walking across Three Mao Bridge, we found ourselves in the midst of the mountain market. Alongside the road, under the trees, peddlers put out their wares as densely as clouds. They each set up a streamer, on which was written either "South Mountain Shop" or "North Mountain Shop." Sweet ale and tasty cooked meats were displayed in disarray. Men and women were cheerful and easy, with no suspicion or apprehension. I thought of Master Yang Peiyuan's remark that "human relations are particularly warm in a mountain village." It was not without some truth. I composed the following poem:

Surrounded by mountain mist, azure on all sides:
A bridge leads to the marketplace.

Voices are clamorous day and night;
Mountain wares gather in abundance.

Rustic elders cheerfully chat on;
In the shed beside the stream, so easy to get tipsy.

If I could just have a loan of a small room here,
I would be happy to live at leisure on the mountaintop.

....

111   Li Bai (701–762), the famous Tang poet, wrote a well-known poem titled "Visiting Tianmu in a Dream."
112   An illegible line was scribbled in the margin here in the manuscript.

It was indeed on that very day that I had first begun to entertain the idea of retiring to this place, hence the last couplet.

I spent that night at Clear Stream Village. I had planned to visit Guoqing Temple, but was unable to. The next morning I crossed the Hundred Pace Range, and paid my respects to the Shrine of Zhang the Perfected Being. I lingered there until dusk and could not bear to leave, so I ended up staying overnight. The next day I approached the Yankeng Range.

The range was high and perilous; it also had many strange cliffs and weird trees that soared into the clouds and blocked the sun. It was dark and gloomy, like a ghosts' cave. By this time Yatou had taken his leave at Tiantai. I had no choice but to exert myself as much as I could and climb alone. Halfway up, a wind began blowing, and I seemed to perceive the sound of music. Taken by surprise, I looked around, and realized it was the cracks and holes of the rocks that were reverberating. Then the mountain became more and more steep. I sat down, closed my eyes, and thought I would die there. Suddenly I heard a sutra recitation coming from the forest. Following the voice, I groped my way along and found an old man reciting Buddhist scriptures in a thatched hut. I asked him for some water. The old man was very kind. He told me to sit down and handed me a bowl of rice to eat. He also gave me directions to a level road. Once I got there, after a mere dozen paces, I made it to the other side of the mountain. I felt that the old man must have been a god or a Bodhisattva.

After crossing the Yankeng Range, one was in the territory of Xianju. The conifer known as "Arhat pine" was growing everywhere; its branches hanging like the willow, its dark green touched the sky. Far and near the cries of gibbons were mixed with the sobbing of the streams. As I closed my eyes and listened to it while resting, it produced a deep melancholy in my heart. Then I thought to myself: although my talent could not compare with that of Shaoling, our circumstances were not that different; it was certainly hard to trudge on the road to Shu, but it was a rare life experience nevertheless.[113] Thereupon I chanted this quatrain out aloud:

....

113 Shaoling refers to Du Fu, who traveled to Shu (modern Sichuan) for the sake of livelihood. "Hardship of the Road to Shu" (Shu dao nan) was a ballad title.

This haggard face of mine—
    no need to feel sad for it;
Even just for the sake of seeing the mountains,
    I would still come.
As long as one can enjoy the finest mood
    of all one's life,
Who cares if these feet
    tread the dark moss?

Soon afterward I crossed the Boundary Range and passed through White Water Field. The mountains began to open up. In another forty leagues I reached the county seat, paid my respects to my host, and stayed with him. I must have looked quite worn out.

Friends at Xianju

Close to the county seat of Xianju there was a South Peak. As I got along well with Yuan Jichuan and Li Xiaju, the three of us often climbed South Peak together, chatting over a picnic and having a good time. Jichuan showed me a territorial map of Xianju that he had drawn himself. He made the map in the *guiwei* year [1883], when Xianju was besieged by bandits, in order to identify the bandits' locations. That was when the bandits Pan Xiaogou and Wang Guangdong were captured. I wrote a long poem in the upper part of the map:

A vast wind blows along the far-stretching road;
Tipsy with wine, I tap the pottery basin, and sing a song.
When the time is right, with a long sword
    one leans against the sky,
Alone, with one's own hands,
    trying to hold up heaven and earth.
From antiquity this has been the intent of all heroes,
With a sincere heart, they rise above a thousand ordinary men.
Riches and fame of this world—what do they matter?
They are not worth a chuckle, or even a faint smile.

Mr. Yuan of Shanxi, a real man,
Shows me a map of this mountain town.

He tells me there used to be
      many jackals and tigers at this place,
Calling out to one another and gathering together,
      the beasts must be destroyed.
The year before last, in the fifth month, an alarm was sounded:
The fox demons of the Gelao Society had risen.[114]
Mr. Yuan has been sheriff here for twenty years—
Mountains and forests are all stored in his mind.
Drawing this map himself,
      he presented it to the one in charge,
      That is, the military commander Liu Youzhi.
With which the one in charge could supplement
      his military strategies.
Organizing and directing the defense forces,
Mr. Yuan revealed the whereabouts of the bandits—
Even if they were ghosts and spirits,
      they would have a hard time getting away.

Upon hearing the story, I heave a long sigh.
Unrolling the map, I rise to my feet, and stare at it intensely:
Tall cliffs and huge crags pierce the sky,
With a thousand bends, ten thousand curves, they wind and coil.
A solitary town, so small, at the foot of the mountain:
A single leaf floating on rivers and lakes.
Like an ox's hairs or a silkworm's threads,
      walled villages in array;
Like the head of a fly or the tail of a scorpion,
      farmhouses are laid out.
Far and near, all twists and turns are clear
      like the palm of one's hand;
The size of a grain of rice,
      but no different from the real.
What kind of divine art is this on display?
When the spirit understands, heaven and earth are complete in it.

....

114   The Gelao Society was the most widespread secret society in the nineteenth cen-
      tury.

There are level roads within the four seas,
　　but those who know them are few;
You, my dear friend, have soared
　　to the path in the clouds.
Looking down at the mortal world, so vast,
　　you see as far as its Eight Extremes,
Gesticulating while discoursing,
　　you have mapped out a plan.

Your home, the region of Fen River,
　　was like paradise;
Not to mention your family had business dealings
　　with the Tartar merchants.
　　Mr. Yuan's family had traded silk and tea with Russian merchants for
　　generations.
Wind and sand stretched on and on
　　to the edge of the sky,
You had traveled ten thousand leagues,
　　all the way to the Dragon Court.[115]
　　Mr. Yuan visited Mongolian territories when he was young, and knew
　　their language.
Why didn't you live in peace, eat your fill,
And easily manage the frontiers for the Son of Heaven?
Giving it all up for this office that is as tiny as a bean,
You hustle and bustle in cap and gown, running around in vain.
Moving away the firewood, making the chimney crooked:[116]
　　you have accomplished a remarkable feat;
And yet your title remains the same as before.
When depression strikes, you laugh it off,
　　and suddenly get up and dance—
The vulgar crowd is taken aback,
　　calling you a crazy fellow.
I offer you ale and urge you to drink up a hundred cups:

....

115　Dragon Court was the site where the Xiongnu people made sacrificial offerings to
　　Heaven. It is used here as a general reference to the northwestern frontier.
116　This saying, which describes measures for preventing a fire, refers to taking pre-
　　cautions before a disaster happens.

You see, from the ancient times,
there have always been repressed men.

I have not seen Mr. Yuan for a long time, and now he has been dead for more than a year. At night, when wind and rain were beating the windows, recalling the good old times we had shared together, I could not help my tears.

Pan Honggui, whose courtesy name was Yiting, was from Liuzhou of Guangxi. At first, he had joined the Longhairs, and was even enfeoffed as a "king." Later on, he came over from the rebels' side, and was made an assistant brigade commander. He was a capable and vigorous man, reserved, fierce, with long, slender fingers like white marble. In the disorder of the *guiwei* year, there was a bandit named Pan Gongniu. He was their "great captain-general," and there was no match for his strength and quickness. Honggui captured him with his own hands, and thereupon the bandits collapsed.

Honggui had come to Tiantai because he knew the magistrate. The magistrate reported his achievements to the superiors, but Honggui received no recognition. After he got to know me, every time he talked about it, he would sigh ceaselessly. I said to him, "Forget it. When a man is beaten down and dies, he just accepts it. What's the point of ranting and raving? Don't you see Mr. Yuan's example?" Honggui nodded his agreement. He thereafter left Tiantai for Xuanzhou, making a living by farming. I once wrote a poem in remembrance of him.

In old age, he becomes a guest at Xuanzhou;
Lonely and quiet, temple hair turning gray.

Though having a home, he is unable to go back;
What a mistake he has made!

Dream of kings and nobles during a daytime nap—
Large and small melons, in the autumn wind.[117]

....

117 This line refers to the story about a count of the Qin dynasty who subsequently
became a melon grower after the dynasty fell. This couplet is a comment on the
illusory nature of status and radical changes in life.

For years I received no word from him—
At the edge of the sky, shedding tears.

But now I hear that because of poverty, he has attached himself to a wealthy family as their gate keeper. In today's world, if those with talent, smarts, courage, and decisiveness do not grow old in repression and obscurity, it is a strange thing.

The Bandits of Xianju

Banditry is always the most mysterious of matters. If there were no fierce and cunning men to take advantage of a famine to fan the flames and incite people, how could the common folk be willing to risk their lives and become bandits? Lord Chen Wengong of Guilin once said, "Only officials lack a conscience, but nobody from the common folk lacks a conscience."[118] Though a little extreme, this has some truth to it.

Jichuan once said to me, "The incident of the *guiwei* year, in all fairness, was not entirely unprovoked. The real troublemakers were just the several leaders: Cheng Xiangzheng, Wang Zaijin, Xiaogou, and Gongniu. But if not riding on the general resentment, they wouldn't have been able to stir up anything."

I said, "This is quite right. Then again, don't you see the case of Huang Jinman? His debtors brought about the death of his father, and he had no way of redressing the wrong, so he killed his entire family with his own hands and then rebelled. People thought he was a righteous man and followed him. (This had happened during the *jimao* and *gengchen* years.)[119] If the government had dealt with his case earlier, it would have been resolved by a few words. Fortunately, he accepted the amnesty, the whole thing was contained, and his wrong was set right. Now, could bandits such as Cheng Xiangzheng and his like have suffered from some sort of injustice? But you guys just chased them down and finished them off. I am afraid you were just trying to make a name for yourselves."

....

118 Lord Chen Wengong was Chen Hongmou (see note 22).

119 The sentence in the parenthesis appears in a smaller font in the original text, indicating that it is a note added by the author. The *jimao* and *gengchen* years were 1879 and 1880.

Jichuan laughed heartily, and replied, "The root cause of banditry is the 'Cult of Eating,' and government officials should, in truth, also take responsibility.[120] But taking this case as an example, I must say that we cannot blame the local officials for everything. Local officials, though dealing with the common folk directly, have no reason to abuse them all the time. In fact, even if they do, some ignorant folk do not even know about it. However, the common folk suffer from the 'traveling merchant tax' every day, and they all know *that*. Even after they capture a thousand offenders, the officials in charge, their underlings, and the soldiers on patrol never let go of a hundred; and even after they capture a hundred, they never let go of a single one. Those peddlers do not make much money to begin with, so how can they bear such a heavy burden? Therefore, the common folk hate the 'traveling merchant tax' much more than they hate bandits. Now, if you consider the entire country, you will see that there are people everywhere and there is this 'traveling merchant tax' everywhere—and that is what I feel concerned about. As for the 'Cult of Eating,' at first it is no more than one or two wicked persons trying to exploit people. If the officials in charge, upon uncovering their doings, punish them and disband them, they are extremely easy to handle. But the officials are slack and sluggish, and let them be. Then, by the time those people grow in numbers, the officials regard all of them as 'bandits' without distinguishing between good and bad, extort money from them, and dispose of them. Under such circumstances, who would not become desperate and make a reckless move? This is all because in times of peace the officials never spend any time worrying about the common folk; then, at a moment of emergency, they rely on clerks and servants to deal with the crisis, until the common folk are finally ruined by a disaster, and the officials themselves are unable to preserve their own lives and families. Thus both sides come to a bad end."

I said, "How poignant your words are! But perhaps the superiors are not aware of this situation. Why don't you let them know about it?"

Jichuan said with a chuckle, "Didn't you say in your poem that I have an office as tiny as a bean? If I do speak to them about it, they will not only ignore me but might also grow suspicious of me. I, too, have a life and a family—why should I put them on a hot stove? Besides, I have done

....

120 The "Cult of Eating" was a derogatory term for Christianity.

everything in my power for my country and for my people; I will continue to perform my duty, and that's about it. What else can I do?"

Thereupon we both sighed and left it at that.

The bandit Cheng Xiangzheng was from Hu'nan. He was eventually captured at the "traveling merchant tax" checkpoint of the Guan Range, and was subsequently executed. Wang Zaijin, who was their counselor, was captured in Shaoxing, thanks to the information acquired by Jichuan. I do not know where Wang originally came from.

Xianju was known as the haunt of bandits. Whenever a bandit was captured, as soon as he confessed, he would be executed. There was no hope for clemency or postponement. It happened almost every month. Once I was taking a stroll in the suburbs outside the eastern city gate. At that time I had not yet learned anything about Xianju's bandits. Just as I was walking casually, all of a sudden I saw a corpse with two tightly clenched fists dancing around. I was so shocked and terrified that I fled for my life. I asked the local sheriff about it, and it turned out to be a bandit who had been executed on the previous day and had not yet been buried.

The sheriff told me that the body of a beheaded criminal will always leap up in about a day; even the body of a puny person will shiver and shake without exception. The reason, he said, was that when a person's head was abruptly cut off, he suffered the greatest pain, and his soul would escape from his body, but his heart had not stopped beating yet; in twenty-four hours, as a cycle was completed and the *yang* energy returned to a hundred arteries and veins, one's blood became dried up, but one's vital energy was circulating, and so one would feel the pain intensely, and expire completely only after one last spasm. This, according to him, was nothing strange, and people found it bizarre simply because they had rarely seen it. How remarkable the principle is, and yet how subtle and accurate. "When there are doubts about a crime, the penalty should be as light as possible."[121] And, "once you understand the motives behind any crime, you should feel grieved and compassionate for the accused instead of complacent and joyful [about your own ability]."[122] I wish those who are in charge of law and punishment would think about the cruelty of it all and feel some compassion.

....

121 This quotation is from the *Classic of Documents*.
122 This quotation is from the *Analects* 19.19. See note 56 of part 1.

In managing a chaotic country, one should apply the penal code strictly, but execute only those who are truly guilty and whose crimes fully deserves such a sentence, so that the execution of one man serves as a warning to a hundred. Who would have expected that government officials might be as fierce as fighting cocks and indulge in their wrath to destroy the lives of the common folk? Moreover, they have embarked on their official careers by studying the *Classics*; shouldn't they know the saying that "the common folk are not intimidated by death, so wherefore try to intimidate them with death"?[123] I once met an official who believed that every resident of Xianju was doomed to spill blood. He claimed that if they were not executed, there would certainly be armed combat, and tens and hundreds would die that way; and that it was much better to have them killed off by the government, so that the custom of getting into fights among themselves might be mollified. If this had been true, then in order to "transform the vicious and thereby do away with the death sentence," we would have needed *evil* men to govern the country for a hundred years.[124] How outrageous! If everyone thought the way that official did, I simply would not know what to do.

An elder of Xianju once asked me, "You, dear sir, have been here for several months now, and you have witnessed a fair number of captured bandits. Have you ever seen one as strong as a tiger or leopard, and faster than a monkey or gibbon?"

I said, "No, I have not."

The elder said, "A real bandit always hides his tracks in the deep mountains and great marshes. Like a kraken or a snake, he is elusive. When he comes out, he carries small weapons and firearms. When he finds a wealthy household, he will get together with one or two of his comrades and coerce a dozen poor people to go with them, giving each of those people about a hundred cash. He himself will break in first, and tell the man of the house not to make any noise. Then he will order those poor people to carry away the loot for him. When he runs into bailiffs, he will be the first to take flight. He excels in running and leaping over

....

123   This quotation is from Laozi's *Dao de jing*.
124   This is from the *Analects* 13.11. The original remark is as follows: "The Master said, 'If good men were to govern the country continuously for a hundred years, they would be able to transform the vicious and thereby do away with the death sentence.'"

highs and lows, and his martial arts skills are good enough to fend off dozens of men. Besides, in peacetime he makes friends with officers and associates with clerks; throughout the year he regularly bribes them and enters into a bond with them like brothers or father and son. So even if they see him, they do not arrest him. When being pushed by their superiors, they will apprehend one of those poor people hired by real bandits, since he has indeed participated in the raid after all. The 'bandits' whom you, my dear sir, have seen are none other than those poor bastards."

I said, "Then why don't they report it to the officials as soon as they are pressured to join the bandits?"

The elder said, "They are too stupid to do that. Even if they do, half of the bailiffs side with the bandits—who would forward their report to the officials?"

I said, "But when they are captured, why do they admit to being a real bandit?"

The elder said, "Dear sir, you are truly a nice man. Don't you know that the officials have the 'scales'?[125] Besides, the bandits have their code of righteousness: when one of those poor people confesses to the crime and submits to execution, they will provide for his parents, wife, and children for the rest of their lives without fail. Therefore, banditry in our place will never be purged even for a hundred generations. Fortunately, these bandits carry on only small-scale stealing and robbing, and do not have any grand aspirations."

If this was true, perhaps there was, after all, a grain of truth to the theory that everyone in Xianju was doomed to spill blood? It is so sad.

Xianju's real bandits, on the other hand, had a strong sense of shame. If one of them robbed a local family, then the others would look down on him and regard him as a Licentiate Scholar, since he only knew to exploit his fellow townsmen. Therefore many bandits took to the sea. Occasionally they would raid Linghai, Huangyan, Taiping, and Ninghai, but they would never go near Tiantai, because Tiantai was Xianju's close neighbor, and also because they felt sorry for the Tiantai people's poverty as well as admired their kindness. When captured, they would take all of the blame on themselves and never wrongly implicate an innocent person, for they believed that a real man must not leave behind a bad reputation.

....

125   The "scales" is an instrument of torture.

They would not violate the old or weak, rape women, harm the crops, or take farming tools, and in all these aspects bandits from other places were inferior to them. To say that they had no conscience was not necessarily true. If a magistrate could act as a worthy parent to the common folk, clothe them, feed them, teach them the way of being good, and give them encouragement, these bandits would make excellent defenders of the country. If only the officials could put this into widespread practice and help rectify the contemporary political situation, wouldn't they be able to share the glory and the honor? Instead, they hang someone's head on a pole in the morning and call him a bandit, and cut off someone's foot in the evening and call him a bandit—wouldn't real bandits burst into laughter at this? Alas, all these "bandits" are but the little children of Our Imperial Majesty!

Governing is not easy, but it is not difficult either. The key is to establish the foundation well. If one does not cultivate the root and engages only in pursuing the branches, the more one tries to govern well, the less well-governed a place becomes. Insisting that the common folk are hard to manage—how could this be the initial intention of a worthy parent to the common folk? I am afraid that when the officials say this, it is simply because they have not given it much thought. For this reason the common folk are in dire straits, and have no way to recover from their hardships on their own. I will explain what I mean.

Those in positions of power say that of the four kinds of people, scholars are of the first and foremost importance;[126] and that in order to improve customs, one must begin with setting up schools. This is quite right. However, they do not care about a scholar's virtue, but look only to his cultural skills. Little do they know that it is indeed possible for cultural learning to harm the Way. Some scholars try their best to cover up their failings and show off their strengths; they are also capable of catering to officials' tastes and charming them. Thereupon black is turned into white, and yellow is regarded as brown. Ignorant people have never seen the least bit of filial piety or brotherly love in those scholars while clever people are all too ready to emulate their shamelessness. If one wants to improve customs by employing these scholars, how could it be possible? Not only that, but they also get involved in lawsuits, form

....

126　The four kinds of people refer to scholars, farmers, craftsmen, and merchants.

cliques, and basically stop at nothing in their transgressions. In a remote and backward place, when someone becomes a Licentiate Scholar, the whole village panics; when someone purchases the status of a National University Student, all of his neighbors are alarmed.[127] From this one can tell just how wild and overbearing those scholars are.

Those in positions of power say that the common folk regard food as their heaven; and that to give them a good life, we must first pay attention to agriculture and sericulture. This is quite right. However, they do not teach by example, but by rules and regulations instead. Little do they know that as soon as a clerk receives an official notice, he immediately follows up with exhortation and censure. The common folk are startled, and have no idea what is going on. As a result, before one even sees mulberry and hemp growing in the field, there are already no roosters or dogs left in the village. Under such circumstances, how could they become wealthy and well provided for? Not only that, but the clerks also take advantage of the opportunity to engage in all sorts of wrongdoing, such as threatening and defrauding. In broad daylight, they stir up trouble whenever possible, abuse their power and influence, swindle people out of their money, and violate their wives and daughters. The damage they cause the common folk is immeasurable.

Those in positions of power say that the horse harming the herd must not be tolerated, and that to bring peace to the common folk we must first punish the local strongmen. This is quite right. However, they do not pay much heed to the matter during peacetime, but suddenly decide to get rid of these people one morning. They ask their assistants to be their eyes and ears, and entrust confidential information to their kin. Little do they know that those strongmen, who are capable of wily schemes like ghosts and demons, have enough influence to bring about disasters and enough money to buy off gods. If in exposing them one does not exercise caution, one may hurt one's own reputation instead, and, what is worse, may even incriminate innocent people and mete out unjust verdicts. When that happens, will regret do any good?

Those in positions of power say that one must not be opinionated and

....

127   National University Student (*jiansheng*) was a common generic designation of students admitted to the National University (*taixue*) maintained by the Directorate of Education (*guozijian*) in the Qing dynasty.

regard oneself as infallible, and that to placate the common folk, one must first deal with legal cases at hand and clear them up. This is quite right. However, they do not attempt to gain insight into the hearts of the folk, discover their secrets, and pass judgment based on human nature and common sense. When those ignorant men and women step into the courtroom for the first time in their lives, they are so scared that their spirits have already left their bodies, which makes them look as if they had a guilty conscience. The crafty ones, on the other hand, put on an honest and pitiful face instead, and sometimes even deliberately muddle their words to bring about further interrogation, so that they may have a chance to present their argument and demonstrate their innocence. Even an official with the acuity of the Qin mirror cannot but be deceived.[128] How, then, can they expect justice to be served?

The problems described above are all due to the fact that the foundation has not been established at the outset.[129] Once the foundation is established, everything will be on track, and governance is not so difficult after all. What, then, is the foundation? I say: it is to be public-minded and sincere; it is to avoid being greedy, hypocritical, eager for instant success, or fearful of getting in trouble; it is to treat people gently and generously, so that the common folk will come to you; it is to be astute and discerning, so that the common folk will trust you. If one can act like this, there is no reason why he should not be honored in life and enjoy sacrificial offerings after death. Is there in the world any worthy parent to the common folk who might be so inclined? Alas, how sad! Alas, how sad!

....

128 The Qin mirror is a legendary mirror possessed by the First Emperor of Qin (259–210 bce) that could supposedly reflect the internal organs of a person.

129 This sentence was crossed out in the manuscript and changed to "Therefore, the foundation must be established at the outset."

CHRONOLOGY

JANUARY 29, 1854 (the first day of the first month in the *jiayin* or fourth year of the Xianfeng era): The author, Zhang Daye, is born at South Qinghe/Yuanjiang (in Huai'an, Jiangsu), where his father is serving in public office

1857: Author begins schooling

FEBRUARY 20, 1860 (the 29th day of the first month in the 10th year of the Xianfeng era): The Nian rebels press close to Huai'an of Jiangsu, and the director-general of the Grand Canal flees; at about the same time, author escapes with his three mothers (his "birth mother," "legal mother," and "concubine mother") and young servant Zhou, and goes to family residence at Shaoxing

AUGUST OR SEPTEMBER, 1860: Author's "legal mother" Madame Chen goes back to Yuanjiang to join his father; author stays behind at Shaoxing along with his "birth mother" Wang and "concubine mother" Lou

OCTOBER 29, 1861 (the 26th day of the ninth month in the *xinyou* or 11th year of the Xianfeng era): Author flees from Shaoxing to Black Stone Village with the help of hired hand Lu Sanyi, just before Shaoxing falls to the Taiping army

NOVEMBER 1, 1861: Taiping army captures Shaoxing

NOVEMBER/DECEMBER 1861: Author flees to Tiaomachang, south of Black Stone Village, via Cuangong

DECEMBER 28, 1861 (the 27th day of the 11th month): Taiping army attacks Tiaomachang

1862: Author goes to Lu's Dyke (his fourth sister's married home), where he witnesses the dismembering of a woman; then to Diankou (hometown of his "legal mother") and on to Pig's Jaw; then to Ding's Port, and comes down with malaria; then back to Diankou

SUMMER 1862: Author suffers from acute dysentery at Diankou; goes back to Ding's Port, then is taken by Wenjing to Houbao, where he receives news of Zhou's death; paternal aunt gets married to Mr. Lu at Dragon's Tail Mountain

JULY 27, 1862: Bao Village is captured and slaughtered by Taiping army; author's maternal cousin Xiong and his wife die

LATER 1862: Author flees to Temple's East, where he watches family tailor's son Feng Zhihua retrieve his brother Feng Zhiying's head; in early autumn, he and mother briefly seek refuge at Cypress Lodge, where his ancestral shrine is; then to Tao's Weir; then to West Port (aka Roosting Duck Village), where cousin Xiaoyun's wife née Wang commits suicide; her infant son Ren dies shortly afterward; author, mother, and old family servant Ah Zhang flee to Dragon's Tail Mountain and join author's aunt, now Mrs. Lu; mother is ill; author is cared for by Ah Zhang for six months

SPRING 1863: Author's mother gradually recovers from illness

MARCH 17, 1863: Taiping army leaves Shaoxing

MARCH 18, 1863: Cousin Xiaoyun returns to Shaoxing to look at family residence, finds everything intact, and leaves

MARCH 25, 1863: Cousin Xinquan goes back to Shaoxing's family residence and finds it robbed clean

OCTOBER–NOVEMBER 1863: Author and mother go north and join his father at South Qinghe/Yuanjiang of Jiangsu, and subsequently witness the Nian rebels' attack of Yuanjiang

1870: Author's father passes away; author escorts father's coffin back to Shaoxing; pays respects to Lu Sanyi's grave; sees Ah Zhang for the last time

1871: Author visits Tiaomachang and sees Old Woman Tang

OCTOBER/NOVEMBER, 1874 (the ninth month of the *jiaxu* or 13th year of the Tongzhi era): Author begins trip to Jinsha (in Nantong, Jiangsu) (Yuanjiang—Huaicheng—Baoying—Gaoyou—Shaobo—Yangzhou—Tai Zhou—Rugao—Jinsha)

1875: Author returns to Yuanjiang from Jinsha

APRIL 22, 1875: Cousin Xuequan dies

NOVEMBER 28–DECEMBER 27, 1875 (the 11th month of the *yihai* or first year of the Guangxu era): Author goes to Shaoxing for father's permanent burial (Yuanjiang—Danyang—Changzhou—Wuxi—Suzhou—Pingwang—Jiaxing—Shimen—Hangzhou—Shaoxing)

SPRING 1876: Author stays at Shaoxing and tours nearby sites; returns to Yuanjiang (Shaoxing—Xiaoshan—Hangzhou—Shimen—Jiaxing—Pingwang—Suzhou—Wuxi—Changzhou—Zhenjiang—Yangzhou—Shaobo—Gaoyou—Yuanjiang)

AUGUST 11, 1878 (the 13th day of the seventh month in the *wuyin* or fourth year of the Guangxu era): Author goes to Hangzhou for livelihood

[DATES UNKNOWN]: After leaving Hangzhou, author spends seven months at Songjiang (Shanghai), followed by several years at Suzhou; also, some time between 1878 and 1893, author's family moves to Ningbo

APRIL/MAY 1885 (the third month of the *yiyou* or 11th year of the Guangxu era): Author goes on trip from Suzhou to Jingkou (at Zhenjiang, Jiangsu)

MAY 3, 1886 (the 30th day of the third month of the *bingxu* or 12th year of the Guangxu era): Lü Xiuliang dies

JANUARY/FEBRUARY 1887 (first month of the *dinghai* or the 13th year of the Guangxu era): Author leaves Suzhou for Hangzhou, and visits Yu Simeng on the way there; at Hangzhou, decides to go to Xianju seeking employment on Commissioner Xu's recommendation

APRIL/MAY 1887: After visiting Shaoxing briefly, author goes to Xianju (Shaoxing—Sheng County—Xinchang—Banzhu—Tiantai—Xianju)

AUTUMN (1887 or later): Author leaves Xianju

APRIL 8, 1893 (the 22nd day of the second month in the *guisi* or 19th year of the Guangxu era): Yuan Jichuan dies

MAY 21, 1893 (the sixth day of the fourth month): Author sets out from Ningbo to Shaoxing (Ningbo—Fenghua—Xinchang—Banzhu—Tiantai—Shaoxing)

MAY 28, 1893 (the 13th day of the fourth month): Author arrives at Shaoxing; he pays his respects to Yuan Jichuan's spirit tablet on May 29; leaves Shaoxing on May 30, arrives at Huangyan on May 31, and stays overnight

JUNE 1, 1893 (the 17th day of the fourth month): Author visits his "birth mother" Madame Wang's family graves at Huangyan, returns to Shaoxing on June 4 (the 20th day of the fourth month)

JUNE 5, 1893 (the 21st day of the fourth month): Author bids final farewell to Yuan Jichuan's spirit tablet

JUNE 6, 1893 (the 22nd day of the fourth month): Author sets out for Ningbo (Haimen—Dinghai/Zhoushan—Zhenhai—Ningbo)

JUNE 9, 1893 (the 25th day of the fourth month): Author returns to Ningbo

1894: Author writes the last sections of part 3 some time after the one-year adversary of Yuan Jichuan's death ("now he has been dead for more than a year")

APPENDIX

A LIST OF AUTHOR'S CONNECTIONS

1. Family

father (1809–1870), name unknown

mother ("birth mother," father's concubine, d. after 1893/1894), née Wang, native of Huangyan, Zhejiang

mother ("legal mother," father's principal wife, d. between 1875 and 1893), née Chen, native of Zhuji, Zhejiang

Madame Lou/Deng, father's concubine from Guangdong

Madame Li, grandfather's concubine

sisters/female cousins (the author refers to all of his female cousins as "sisters" and sometimes it is impossible to know whether a "sister" is his sister or his female cousin; when we do know for certain, we list the name under "paternal uncles and their wives, sons, and daughters" below):

"elder sister," married to Zhou Shengjie

"fourth sister," lived in Lu's Dyke, presumably married to a Mr. Ni there

maternal uncles (i.e., brothers of "legal mother" Madame Chen):

uncle (name unknown), son, son's wife née Feng, and grandson Chen Youqiao (b. 1853), living at Diankou in Zhuji

fifth uncle Chen Yiting, named Jing, who had a villa at the Sweetness Range in Zhuji

maternal cousin: Xiong and his wife (d. 1862)

paternal aunt, married to a Mr. Lu at Dragon's Tail Mountain paternal uncles and their wives, sons, and daughters:

second uncle, wife (d. 1862); son Xinquan, his wife née Hu, and their son Anxuan (still living in 1893/1894); daughter ("ninth sister"), married to a farmer, name unknown

fifth uncle, wife, two daughters ("eighth sister" and "little sister," d. 1862)

sixth uncle Kuisheng (d. 1862); sons Jingquan, Wuquan (whose only son, name unknown, was still living in 1893/1894), Xuequan (named Wentao, 1848–April 22, 1875), Puquan, Zi, You, and Liquan (the only one still living in 1893/1894)

seventh uncle (d. 1862); wife née Yang (d. 1861); son Xiaoyun and his wife née Wang (d. 1862) and infant son Ren (d. 1862)

eighth uncle Shaozhu, son Qinquan (named Wenzhi) (both died in early 1870s)

2. Friends

(Note: Unless otherwise noted, the local place names in this and the next two sections are all Zhejiang place names.)

Chen Yuyu, native of Tiantai residing in Ningbo

General Liu Tianxing, studio name Youzhi, stationed at Shaoxing, in charge of the banner garrison

Lan Youzhi, named Yan, grandson of Lan Dixi (1736–1797), director-general of the Grand Canal

Li Xiaju, named Chengqi, native of Jiangning (in Jiangsu), secretary to General Liu Tianxing

Lü Xiuliang, named Jinshou, native of Suzhou (in Jiangsu), carpenter

Pan Yiting, named Honggui, native of Liuzhou (in Guangxi)

Qian Bochui (1867–1931), named Qian Zhenxun, native of Leqing, poet

Qian Jufu (d. 1875), named Qixin, native of Xiushui, minor official

Wan Qingxuan (1818–1898), native of Nanchang (in Jiangxi), official, a friend of author's father

Wang Kanghou, named Jin, aka "Elder Brother Thirty," author's classmate

Xu Yingheng (1820–1891), "Commissioner Xu" (?), native of Panyu (in Guangdong), provincial administration commissioner of Zhejiang

Yan Chiya, named An, residing in Changzhou (in Jiangsu)

Yang Chunhua, residing at Shaobo (in Jiangsu)

Yang Peiyuan (1835–1907), named Baoyi, native of Yanghu (in Jiangsu), painter

Yao Gusheng, residing in Songjiang (in Shanghai)

Yu Lang, courtesy name Xingru, native of Shanyin

Yu Mosheng, named Zhixiang, native of Zichuan (in Shandong)

Yu Simeng, named Long, native of Wucheng

Yuan Jichuan (1839–1893), named Shunjin, native of Fenyang (in Shanxi), district jailor of Xianju, Zhejiang

Zha Changqing, named Youchun, native of Haining, a friend of author's father

Zhang De, courtesy name Wangzong, author's first teacher

3. Casual Acquaintances

Chen Yuan (b. 1837), native of Linhai, bamboo carver, met during trip in part 1

Fang Hao, a former soldier, met at Jinhua

Gu Baotang, native of Shangyu, travel companion of Zhou (see under "Servants and Hired Hands")

Lady Scribe of the Jade Capital, née Qi, great-granddaughter of Qi Cifeng (1703–1768), native of Tiantai, met during trip in part 1

Minxi, studio name Huafeng, abbot of Temple of True Enlightenment at Tiantai, met during trip in part 1

Mr. Feng, author's family tailor, who had two sons, Feng Zhiying (d. 1862) and Feng Zhihua (d. 1862)

Mr. Pan, native of Tiantai, travel companion in part 1

Old Man Xu (b. 1830s), Xu Dingmu, studio name Zhiting, owner of restaurant at Dragon King's Lake of Xinchang, met during trip in part 1

Old Woman Tang (b. 1790s), native of Tiaomachang, who helped author in Taiping Rebellion

Qiutan, Buddhist monk at Tanhua Pavilion on Mount Tiantai, met during trip in part 1

Xiaoran, Buddhist monk at Guoqing Temple of Tiantai, met during trip in part 1

Yunya, Daoist priest at Weiyu Mountain, met during trip in part 1

Zhu Changchun, filial son of Jieshou Village, met during trip to Jinsha in part 3

4. Servants and Hired Hands

Ah Zhang (ca. 1800s–after 1870), native of Little Bitter Village, family servant from 1840s until 1870

Chen Laomo and his wife, natives of Zichuan (in Shandong), servants at the South Qinghe residence

[Chen] Wenjing (d. 1862), hired hand, also a clansman on the side of author's "legal mother"

[Chen] Xiaofu, hired hand, also a clansman on the side of author's "legal mother"

Elder Zhang, hired to watch author's father's temporary gravesite

He Xi, maternal cousin's wife Madame Feng's servant

Lu Sanyi (d. ca. 1870), hired hand, native of Black Stone Village

Yatou, native of Tiantai, hired to carry luggage during trip to Xianju in part 3

Ye Ahsheng, native of Tiantai, hired to carry luggage during trip to Tiantai in part 1

Zhao the Six, author's father's grave keeper

Zhou (1844–1862), an orphan from Licheng (in Shandong), taken in by author's father in 1853

WORKS CITED

Caruth, Catherine. *Unclaimed Experience: Trauma, Narrative, and History.* Baltimore, MD: Johns Hopkins University Press, 1996.

Freud, Sigmund. *Beyond the Pleasure Principle.* New York: W. W. Norton, 1961.

———. *On the History of the Psycho-Analytic Movement.* New York: W. W. Norton, 1966.

Gilmore, Leigh. *The Limits of Autobiography: Trauma and Testimony.* Ithaca, NY: Cornell University Press, 2001.

Guo, Tingyi. *Taiping Tianguo shishi rizhi* [A daily account of the historical events of the Taiping Heavenly Kingdom]. Shanghai: Shanghai Shudian, 1986.

Henige, David P. *Oral Historiography.* New York: Longman, 1982.

Herman, Judith Lewis. *Trauma and Recovery.* New York: Basic Books, 1992.

Huntington, Rania. "Chaos, Memory, and Genre: Anecdotal Recollections of the Taiping Rebellion." *Chinese Literature: Essays, Articles, Reviews* 27 (Dec. 2005): 59–91.

Idema, Wilt, Wai-yee Li, and Ellen Widmer, eds. *Trauma and Transcendence in Early Qing Literature.* Cambridge, MA: Harvard Asia Center, 2006.

Kao, Karl S. Y., ed. *Classical Chinese Tales of the Supernatural and the Fantastic: Selections from the Third to the Tenth Century.* Bloomington: Indiana University Press, 1985.

Ko, Dorothy. "The Subject of Pain." In *Dynastic Crisis and Cultural Innovation: From the Late Ming to the Late Qing and Beyond*, edited by David Der-wei Wang and Shang Wei, 478–503. Cambridge, MA: Harvard Asia Center, 2005.

Krystal, Henry. "Trauma and Aging: A Thirty-Year Follow-Up." In *Trauma: Explorations in Memory*, edited by Catherine Caruth, 76–99. Baltimore, MD: Johns Hopkins University Press, 1995.

LaCapra, Dominick. *Writing History, Writing Trauma*. Baltimore, MD: Johns Hopkins University Press, 2001.

Lavely, William, and R. Bin Wong. "Revising the Malthusian Narrative: The Comparative Study of Population Dynamics in Late Imperial China." *Journal of Asian Studies* 57, no. 3 (Aug. 1998): 714–48.

Liu Yiqing. *You ming lu* [Records of worlds of darkness and light]. In *Han Wei liuchao biji xiaoshuo daguan* [A comprehensive compilation of short narratives from the Han, Wei, and Six Dynasties]. Shanghai: Shanghai Guji Chubanshe, 1999.

Moss, Bruce M. *Remembering the Personal Past: Descriptions of Autobiographical Memory*. Oxford: Oxford University Press, 1991.

Owen, Stephen, ed. and trans. *An Anthology of Chinese Literature: Beginnings to 1911*. New York: W. W. Norton, 1996.

Platt, Stephen R. *Autumn in the Heavenly Kingdom: China, the West, and the Epic Story of the Taiping Civil War*. New York: Alfred A. Knopf, 2012.

Ricoeur, Paul. *Hermeneutics and the Human Sciences: Essays on Language, Action, and Interpretation*. New York: Cambridge University Press, 1981.

Spence, Donald R. *Narrative Truth and Historical Truth: Meaning and Interpretation in Psychoanalysis*. New York: W. W. Norton, 1982.

Spence, Jonathan D. *God's Chinese Son: The Taiping Heavenly Kingdom of Hong Xiuquan*. New York: W. W. Norton, 1996.

Strassberg, Richard E., trans. *Inscribed Landscapes: Travel Writings from Imperial China*. Berkeley: University of California Press, 1994.

Struve, Lynn A. "Confucian PTSD: Reading Trauma in a Chinese Youngster's Memoir of 1653." *History and Memory* 16, no. 2 (2004): 14–31.

———. *The Ming-Qing Conflict, 1619–1683: A Historiography and Source Guide*. Association for Asian Studies Monograph no. 56, 1998.

Tian, Xiaofei. *Visionary Journeys: Travel Writings from Early Medieval and Nineteenth-Century China*. Cambridge, MA: Harvard Asia Center, 2011.

Wang Xingfu. *Taiping Tianguo zai Zhejiang* [The Taiping Heavenly Kingdom in Zhejiang]. Beijing: Shehui Kexue Wenxian Chubanshe, 2007.

Xia, Chuntao. "Ershi shiji de Taiping tianguo shi yanjiu" [The study of the history of the Taiping Heavenly Kingdom in the twentieth century]. *Lishi yanjiu* [Historical studies] 2 (2000): 162–81.

Zarrow, Peter. "Historical Trauma: Anti-Manchuism and Memories of Atrocity in Late Qing China." *History and Memory* 16, no. 2 (2004): 67–107.

Zhang Daye. *Weichong shijie* [The world of a tiny insect]. In *Qingdai gaoben baizhong huikan* [A collected series of a hundred Qing dynasty draft manuscripts], vol. 55. Taipei: Wenhai Chubanshe, 1974.

———. *Weichong shijie jielu* [Excerpt from *Weichong shijie*]. In *Jindaishi ziliao* [Modern history materials], no. 3, ed. Zhongguo Kexue Yuan Lishi Yanjiusuo Disansuo [The Third Branch of the Institute of History at CAS], 87–92. Beijing: Kexue Chubanshe, 1955.

Zhang Maozi. *Yusheng lu* [A record of life beyond my due]. Translated by Lynn A. Struve. In *Hawai'i Reader in Traditional Chinese Culture*, edited by Victor H. Mair, Nancy S. Steinhardt, and Paul R. Goldin, 531–38. Honolulu: University of Hawai'i Press, 2005.

Zhao Erxun et al., eds. *Qing shi gao* [The draft of Qing history]. Taipei: Dingwen Chubanshe, 1981.

INDEX

A

Academy of Master Stone Case, 134
The Account of Famous Sights, 47
"Account of My Southern Journey" (Sun
   Jiagan), 147
"Account of Peach Blossom Spring" (Tao
   Yuanming), 101
Account of Ten Days in Yangzhou, 30
Account of the Jiading Massacre, 30
age of no doubts, 13, 79–80
Ah Zhang, 32, 85, 91–92, 104, 105
alum story, 80
An Lushan Rebellion, 25, 139*n*60
Analects, 13, 46*n*22, 62*n*56, 172*n*124
ancestral shrine, 104
ants comparison, Taiping soldiers, 24
Anxuan, 85, 92
Arhat pine, 164–65
atractylodes, 70
aunts, 81, 91, 181–82
autobiographical narrative, overview:
   childhood perspective, 3–4, 23–24; and
   cultural memory, 28–31; local focus,
   6–7, 28, 30; manuscript copy, 5, 8,
   27–29; opening journey summarized,
   9–13; philosophical aspect, 7; Rebellion period perspective, 13–14; structure of, 5–6, 8*n*3, 9, 14–16; translation
   approach, 31; as trauma writing, 7–8,
   16–26; travel theme, 7–8, 14–16; util-
   ity expectation, 6–7, 35–36. *See also*
   specific topics, e.g., landscape *entries;*
   poems *entries;* violence memories

B

Bai Juyi, 112*n*6, 124, 150*n*90
"The Ballad of Pipa" (Bai Juyi), 112*n*6,
   150*n*90
bamboo, 56, 99, 163
Bamboo Leaf Green, 136
Ban Gu, 79
bandits: attacks on water, 103, 104;
   explosion ambush, 102–3; at Peach
   Blossom Spring, 101; Suzhou problem,
   148–49; Taizhou, 61–62; Temple's
   East, 104; Tiantai city, 64; Xianju area,
   73, 74, 165–66, 169–74; Zhejiang, 49,
   50. *See also* Longhairs; Nian uprising;
   Shorthairs; violence memories
Banshan, 138
Banzhu, 39
Bao Lishen, 86
Bao Shenbo (Bao Shichen), 67
Bao Shu, 51
Bao Village, 23–24, 86–87, 93, 96, 102–3
Baoying, 121
Bay of Avoiding Summer Heat, 150–51
beauty, scenes of. *See* landscape *entries*
beaver, hawk-capturing, 98–99, 99
Benniu, 138
"Big Sister, Go Pick Tea Leaves" bird, 76,
   77–78
biji form, as memory shaper, 8*n*3
birds, 13, 39, 44, 76–78, 82, 99, 159
birth mother. *See* Wang, Madame (birth
   mother)
bitter nut, 99

Jiujianlou, 39
Junior Guardian Qi, 58
Junior Tutor Yao (Yao Guangxiao), 125

K

Kaiyuan era, 139
kalpa fire, 145
Kangxi Emperor, 58
Kaogong (Xia Yunyi), 145
King Python, 136
Kingdom of Virtuous Men, 49
krakens, 65, 156
Kuisheng, 117
Kuocang Mountain, 100

L

LaCapra, Dominick, 16
Lady Scribe of the Jade Capital, 47
Lai Junshu (Lai Xi), 115
Lai nan lu (Li Ao), 25
Lai Wenguang, 112–13
Lake Tai, 152
Lan Suting (Lan Dixi), 140n64
Lan Youzhi (Lan Yan), 140–41
land of Zou and Lu, 60
landscape descriptions: during burial
    journey for father, 125–26, 131; child-
    hood memories, 101–3; Gaoyou, 121,
    122; Haimen sea route, 58; Hexia, 116;
    Lake Tai region, 150–51; Lion Hill, 134;
    literary effects summarized, 24–26;
    near Haizhou, 142; philosophy in, 107;
    Shaoxing area, 54, 128; Spoon Lake,
    121; Square Hill, 55; Suzhou area,
    146, 151–52; Tai Zhou, 125; Taizhou
    counties, 63; Xianju journey, 161–65;
    Yuanjiang journey, 137–38, 139, 140; at
    Yu's Mausoleum, 133–34
landscape descriptions, Tiantai: Shaoxing
    area, 53–54, 56–57; surrounding area,
    43, 44–45, 46–47; during travels from,
    48–49; during travels to, 38–39, 40–42
Lanting, 133n45
Laoyue Temple, 130–31
Laozi, 118n20
laughter: dismembered woman episode,
    18, 96–97; shackle episode, 23, 101;
    with Yuanjiang friend, 141
lawsuits, 72, 73, 130

Lean Buffalo's Back, 134
legal mother. *See* Chen, Madame (legal
    mother)
Li, Brother, 159
Li, Madame (grandfather's concubine),
    81, 83, 91, 105
Li, Madame (Yuan Jichuan's wife), 51
Li Ao, 25
Li Bai, 163–64
Li Hongzhang, 116n15, 121n25
Li Ruzhen, 49n29
Li sao, 153
Li Sixun, 59
Li, Xiaju (named Chengqi), 49, 51, 56–57,
    58, 165
Li Xiucheng (Loyal Prince), 148–49
Li Yangbing, 146
Li Yuan, 107n29
Li Zhaodao (Li the Junior), 59
Li Zhaoshou, 115–16
Liang dynasty, 141
Liang Hong, 141n66, 147
Lianshupu, 88–89
Liao Zongyuan, 82n11
Licentiate Scholar, defined, 39n2
life and death, contemplations, 43,
    116–17, 123–24, 132, 141–42, 149–50
life expectancy, Chinese men, 13
Lihai, 92
The Limits of Autobiography (Gilmore), 17
Ling, King of Zhou, 45n17
Ling shan (Gao Xingjian), 25
Linhai county, 63
Linpu, 86
Lion Hill (Hou Hill), 134–35
Lion's Grove, 147–48
Liquan, 92
Litoupo, 136
Little Bitter Village, 91
Little Western River, 127, 137–38
Liu Ao, 61n55
Liu Bang, 47n25, 142n67
Liu Chen, 9–10
Liu Chong, 138
Liu Guo, 107
Liu Tianxing (studio name Youzhi), 49,
    52–53
Liu Yong, 40n7
Liu Zongyuan, 63n59

CPSIA information can be obtained
at www.ICGtesting.com
Printed in the USA
FSOW01n1857251116
27780FS